# THE STORY OF
# BILLIARDS &
# SNOOKER

# THE STORY OF BILLIARDS & SNOOKER

## CLIVE EVERTON

**CASSELL**
LONDON

CASSELL LTD.
35 Red Lion Square, London WC1 R 4SG
and at Sydney, Auckland, Toronto, Johannesburg,
an affiliate of
Macmillan Publishing Co., Inc.,
New York.

First published 1979

ISBN 0 304 30373 9

Design and Production in association with
Book Production Consultants, Cambridge.

Printed in Great Britain at the Burlington Press,
Foxton, Royston, Herts.

# Contents

**Tables**

# Introduction

The Story of Billiards and Snooker is an attempt to repair a gap in the recording of sports history: there has never been a lengthy chronological account of our two most popular billiard table games. Billiards, the parent game, is still played in the English version in all Commonwealth countries and a few miscellaneous outposts besides; the continental pocketless version, which sprang from the same roots but which is otherwise outside the scope of this book, is played on the continent, in the United States, South America and parts of Asia.

Snooker, now by far the more popular, with some four million participants in the British Isles alone and at least double this number world wide, is also played wherever British influence has been felt and has recently taken off in the most spectacular fashion as a television sport.

Unlike Billiards, whose roots are buried in antiquity, Snooker is of recent origin. It was invented only in 1875 and it was another half century before it began to make any significant impact on the competitive game which has been my prime concern in this book. It is not therefore until Chapter VIII that Snooker rates more than a fleeting mention.

Those readers who are primarily interested in Snooker will not, I hope, discount the earlier chapters, for without the Billiards pioneers Snooker would never have existed. Indeed, had those early giants of the green baize, and those who succeeded them, not by degrees become so very good that the possibilities of Billiards were gradually exhausted, no need or demand for Snooker might ever have been created.

Through study at the British Musuem Newspaper Library and elsewhere, notably through the kindness of private collectors like Ron Archer, Norman Clare and John Silverton, my priorities have been to establish and present the true sequence of events, an operation which inescapably involves a degree of statistical detail which some, though not all, may find indigestible. Had there been a previous study, my inclination would have been to cut some of this detail short; as there had not, I hope it will not convey the impression that the players were merely the sum of their statistics rather than the richly varied human beings they were.

The greatest of them all, Joe Davis, second only to Walter Lindrum as a Billiards player and to no one at Snooker, read all but the last chapter of my manuscript shortly before he died and from over sixty years' experience contributed some pertinent anecdotes and valuable corrections. Without him, indeed, this book would never have been written not merely in the sense of his role in the games' development but through my boyish impression of him in his prime all those years ago; his mastery of every phase of all the arts of the billiard table created in my mind an image of style and perfection which has remained at the heart of my love for the games.

Clive Everton,
*Snooker Scene*,
Poulton House,
197 Hagley Road,
Edgbaston,
Birmingham B16 9RD

October 1978

# CHAPTER I

# The Origins

About 1560, William Kew, a London pawnbroker, was fond, so it has been claimed, of taking down the three balls which identified his profession and pushing them about with a yardstick on his countertop or even the floor. Hence Bill-yard. And the stick, of course, became known as a kew and hence cue. The term "marker", the keeper of the scoreboard, derived from his additional responsibility of warning the players of the approach of an angry wife: "Mark her." Clergymen from nearby St. Paul's became partial to this strange game and thus "canon", or "cannon", became the term used to describe a shot in which one player's ball made contact with the other two.

Inconveniently, the words "cannon", "cue" and "marker" did not become current until the eighteenth century so this picturesque version of the origins of Billiards must be discarded in favour of a series of more fragmentary clues which have been documented in a most scholarly way in *A Compleat Historie of Billiards Evolution* by the American William Hendricks in a privately published pamphlet which is concerned with the origins of the game and development of its equipment.

The evidence suggests that "billiard" is a word descended both from "ball" words like pila (Latin) – billa (Medieval Latin) – bille (French) and "stick" words like bille (Old French) – billette (French) – billart (Old French). "Cue" comes from "queue", the French word for a tail, which refers to the early practice of striking the ball with the "tail" or small end of a mace when the ball was under a cushion.

Even the Greeks and Romans played many games with balls and sticks but it is not until the 1340's that the evidence hardens into a recognisable form of Billiards played, like Croquet, on a lawn with a stick very similar to the French billiard maces which are familiar in engravings and woodcuts of the 1600's and with an arch and pin in the playing area which was to become a common feature of early Table Billiards.

Louis XI of France (1461–1483) had a billiard table of sorts and such an item of furniture shortly became quite common among the French nobility. Ground Billiards survived into the 1600's but Table Billiards grew in popularity among the French and English nobility.

Mary, Queen of Scots, only months before she was beheaded, complained bitterly that her "table de billiard" had been taken away by her captors who were to add insult to injury by ripping the cloth off the table and half covering her beheaded corpse with it.

In 1588 the Duke of Norfolk owned a "billyard bord covered with a greene cloth . . . three billyard sticks and eleven balls of yvery". Public tables became quite common, as Spenser, Jonson and Shakespeare record, in London, and in Paris fifty-seven "billardiers paulmiers" (billiards and tennis court proprietors) were offering Billiards to their patrons. By 1727, Billiards was played in virtually every Paris café. In England it had come to be one of those games of skill and chance which it was the done thing for gentry and aspiring gentry to indulge in.

Around 1670, the thin end of the mace started to be used not merely when the ball was under a cushion rail – originally of course designed merely to prevent balls running out of play – but for the other shots as a matter of preference. The complete change from mace to cue took until about 1800 to complete.

With the mace, the idea was for players to push rather than strike. Skilful exponents of trailing or raking could achieve more or less unfailing accuracy but the cue introduced a greater variety and new skills. Cushions began to be stuffed with flox or cotton so that balls would actually rebound.

In England's inns, taverns, coffee houses and public gaming rooms, only the better players were at first allowed to use cues for fear of damaging the cloth, but in both France, slightly sooner, and England the cue gradually took over.

At the turn of the eighteenth century, Billiards was still largely the pursuit of the French, English and indeed Americans. The game had almost certainly been exported in the 1600's by the early English colonists – the nobility and well-to-do – but by 1800 there were enough public tables in French cafés, English ale houses and everywhere in America from private houses to the toughest frontier outposts to justify the claim that it was now a game for all classes.

The demand for tables and equipment was first met by furniture makers, carpenters and the like but some of these, like John Thurston (established 1799), went over entirely to this new specialist trade (1814).

The very earliest balls had been made of wood but ivory was preferred by the rich, who could afford them, and came to be accepted. The art of ball-making was to get the centre of the elephant tusk as the centre of the ball. By 1820 the mace was rapidly becoming extinct though almost until the end of the century it was still permissible to strike the ball with the butt of the cue.

References in the early games to "the arch" (like a Croquet hoop), "port" (another hoop) and "king" (a pin or skittle near the hoop) imply their lack of resemblance to the modern game but, about 1770, two variants, the "winning game" and the "losing game", introduced two of the three scoring elements of modern Billiards, pots and in-offs.

The "winning game" was a 12-point contest played with two white balls. The player who could get his ball nearest the opposite cushion without lying against it began the play, a rule which has reached the twentieth century in the custom of "stringing" for break, that is, sending the two cue-balls up the table and back to the cushion, the player whose ball finishes nearer the cushion having choice of break and ball.

A player who pocketed his opponent's ball scored 2 points – as he still does – and a player missing his opponent's ball had one point (still the penalty for a miss) added to his opponent's total. He conceded 2 points if his ball went into a pocket after contacting his opponent's ball and 3 points if his ball entered a pocket without striking the ball at all.

The "losing game" was, of course, the opposite to the "winning". The terms "winning" and "losing hazard" still remain in the official rules the approved terms for "pot" or "in-off" although they have long since dropped out of colloquial usage.

The third element of modern Billiards, the cannon, arose from the game of Carombole which reached England from France. A red ball was added to the two whites (stained balls were being sold in London as early as 1771) and counted three, but the object of the game, it appeared, was for a player to hit the other two balls with his own ball, a carombole (later a cannon or carom) counting 2 towards the game total of 16. The skill involved in these games helped the cue to retire the mace.

Around 1810 the French started to make their tables without pockets so that games consisted entirely of caroms (cannons). Some of these tables reached America, but the English influence was also apparent there in that 15-ball Pool, with the balls initially in the characteristic Snooker pyramid, was being played in the 1860's and led to the first American Pocket Billiards tournament in 1878.

In the early days of the cue, before cue-tips had been invented, the idea was to strike the cue-ball as centrally as possible to avoid a miscue. Striking low (to bring the cue-ball back from the object-ball) or high (to make it follow through) were two skills discovered before tips were used but which were naturally used much more extensively when a French infantry captain, Mingaud, studying Billiards during his sojourn in a Paris prison, experimented successfully with a leather tip in 1807 and astounded all and sundry with his cuemanship on his release.

In pre-tip days it was common for players to twist the points of their cues in a wall or ceiling so that a round chalk like deposit would at least partially guard against a miscue. Ordinary chalk also came to be used but the first systematic marketing of chalk was done by John Carr, a marker in John Bartley's billiard rooms at Bath.

Between 1818 and 1823 either Bartley, who subsequently showed Carr, or Carr himself discovered the positive uses of sidespin, or side. Carr attributed the strange new effects he was producing to a special brand of "twisting chalk" which was actually ordinary chalk in small boxes but which he was able to sell at prices more commensurate with a substance of magical properties!

"English", the American term for "side", is a clue that this was an English discovery just as "masse", the French word for mace, points to the French origins of this stroke. Mingaud it was who discovered that, by raising the cue almost vertically (in fact into the position adopted for the mace), extraordinary close spin effects could be obtained by striking a glancing blow across the left or right of the cue-ball.

By 1840, slate had generally succeeded wood as the table bed surface on which the cloth was laid. Slate is naturally found in flat layers which make it ideal for the permanently and perfectly flat surface necessary for the game to be played to its best standards.

Thurston, who began experimenting with slate in 1826, was responsible for many of the improvements which brought the manufacture of tables near enough perfection. The early cushions were layered strips of felt but, after trying hair, list, Russian duck, white swanskin and other substances, rubber was introduced in 1835. There were all sorts of problems. Cold weather caused rubber to lose all its elasticity, a contingency which Thurston's met temporarily with cushion warmers – metal pans or tubes to hold hot water. But the real breakthrough was the development of the vulcanizing process, raising the temperature of the natural rubber and combining it with sulphur to produce a substance more resistant to temperature changes. In 1845, Queen Victoria received the first set of these new cushions.

The quality of cloth began to be improved when machines were developed to mow the previously long nap.

The expense of ivory balls made a synthetic substitute necessary. In 1868 John Wesley Hyatt, a New York inventor, discovered that collodion (nitro-cellulose, camphor and alcohol), which printers brushed on their fingers to protect them from cuts and grazes hardened when it was dry and could be made into balls. Hyatt and his brother Isaac patented their process in 1870 under the trade name of celluloid, the world's first commercial synthetic plastic. They used it to make not only billiard balls but false teeth and piano keys. Among the teething problems of the new ball was that celluloid was highly flammable and, if struck too hard, a ball could explode! Nevertheless, this initial discovery led directly to the cast resin and cast phenolic balls which are used today.

Many refinements were to follow but by the latter part of the nineteenth century the essentials of the modern game were in being.

# CHAPTER II

# The Age of Roberts
*(Professional Billiards 1820–1900)*

In its early days Billiards was either a gambling activity, as most games were, or a leisurely relaxation for the gentry. The twin traditions of Billiards were epitomised by the country mansion and the tavern or public room. The gentry were often great patrons of the game but the best players invariably came from much lower down the social scale even though their successes were sometimes to establish them, eventually, securely in the middle class.

The origins of competitive Billiards are reminiscent of the prize ring beginnings of boxing. Long before any official governing body was set up, there were recognised "champions" whose titles were current on the strength of public opinion. This opinion was largely determined by a series of challenge matches for money.

Edwin Kentfield of Brighton, known as Jonathan Kentfield, was the first player to be recognised as champion, around 1820. He had a top break of 196 which included 57 consecutive pot reds off the spot, no mean feat as the deadness of the cushions – these were pre-rubber days – meant that the spot stroke had to be played either by screwing back or rolling through. Nevertheless, at the very beginning of the game's competitive history, the crucial importance of the spot stroke as a scoring weapon – it still is quite important under current rules – was thus established.

John Carr of "twisting chalk" fame, like Kentfield a marker, challenged him in 1827 but fell ill before the match and Kentfield remained champion until 1849 when he failed to meet a challenge from John Roberts (senior) of Liverpool. The title "champion" meant, of course, champion of England and it was perhaps a reflection of the nation's self confidence that this was simply assumed to be champion of the world. Incredibly, the Billiards Championship was known simply as "The Championship" until 1933.

Roberts, an enormous man with a long thick beard, was a tough competitor. One tale which has survived is of a series of eleven games of 100 up for £20 level with "Old Minchey", a Billiards sharp or, to use the modern term, hustler. Roberts, holding back for bets, let Minchey get to 5–5 with an 87–35 lead in the decider. He left Roberts a double baulk only for Roberts to knock both red and cue-ball off the table, a stroke which then carried no penalty. Minchey bet him he could not do it again but he did – five times. Tactics were obviously highly developed for Minchey gave no less than 18 misses but he then failed to leave his opponent a double baulk and Roberts ran out.

Roberts's highest recorded break was 346 against William Dufton in 1862. He practised hard to perfect the spot stroke and was undisputed number one until he signed to play William Cook for £200 and the title in February 1870. Before the match the leading players of the day and the Billiards trade met to draw up Championship rules. These included a stipulation that pockets should be 3" (as against the usual and modern 3½") and that the red spot should be placed 12½" from the top cushion instead of the then usual 13¼" and the now standard 12³/₄".

Though Roberts was much superior in the all round game, Cook was a spot stroke specialist and the conditions thus appeared much in the champion's favour, but Cook, after a five hour battle, won 1,200–1,083 at the Guildhall in front of the Prince of Wales and many members of the aristocracy to become champion.

Family honour was avenged two months later when John Roberts (junior) beat Cook in three hours four minutes by 1,200–722. This defeat seemed to bring home to Cook what now appears obvious – that there was an enormous difference for a spot stroke player between the ordinary 3½" pockets and the 3" Championship pockets.

Cook steadily improved his best break to 936 (including 262 spot strokes) but had the foresight to introduce the "spot barred" game which stipulated that the red could not be potted twice in succession from its spot, a rule which ensured that Billiards would be a varied three-ball rather than a repetitive two-ball game.

The Championship, of course, remained "all in", albeit under the more difficult Championship conditions, and Cook, after his success by a mere 15 points over Roberts in May 1871, repelled three further challengers until beaten by Roberts in May 1875. In these days Burroughes and Watts, Thurstons and Cox and Yeman would draw lots as to which firm provided the Championship table and *The Sportsman* acted as general arbiter in the absence of any governing body.

Roberts retained the title until November 1880 but was by then good enough to concede start to his rivals and opted out of the Championship to go East when, in the course of his travels, he set up a billiard table factory in Calcutta. Cook claimed the title but also resigned it to go East and Joseph Bennett became champion. Bennett made a Championship record break of 125 in his successful title defence against Tom Taylor in January 1881 but then broke his arm when he was thrown out of a gig and resigned the title.

Roberts billed himself as "Champion of the World" but stated that he had no intention of ever again playing in the Championship under the rules then appertaining and, more or less by default, Cook held the title for the next three years.

Roberts conceded starts to all and sundry both at "spot barred" and "spot in" and the situation was – as it was to be many times in the future – that the players whom the public knew to be the best devalued the Championship by not playing in it. In short, the personality of the top player was stronger than the game's administration.

William Mitchell became the first player to compile a thousand break in public with an effort of 1,055 (including 365 spot strokes) against W.J. Peall at the Black Horse Hotel, off Oxford Street, a feat which he repeated identically the following week. Peall, however, soon began to eclipse everyone at the spot stroke and in May 1884 he inflicted a break of 1,989 on Mitchell which included 548 consecutive spots.

Peall did not figure in the first professional circus which Roberts, feeling his strength as a Billiards impressario, took round the British provinces in the same year, offering short games on handicap on the American tournament system with nine players, but Peall did manage to beat Roberts (receiving 2,000 in 10,000 "all-in") by 598 in a challenge match at the Royal Aquarium.

Roberts was now so good that he played several matches in which opponents were allowed to play "all-in" while he himself was restricted to "spot barred". In late 1884, he took the "spot barred" break record from 309 (by Cook) to 322, 327 and then 360.

He developed the top of the table technique in which, by manoeuvring the object-white into position by the red spot, he was able to compile breaks with an alternating sequence of cannons and pot reds and, with his showman's instinct, started to refine the art of "accidentally" losing position so that he could astonish the crowd with a spectacular (but usually not as difficult as it looked) recovery shot. He was a master of all phases of the game, including nurseries (though with the aid of the push shot) but never singlemindedly favoured one method of scoring. He thus remained incomparably the most attractive and exciting player of his day.

By now, there was a generally appreciated need for a universal set of rules and to this end a meeting took place in February 1885, attended by the leading professionals and leading figures in the trade, at which the Billiards Association came into being and (after one further meeting) an official set of rules was agreed.

Roberts, who had been in the chair at this meeting, now decided to play for the Championship again. Cook did not reply to Roberts's challenge within the stated time but immediately challenged when the cup went to Roberts. The match itself, when it came to be played at the Billiard Hall, Argyll Street, turned into a close one in which Roberts made a Championship break record of 129 and won by a mere 92 (3,000–2,908) a surprisingly slender margin in view of the fact that immediately afterwards he (conceding 2,000 in 12,000) beat Cook by no less than 2,759,

After retaining his title against Bennett in June, in which he made breaks of 147 and 155, a new Championship record, Roberts played weekly matches at the Billiard Hall, Argyll Street, steadily advancing his "spot barred" record to 506. Peall, Mitchell, Fred White and others were all capable of thousand breaks with the spot stroke and Peall indeed defeated Roberts 16,734–11,924 for a £200 purse in an extraordinary match in which each player, at the start of a break, could place the cue-ball where he pleased.

Peall also beat Roberts in a match in which he was restricted to 100 spots in any break, a condition which was misunderstood by Peall's faithful backer, Billy Shee, who laid £500 to £1 that Peall would make 100 consecutive spots in the course of the match. After a few days, Shee could not fathom why Peall was frequently making 97, 98 or even 99 consecutive spots without making 100. When Peall told him, his consternation was considerable but by then Peall was so far ahead that he could afford to sacrifice one break in order to save Shee's money.

Shee, incidentally, was arguably the worst player of his day. Playing once for £500, he needed only two for game with the cue-ball in hand and the two object-balls almost touching each other just outside baulk. The cannon could have been made by any player with a tipless cue but in his excitement Shee thought both balls were in baulk and played up the table with the butt of the cue, a stroke then permissible, and lost the game.

Receiving 2,000 in 10,000 Peall also beat Roberts by 441 on the strict Championship table, 3″ pockets and all, making a break of 445 including 128 spots. Roberts never made more than 16 consecutive spots on the Championship table.

Peall, in fact, called himself Champion of Ordinary Billiards after Roberts had refused a £100 match all-in challenge unless there was also a second match, Peall to receive 4,000 in 12,000, spot barred. Secure in his spot barred supremacy, Roberts was quite content to let Peall and Mitchell indulge in spot stroke orgies, knowing full well that in no sport will the paying public tolerate a high degree of repetition. It was a problem Billiards was to be faced with time and time again.

As had happened before and was to happen many times again, internal strife was to interfere with the Championship which, despite the promise which the formation of the Billiards Association had seemed to indicate, fell into abeyance between 1885 and 1899 for no other reason than that Roberts was supreme at spot barred but would not play all-in.

Peall, who had pocketed £50 from Mr Wright, of the Billiard firm bearing his name, for the first 2,000 break, 2,413 in 1,886 won four spot stroke Championships between 1887 and 1891 with five breaks over 1,000 including one of 2,031. Less than five feet tall, Peall was an amazingly consistent and accurate potter, particularly if we take into account his semi-upright stance. A popular and cheerful man, he was an enthusiastic cyclist and motorist when these activities were in their infancy. Once, when he appeared in court at Reigate to answer a summons for exceeding the twelve mile per hour speed limit, he was tetchily told to stand up and was thus able, in all innocence, to utter the immortal words: "I am standing up, sir." He lived until he was over ninety and continued to play with great keenness until shortly before his death. Once, having missed a pot red from its spot, he exclaimed in some irritation: "I'd have got that with my eyes shut fifty years ago."

The Billiards Association eventually tried to break the deadlock caused essentially by Peall wanting to play on the ordinary table (whose relatively generous pockets favoured the spot stroke) used by the public while Roberts wanted the "championship table" which had 3″ pockets. The Association decided to award cups for both "all-in" and "spot barred" matches to be played on a "standard" table whose pockets measured strictly 3⅝″ at the fall of the slate, these to be tested by an official template before each match.

The "all-in" event carried the further interesting condition that a new cloth had to be fitted each day as the potting of the red from its spot several hundred times gradually created a channel which made these shots easier. Peall won the "all-in" title easily and Mitchell the "spot barred" just as easily but a clash between Peall and Roberts was as far away as ever.

Roberts so clearly was Billiards that he could override the Billiards Association with impunity. Arrogant, assured, immaculate, Roberts made tables and sold cues, chalk, balls, books, cushions and even cigars and crockery. He said that he could not regard "a letter from the secretary of a moribund association as other than a gross impertinence." He grandly offered the Association a venue, a table and a trophy for their Championship – but declined to play in it.

There were some diversions: Tom Taylor made a break of 1,467 (729 cannons) through getting the two object-balls jammed in the corner pocket entrance and Taylor and J.P. Mannock attempted an amalgam of the French, American and English games by playing on a four pockets table, the push shot, a prominent feature of the day, being barred.

Quite a few cannon breaks started to be compiled with the balls jammed but none more dramatically than one by Frank Ives, the American champion, against Roberts. Playing 6,000 up for £1,000 at Humphrey's Hall, Knightsbridge, on a table with 3¼" pockets (smaller than usual) and 2¼" ball (larger than usual). Roberts led 3,000–2,243 but, on the fourth evening, Ives jammed the balls in the corner pocket and ran to 1,540 unfinished (770 cannons) to lead 4,000–3,484. Roberts perceived all too clearly that the game was virtually over and offered to concede if Ives would play 2,000 up for another £1,000 – jammed stroke barred. Ives declined and continued the break to 2,539 before breaking the balls up, only to jam them again on the final evening in compiling an 848 in winning 6,000–3,821.

A return match for £400 at the Central Music Hall, Chicago, varied the original conditions in that a baulk line 7" long was drawn across each of the corner pockets inside which only two strokes could be fairly made before sending one object-ball out of baulk. Ives won 6,000–5,243, making a best break of 432 and Roberts 166.

Roberts – he who had been insisting on 3" pockets to play Peall – had the pockets increased from 3¼" to 3⅝" for his match against Ives in New York. Ives gave a classic exhibition of nurseries (a sequence of cannons in which the cue-ball nursed, an inch or so at a time, the other two along the cushion) with breaks of 651, in which he took the balls past four pockets, and 516, but Roberts won 10,000–8,738.

Roberts also played the American Pool champion, Alfredo De Oro, at Madison Square Garden at Pyramids and Pool and was beaten 1,000–924. Regrettably, this was more or less the last attempted fusion of the British and American games and Peall and Charles Dawson, engaged for a short season at the Folies Bergère, failed to interest French spectators either in Billiards or Pyramids.

On his return, Roberts encamped at the Egyptian Hall, Piccadilly, and pushed up his personal record by stages to 867 until in May 1894 at the Gentleman's Concert Hall, Manchester he compiled a 1,392 against Edward Diggle in Manchester, the first ever thousand to be made unaided by specialist repetition strokes, albeit on an "ordinary table".* The best break on a "standard table" was one of 985 by Diggle, a Manchester professional, against Roberts in January 1895.

Diggle, Dawson, Peall and Mitchell all kept well in the public eye but Roberts was still undisputed king, not only at the table but away from it. At his Regent Street rooms, he introduced a new pneumatic rubber cushion bearing

---

*There were 54 nurseries at 700 and a cheer from the press benches when he passed the previous spot barred record of 867. He finished the session in play with 1,033 and left the red on the edge of the pocket when he broke down.

his name and also, in October 1895, brought out the game's first magazine, *The Billiards Review*.

The first issue carried an article by Mitchell calling for the outlawing of the push shot which developed into a crusade by *The Sportsman*. Roberts persuaded Diggle and Dawson to support him in a letter to *The Times*, resenting a point of law being decided by "a clique of sporting journalists and second class professional players." *The Sportsman*, unrepentant, continued its campaign; Roberts complained of dwindling attendances when he played push barred and went back to playing push in, as indeed did most, though Mitchell issued a standing challenge to play anyone except Roberts level "push barred". Then, in 1898, Roberts again changed his views and the "push and spot barred" game started to be generally accepted.

The Billiards Association weighed in with official rule amendments in October 1898 outlawing the push shot and stipulating that the red, after being potted from its spot twice in succession, should be placed on the middle spot.

With these rules in force, the Championship was again held in 1899, Dawson beating Joe North. More significantly, Dawson's backers challenged Roberts on level terms for £100, the whole of the gate money to go to the winner. The form of Roberts, who was starting to play with bonzoline, was thought by disinterested judges to be marginally deteriorating but he won the match, of a fortnight's duration, by 1,814. Roberts took the £100 sidestake and the whole of the gate, £2,154.

The stories told of Roberts were legion. George Nelson, the Yorkshire professional champion, was once doing comparatively well against him in a week's match and thus felt able to venture the opinion that the ivory set of balls they were using was a particularly foul set.

"What's the matter with them?" he demanded peremptorily.

"They run off badly."

"You shouldn't let them run off."

As there was no such thing as a perfect set of ivories, Roberts perfected the drag shot for length of the table strokes, sticking his cue through the cue-ball as if he was screwing back in order to prevent it running off before it contacted the object-ball.

Roberts, who played many times for royalty, was once involved in a bizarre game with Lily Langtry, one of the great Music Hall personalities of the day, when the Prince of Wales matched them to play 50 up, Miss Langtry to score all she could by normal methods while Roberts played strokes nominated by the Prince. Not all these were as impossible as the Prince thought, for Roberts, while ensuring that his opponent won the game, was able to display his skill in a manner which earned him many other society engagements.

For the first of his many tours of India, he decided to augment his playing income by taking some tables with him to sell. On his arrival, he heard that the Maharajah of Jaipur was a keen sportsman and therefore, in the absence of a railway, chartered some elephants to carry some tables to show him. The Maharajah ordered half a dozen and created Roberts Court Billiards Player for life with an annual salary of £500 with full expenses for coming to India one month a year.

Roberts and his wife were housed in a palace of their own with a hundred servants at their disposal and the champion gave his Highness tuition and occasionally arranged entertainments. Once, he had Roberts describe how a professional tournament worked and decided there and then to hold one himself in his palace the following season. For Roberts it was unthinkable "to bring eight players all these thousands of miles by rail, boat and elephant . . .", but the Maharajah did not perceive any disproportion and the tournament was arranged.

The expense of about £5,000 was, it seemed, only petty cash and the tournament began with Roberts playing a clever but somewhat touchy player, S.W. Stanley. At his first visit, Roberts gained spot stroke position (the spot stroke then being allowed) and proceeded to pot the red some twenty times. The only spectator, the Maharajah, quickly bored, descended from his throne, picked up the balls and declared: "We will have the next game. Mr. Roberts is the winner." Stanley, having travelled ten thousand miles only to play one safety shot, never forgave Roberts and, reputedly, was scarcely the same again.

Roberts played everywhere from Indian palaces on all ivory tables to Australian mining towns on a makeshift board. Wherever he played his determination was prodigious. When an old man, he was engaged to play Mitchell in Manchester. He had malarial fever and ague but came over from Sale, where he was staying with his brother-in-law, in a brougham, smothered in rugs and wraps. He was conceding 200 in 1,000 but could scarcely walk round the table and Mitchell got to within 40 of game before Roberts amazingly ran out with 600 unfinished.

When electric light was in its infancy, a special motor plant and the new light was installed for a match at the Palais Royal. One day, though, the bulbs exploded and crashed on the table. Marker and spectators set about clearing up and the show went on, Roberts immediately compiling a 400 plus despite burns, cuts and lingering minute pieces of glass. Roberts did not trust electricity again. A new cloth was fitted, the plant was removed and gas again illuminated the scene.

No statistics could even hint at Roberts's stature. When he was billed by *The Sportsman* as "ex-champion" on the authority of the Billiards Association he sued for £1,000. His henchman, Tom Taylor, who had borne the brunt of Roberts's wrath when the terms he agreed for the great man's match against Ives actually played into the American's hands by favouring his cannon mastery, had another unfortunate lapse in the witness box when cross-examined by counsel for the defendants.

After counsel had courteously outlined Roberts's claims to greatness he said:

"Surely, Mr. Taylor, you cannot think that such a great player as we all know Mr. Roberts to be could be damaged by a statement in *The Sportsman* that he is not champion."

"Oh dear no", agreed Taylor happily. "It couldn't do him any harm; in fact, it would rather do him good as an advertisement."

This scarcely endeared Taylor to Roberts – especially when the case went against him – but what Taylor said was right enough: everyone knew who was boss. Once, Cecil Harverson was deputed by the professionals competing against him in a tournament to approach him.

"We hear", said Harverson, "that you are being paid to play with the balls we are using and the other players are under the impression that they should have their share of the money."

"That impression will wear off. Good morning, Mr. Harverson."

# CHAPTER III

# After Roberts
## *(Professional Billiards 1900–1914)*

Roberts's defeat of Dawson nevertheless presaged the end of the Roberts era. There was no one of remotely similar stature but his retirement did give the Championship a new reality. Dawson, already the titular champion by virtue of his win over North at the Gaiety Restaurant in 1899, when the profit only just covered the cost of crockery breakages, was, in a sense, the man in possession.

A dour, stubborn man from Huddersfield, Dawson possessed a fine match temperament. In 1890, playing Joe Watson of Newcastle 6,000 up for £100 a side, he needed only 194 for game when Watson got on the spot and made 1,075 before breaking down. The applause was such that it was ten minutes before order was restored. When it was, Dawson imperturbably ran out with 194. The same Watson was involved in another close finish in 1895 when receiving half the game in 12,000 up from Roberts. Roberts needed no less than 4,148 to win on the Saturday and scored all but 17 of them when midnight struck and the match had to be abandoned because of the stringent regulation against Sunday play.

The main threat appeared to be Diggle, originally a Manchester marker, whom Roberts had nursed into a playing career, largely as his own sparring partner to begin with. A languid, wry man with a casual, half upright style with both legs inelegantly bent, Diggle was generally considered, in the mid-1890's, number two to Roberts, for in 1895 he beat Dawson twice out of three and, receiving 8,000 instead of the customary 9,000, also beat Roberts by 1,381.

When he began to travel less with Roberts, he travelled more with Dawson, an experience he did not always savour. Diggle, who had an easy-going nature, not only disliked practising but even talking about Billiards, while Dawson practised a lot and talked and thought of little else. When asked one day why he was smiling to himself for no apparent reason, Diggle replied that because he was staying in his own home town for the week Dawson would thus be unable to collar him at mealtimes or even in the middle of the night to ask him what shot he would play in a certain position.

When he was asked whether it was really coincidence that so many professional matches seemed to run neck and neck to keep the paying customers interested in a close game, Diggle replied enigmatically: "There's tricks in every trade but ours." Dawson, in 1904, answered the question less humorously when his solicitors announced: "We have been instructed with regard to statements which have appeared in the public press suggesting that the matches now being played are not genuine ones. We are instructed to give the most emphatic denial to such suggestions."

Neither was Dawson overjoyed when, in 1902, Diggle exposed a loophole in the rules. With the object-white covering the spot, Diggle proceeded to keep potting the red off the pyramid spot. Dawson, in some agitation, phoned Sydenham Dixon, later Secretary and President of the Billiards Association, who was then working for *The Sportsman*. "Diggle won't stop scoring off the pyramid spot, Mr. Dixon. Please come and stop him." Diggle made 168 and the rule was revised to stipulate that the red be placed on the middle spot after being potted twice in succession from the pyramid. On another occasion, in Australia, Diggle made a break of 222 off the white. "Why did you do that?" someone asked.

"Well", said Diggle, "they've seen potting the red and in-off the red, I thought I'd shown them in-off the white."

In 1900 Dawson had a bright idea. He was champion and H.W. Stevenson, who by then had accomplished little, challenged. He took Diggle to one side.

"You challenge also, beat him in the preliminary round and then we shall have a nice gate for the final." It was a nice gate all right but it was Stevenson who shared it for he compiled a 600 unfinished to conclude his opening session against Diggle and beat him easily. Dawson then beat Stevenson 9,000–6,775 in the final at the Argyl Hall, but later that year Stevenson confirmed his number two position by beating Diggle with the aid of a 586 break, 18,000–17,013 after being 1,166 behind.

Stevenson duly beat Dawson for the title the following year but, later in 1901, Dawson won it back. To say these two were rivals is to put it mildly: they hated each other. The title of "Champion" in those days carried an annual grant of £100 and when Dawson replied, still later in 1901, that the dates on which Stevenson wished to play him were inconvenient, Stevenson was declared champion and the grant passed to him. Nevertheless, they played a best of three grudge series which Dawson won 2–1, a series which included for the first time a stipulation that two plain balls should be used with a spot marked on one of them. This followed an incident the previous month when the young Melbourne Inman, apparently set for victory against Harverson, saw the spot fall out of his ball. A new set was provided but Harverson won by 163 by running out with 225 unfinished.

There was so much needle between Dawson and Stevenson, though, that another match for the Championship was inevitable. It came about at the National Sporting Club in 1903 but not before considerable negotiation. Dawson stipulated that players should toss for choice of table and that the game should be 18,000 up. The Billiards Association raised no objection (though Stevenson successfully resisted the longer match) but there was a great hue and cry when the players selected a table supplied by a Northern firm, Riley's of Accrington, rather than one manufactured by the magic circle of four firms (all of whom voted as Vice-Presidents of the Association) who had hitherto done so. After this, the billiard table manufacturers withdrew from voting positions on the Association and Stevenson and Dawson both visited Riley's works separately to make sure that a specially tight table was supplied.

The bitter contest, which Dawson won by a mere 300, did not end with the customary exchange of civilities: "So much for the Billiard Association Champion", snarled Dawson as he made the winning shot.

Dawson and Stevenson played a long series of matches totalling 144,000 up in 1904 (the series which necessitated the disclaimer by Dawson's solicitors) which ended with Dawson leading 135,715–134,579. Shortly afterwards, though, Stevenson beat Dawson by 5,269 in a heat of the Burroughes and Watts tournament. Dawson, obsessional as his nature was, experienced this as a humiliation and his rapidly worsening mental troubles started from this date, though it may be more accurate to say that they reappeared in a more serious form than in a bad patch he had had from 1894–1898.

"I can't play drag shots from the 'D' slowly", Dawson had said then. "My cue won't let me." A specially built cue brought him back to form then but this time there was the insuperable handicap of failing eyesight. Soon, he could not see well enough even to play and, despite one or two charitable attempts to alleviate his financial problems, he died in penury. This was not all that uncommon a fate for an old player. Billy Mitchell, second only to Peall as a spot stroke specialist, though second to none in his fondness for a drink, had his old age in his native Sheffield cushioned by twenty enthusiasts who each subscribed a shilling a month which he received through *The Billiard Player*. Uniquely, one group of enthusiasts organised a testimonial earlier in his career to send him to South Africa and another group, in South Africa, organised one to send him home!*

Dawson's decline left Stevenson, still in his twenties, and approaching his prime, as number one, though no Championship was promoted after 1903 until Inman was declared champion in 1908, partly because in 1904 Stevenson had appealed in vain that the choice of tables for Championship matches should rest with the players and not the Association. Roberts was still active until 1906 when he played his last public match against Diggle and in 1905 conceded Stevenson 2,000 in 18,000 at the Caxton Hall for £500 with Stevenson wagering a further £100 that he won by more than his start. Stevenson won by 1,520, so in a sense honours were even – which may not entirely have been a coincidence. The players shared a £2,500 gate for the fortnight.

Roberts's eyesight was not what it had been but in the year of his retirement he made 1,486 in a minute short of two hours against J. Duncan in Glasgow, 23,509 in twenty-four hours and a break of 519 in twenty-seven minutes. Roberts also brought a future world champion into the game in Tom Newman, born at Barton-on-Humber, Lincolnshire in 1894. He made his first century at the age of eleven, a 500 at fifteen and beat Roberts by 2,000 when receiving 5,000 in 18,000 when still in his teens. This led to a three year contract in which he toured with Roberts, though on their trip to Canada the doyen of Billiards suffered a bout of pneumonia which was indirectly to hasten his retirement.

Diggle was still a good player though he had stopped improving and, with players like Tom Aiken, the Scottish champion, obstinately remaining a fraction short of the top, the immediate rising challenge was represented by Inman, originally a Twickenham marker, and Tom Reece, an Oldham knotter, whose first sporting interest was swimming and who came into contact with

---

*One glorious tale survives of Mitchell and Harverson arriving for an exhibition so far gone that their first attempt to hit an object-ball was an abject failure. "There will now be a short interval", declared the harassed promoter, thus bringing to an end the shortest session on record.

Billiards only because he had to pass through a Billiard room on his way to the swimming pool.

Inman, a great competitor and stroke player with a flat stance and thrust-out bridge arm, possessed the gift of irritating his opponents to the detriment of their performances. One aspect of this was his habit of roughing up the nap of the cloth as he was playing and there was a bizarre incident in a match with the easy-going Harverson when the latter went to the table with the table brush in his hand, and a three way wrestle for possession of it between the two players and the referee ensued.

Reece mastered the anchor cannon – discovered by J.P. Mannock, the coach, and one of his pupils, Captain Trevor Key, on Mannock's own table at Buckingham Gate and first exhibited to the public by Walter Lovejoy (see page 29) – to such an extent that he compiled a break of 499,135 against Joe Chapman at Burroughes and Watts, Soho Square, in 1907. With the two object-balls suspended on either jaw of a top pocket (see diagram) Reece went on and on at the rate of about 10,000 per session for some five weeks.

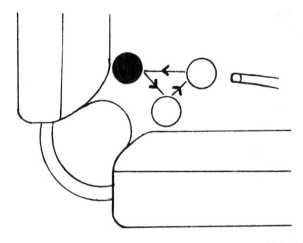

Reece, who was not particularly fond of Chapman, indulged his biting sense of humour by such remarks to his hapless opponent as "What chalk do you use?" until Chapman departed in disgust. An official record certificate was refused on the grounds that press and public were not present throughout the break (although the referee, W.H. Jordan, was), but there is no doubt that it was made. However, the anchor stroke was then barred.

The Billiards Association was governing the game ineffectually, but in 1908, to get the Championship going again, Inman was declared Champion, a title he successfuly defended against Albert Williams, who subsequently settled in Australia, in 1909. Amid the dissatisfaction with the Billiards Association, however, the Billiards Control Club, a new body which, as its name implied, actually operated from club premises, assumed control of the professional game when it declared Stevenson champion in April 1909.

Stevenson, a dapper man from Hull with an attractive all round game, twice justified their opinion, in October 1910 and April 1911, by beating Inman for the title, though their first match for the Championship in April 1910 was abandoned three-quarters of the way through when Stevenson's wife died.

Soon, though, the leading British exponents were forced to yield the limelight for, just as the spot stroke had threatened to dominate the game in the 1880's and 1890's, the Australian George Gray seemed certain to dominate the second decade of the twentieth century through his mastery of in-offs. With a total command of a relatively limited range of shots and the intensity of concentration needed to repeat them endlessly, Gray achieved virtual perfection with the short range in-off into the middle pocket, gauging the strength of the table so well that the red travelled up the table and back off the top cushion to within an inch or so of its original position. When the red dropped short, position was restored by playing an in-off into one of the top pockets and bringing the red round off three cushions for middle pocket in-off position again.

With balls (composition) and cushions (Rileys) of his own selection he could make a thousand break more or less when he liked. Once at Manchester his opponent/road-manager George Nelson wanted to catch a train to get home to his family for the weekend. The last train on Saturday was at nine fifteen and the session did not end until ten o'clock but Nelson made sure that Gray was in play just after nine o'clock and caught his train secure in the knowledge that Gray would play out time.

Gray was so good, in fact, that the general opinion was that the only way to beat him was either to revive the spot stroke (now barred) or to introduce new legislation limiting the in-off game. In the event, neither proved necessary, for a complicated series of wrangles over the make of ball to be used in Championships, and various forms of pressure which tend to build up at the point where a young man realises that there is more to professional sport than simply playing his chosen game to the best of his ability, combined to undermine him when his chance for the title came.

Playing with composition balls (Crystalate), the nineteen year old Gray made 23 breaks over 1,000 in winning all his thirty-one matches in the 1910–11 season. His top break of 2,196 (against Harverson) was some way ahead of his second best, 1,576, but his consistency was phenomenal. In Cardiff he made 289 consecutive middle pocket in-offs.

Gray was simply in a class of his own, beating Inman 16,000–7,231 at the National Sporting Club in a match in which, at one session, he denied his opponent even one shot. In another, he allowed Diggle only three shots in two days. As a parting shot, Inman challenged him to a rematch with ivory balls but no one took his chances seriously.

Gray did, though, in September 1911, encounter an unexpected defeat in England at the hands of a Darlington linotype operator, Willie Smith, who was himself to become champion in 1923. Smith received halfway start in 4,500 and actually scored more points than the Australian. He beat him again, receiving 400 in 1,500, and in an interview in 1975 said: "Gray wasn't a Billiards player at all. He could only play in-offs. He was with George Nelson and Riley's. He had one set of cushions and two table frames he used to take round with him and one roll of cloth which they took a length off every match he played, but we played on a Burroughes and Watts table with a thicker cloth. He couldn't get a long loser."

During the second season in Britain, Gray was, for financial considerations, in the course of adjusting from Crystalate to Bonzoline; and though he was still good enough to beat Stevenson, the champion, level, in two matches out of three, the thousands came less frequently. It did not help that John Roberts, who had originally brought him to England, sued him through his father/manager Harry Gray for breach of contract, Gray having failed to fulfil a commitment to play Diggle. Roberts, it seemed, was contracted to promote with Bonzoline and not Crystalate. Gray's father refused to let the match take place with Bonzoline because, he alleged, Roberts had failed to disclose any such condition when the contract was signed.

Roberts sued for £2,600 and was awarded £1,500. The Grays stalled, were examined under the Fraudulent Debtors Act in a Melbourne court and were declared insolvent until eventually a well known horse trainer brought Roberts and Gray together to agree an out of court settlement. Gray subsequently switched to Bonzoline (when it suited him) to add weight to the view that the breach of contract was a business double-cross instigated by Gray's father.

Still further fogging the issue were ivories which were still the balls chiefly used in clubs and halls and indeed for the Championship itself despite being somewhat unpredictable in throw and angle and inconsistent from set to set.

Stevenson, pleading ill health (but not so ill that it prevented him playing a full British season and a lucrative South African and Indian tour with Gray, making a 1,016 break in sixty-two minutes on his return) chose not to defend the title and Inman won it in 1912 by beating Reece easily.

Reece was Inman's only challenger the following season and gave the holder a much closer match, the penultimate session producing breaks of 535 by Reece (wiping out Inman's lead) and 522 by Inman (restoring it). The amount of safety play can be gauged from the fact that Inman scored 196 by misses and coups and Reece 181, though this only partly accounted for the low averages of 26.9 for Inman and 24.8 for Reece.

Having categorically stated his opposition to ivories, the Championship ball, Gray eventually agreed to play with them and entered the 1914 Championship. Though his top break of 1,199 with Bonzolines was well below his 2,196 with Crystalates, the leading exponents were not a little fearful of the potency of Gray's specialised in-off method of scoring. Inman proposed that if Gray won the Championship the rules should be amended so that after 33 consecutive in-offs the red should be automatically placed on its spot. Stevenson suggested that after 20 red in-offs the next should be played with the cue-ball on the centre spot in baulk.

But, in the event, Gray's switch to ivories made such steps unnecessary for he produced scarcely fifty per cent of his true form in the Championship, Reece forging 1,000 in front after two days, 2,000 after four days and winning very easily. Reece then came from 1,000 behind to beat Stevenson in a semi-final which overran until the Monday morning before he started his final against Inman in the afternoon. Inman, aided by a Championship record of 744 in seventy minutes, won by over 5,000 to retain the title. Gray challenged Inman for £250–£500 with ivory balls level, 18,000 up, but Inman, who later that year beat Stevenson level for the first time, coolly referred him to the next Championship. The outbreak of war meant, however, that the next Championship was not until 1919 so Gray, who had looked certain to dominate the professional scene, never even challenged again for the title.

Tall, quiet, unassuming, Gray suffered, one can now say with hindsight, from the domination of his father. When he was practising, which he was for most of his waking hours, his father was so insistent that the cue should go through horizontally that he administered a sharp blow to his elbow with a walking stick from behind if he should raise the butt by as much as a fraction. With his decent sense of filial duty, Gray seems to have felt keenly that he had let his father down by not winning the Championship. He was never the same again and eventually his game disintegrated completely. Indeed, when he played Fred Lindrum in 1934, he was unable to record a single century in the whole week. His cue arm at the back, just where his father used to rap it with his stick to remind him to keep it down, was uncontrollably unsteady.

# CHAPTER IV

# The Early Amateurs

## (Amateur Billiards 1888–1929)

Until sport ceased to be synonymous simply with recreation or gambling and amateur competitions began to be formally organised and not the outcome of wagers, no one thought it worth while to chronicle the activities of any but the best players, that is, the professionals.

In the beginning, anyone who was good enough was a professional and the rest were amateurs. A little later, when the amateur ethic became a potent force, the upper classes jealously guarded their exclusive empire within the game which they controlled by a rigidly strict definition of professionalism which excluded from amateur competition not only those who made a living from playing but those who, regardless of their standard of play, were associated with the game in any professional capacity, like managing a billiard hall, or who, it seemed, had had any contact at all with a professional.

This kind of distinction was made in every sport in Britain. And moreover because Britain, then standing at the head of an imposing empire, virtually controlled the sporting world, this led to the upper classes controlling not only amateur Billiards but also – partly because the professional players were too busy playing to bother with organisation and administration – the professional game. It was also a time when the professional sportsmen did not command a prestigious position on the social scale and the players themselves thus accepted that it was in the natural order of things for their livelihoods to be governed or at least affected by part time amateur enthusiasts whose attitude towards them was paternal at best, indifferent or even hostile: in short, the narrowly defined GENTLEMEN AND PLAYERS situation.

In fact, the very first Amateur Championship in 1888 was bedevilled by controversy over exactly what constituted amateur status. Orme and Sons, the table makers, had presented a silver cup valued at £100 for an Amateur Championship, the cup to become the property of anyone who won it three times in succession or six in all, but S.S. Christey, who beat W.D. Courtney in the Southern division (the forty-four competitors from England, Scotland and Ireland being divided into four areas) was then objected to by Courtney on the grounds that he was a professional.

Christey had indeed played with professionals at a tournament at the Royal Aquarium the previous year which had been announced as "Open to Amateurs and Markers" but Courtney's objection was nevertheless upheld. Not satisfied with the decision, Christey pursued the matter with the Billiards Association who eventually reinstated him, but meanwhile the players whom Christey had beaten claimed the right to play again. H.A.O. Lonsdale (Manchester) thus became the first champion.

Thence ensued a number of contests on the challenge principle, the challengers eliminating each other until one survived to challenge the champion. Christey, in 1888, made the first Championship century, 136, but it was not until the sixth championship in 1890, that there was another, 114, by A.P. Gaskell (London), a useful spot stroke exponent, who retired the cup (and himself) after his sixth championship in 1890.

Courtney won the title later that year and retained it in 1891 but achieved wider fame that year by replying to a newspaper challenge issued to all and sundry by Inman, later the professional champion but then only an aspiring marker.

Courtney replied loftily: "W.D. Courtney does not profess to know anything of markers' form but to encourage rising talent he will give M. Inman 2,000 start in 8,000 up for £25 a side." Inman won by over 4,000 points and a return match level. "The cost of encouraging rising talent" became a standing joke and the episode finished Courtney as a player.

Orme's had meanwhile presented another trophy. The Billiards Association in May 1892 also decided to run another Championship (all in), won by Christey, and Orme's, after their 1893 event had been won by Arthur Wisdom (Southsea), then amicably left the field to them. Christey, who had had 98 spots in his record 297, was not challenged for all All-In Cup within the stipulated three years and thus retained it.

The regulations for the second 1893 event in March (conducted by the Billiards Association) were a trifle cumbrous in that Wisdom, who had won the cup twice, was required to play S.H. Fry, who had emerged from the challengers, two games of 1,000 up. If Fry won *twice* (as he did by 11 and 315) a further 1,500 up would decide the Championship. This too Fry won.

Yet a third 1893 event had been a new Spot Barred Championship won by an Indian, A.H. Vahid. Subsequent championships were played spot barred but it was not until 1896 that the push stroke was also barred. Fry recorded his second Championship win in that year and held the title only eleven days short of the three years that would have given him permanent possession of the cup. Technically, as the spot barred game had been abolished, he could have refused to play all in as the rules now required. As it was, he was beaten by Wisdom but regained the title the following year.

A first round match in the 1901 event between W.S. Jones and E.C. Breed, later a professional, saw Breed leading 500–489 at the interval, at which point Sydenham Dixon, the Hon. Secretary of the Billiards Association, announced the death of the Queen and stated that there would be no more play until after the funeral. On the belated resumption, Jones won by 5 but lost to Christey in the final.

A.W.T. Good, a red ball specialist, recorded the first two of his four titles in 1902. His victory over Christey, like himself a publican, saw him average 12.6 to Christey's 10.6 so standards were still very modest compared with professionals. Good's Championship record of 155 (153 off the red) was made against A.J. Browne later that year but his overall average was still only 9.1 while Browne, with a top break of 49, managed only 7.6.

Wisdom's fourth title success in 1903 included a 153 break against Christey and a record 18.6 session average but the second Championship of 1903, in December, saw the challengers' tournament become the Championship itself when Wisdom withdrew because of the death of his father-in-law. In this way, the Championship gained one of its most eccentric finalists, C.V. Diehl, whose precarious niche in the world of journalism was that of a weather prophet. Wearing felt slippers and exhibiting an extraordinary wide apart stance, Diehl disposed of Good in some strange way in the semi-final, though he averaged only 8.3 and made a top break of only 54 but failed to recapture even this modest peak in the final when Christey won with 8.4 to Diehl's 6.9 to become champion for the third time.

Christey did not defend in 1905 and Walter Lovejoy, who had a very unorthodox upright style and played with a twelve ounce cue, revealed a much higher standard with breaks of 135 and 103 in a first session average of 17.2 in the final. Lovejoy became the first amateur champion to turn professional and was the first to exploit in public the anchor cannon discovered by J.P. Mannock and perfected by Reece in his 499,135 break. Lovejoy, a very tall man, always argued that the 2'10" from the ground at which the table was set was an unfair disadvantage to such as he and issued an open challenge to play anyone for £500 on a 3'1" table. In 1910, playing Harverson, he fetched a stool and played a series of middle pocket in-offs from a seated position.

In 1905, the Championship, previously confined almost entirely to Londoners with a sprinkling of wealthy provincials, was thrown open to the whole of the United Kingdom with qualifying rounds in London, Manchester and Dublin. George Heginbottom compiled an amateur championship record of 174 in the final but could not prevent Good winning his third title.

Edward Breed won in 1906 in York and turned professional, possibly because Sydenham Dixon, who was the Billiard Association President from 1906 to 1919, was known to favour a definition of professionalism which would have excluded him anyway. Dixon, a sporting journalist, had a pragmatic attitude to organising championships and not only admitted but was wont to boast that the draw was fully "arranged" during his presidency.

Harry Virr of Bradford then won the title six years out of the next eight. Major Fleming, a redoubtable Scot, won it in 1909 and Lonsdale, twelve years after his first success, in 1910, though he made only 1 century to Fleming's 3.

Lonsdale did not defend in 1911 as he thought the final should be played in Manchester in accordance with the previous custom of the holder playing virtually at home but the finals were actually played in Dublin. Relations between Lonsdale and the Billiards Association deteriorated when, on flimsy grounds, the Association autocratically suspended him for professionalism – in fact for having played Stevenson four times for charity. *The Billiards Monthly* ran an article by its legal correspondent stating that the suspension constituted a libel. Lonsdale sued but the court failed to find malice on the part of the Association and also concluded that though Lonsdale was technically in breach of one of its published regulations its suspension did not make him no longer an amateur. Nevertheless, to protect itself against future libel actions, the Association prudently made itself into a limited company.

Virr, a fine red ball player and tough competitor, probably produced his best in 1912 when his four session averages in a heat were 14, 22, 29 and 35. This year produced the closest Amateur Championship final of all time when Virr scraped home only by 7 over Fleming.

J.G. Taylor (Walsall) compiled a new Championship record of 210 (150 off the red) in the Midland section in 1913, only to have this superseded by Fry with 236 in the Championship proper. With conditions altered so that the holder had to play through, Virr had to dispose of Fry in the English final when the second session of their match saw Virr average 33.5 and Fry 31.5, the first occasion when both players had averaged over 30. Virr's semi-final break of 171 was a new red ball record.

The 1914 event was again won by Virr but in this year a rival championship was conducted under the auspices of the Billiards Control Club which attracted some of the leading players, Major Fleming beating Fry in the first round and going on to beat R. Hill-New in the final.

Sidney Fry, a championship class golfer and all round sportsman, and J. Graham-Symes, a London solicitor, between them held the championship from 1916–1922, Fry winning four times and Graham-Symes twice. Fry had reached the final in 1890 and had made a Championship record of 168 in 1899 but this was to be his best period.

In 1921 he disposed of the Australian champion, J.R. Hooper, in the semi-final, 2,000–1,720 though Hooper made a break of 228 all off the red. This meeting of English and Australian champions, foreshadowing future Empire and World Championships, created enormous interest and provided the match of the tournament, Hooper leading 666–332 at the end of the first of the three sessions only for Fry to outpoint him 1,002–579 in a three and a half hour second period to lead by 87. The match was, of course, played with ivories of which Hooper, who had played mostly with Composition, had had little experience. The previous year, incidentally, Arthur Walker, a South African millionaire, had proposed an Empire Championship which the Billiards Association had turned down as impracticable.

W.P. McLeod, a Middlesbrough man with a small plumbing business, beat Fry in the 1922 semi-final but went down to Graham-Symes in the final when the latter had only 1 century and an average of 12.8. McLeod, the first member of the artisan class to cut much ice in the Championship, had had little experience with ivories as he was accustomed to the cheaper Composition ball but he was able to reverse this result in the final of the following year and win again in 1924, though he then toured so extensively that questions were asked about his amateur status. He thus withdrew from the 1925 event to clear his name, and Fry, aged 57, and thirty-two years after his first success, won the title for the eighth time, a record since equalled by Leslie Driffield and exceeded only by Norman Dagley.

In 1926, amid great controversy, Composition balls replaced ivory for the Championship and Graham-Symes, among many others, said that he would not enter. "Amongst the middle and upper middle classes there is very little doubt that ivory balls are in general use", he said. "Then why should these classes be sacrificed for the lower middle and working classes?"

The switch from ivory to Composition and the reduction of the entry fee from £2.2s. to 10s.6d. opened up the Championship considerably.

McLeod had cleared himself of professionalism but was hurt in a motor cycle accident and did not compete, but Joe Earlam, a twenty year old from Runcorn, proved an outstanding champion.

He set a new Championship record of 278 (165 off the red) and 286 (261 off the red) in the Liverpool area and clocked up 435 points in thirty-three minutes but made no secret of his intention of using the Amateur Championship as a stepping stone to a professional career and this was resented in some quarters.

Laurie Steeples, another exceptionally talented newcomer, perhaps more so in the all round sense than Earlam, who was essentially a red ball player, made a 377 break in the Sheffield section against Charlie Simpson, a very fluent left-hander whose family connection with Billiard halls caused him soon to be designated a professional.

The Championship clearly lay between Earlam and Steeples but the B.A. and C.C.'s failure to seed the thirty-two man draw for the competition proper meant that Earlam's victory by 511 in the semi-final (all games except the final were only 1,000 up) with breaks of 273 and 107 made him virtually a certainty for the title.

This was because the bottom half was so weak that C.M. Helyer (Middlesbrough) who had beaten Lewis Stroud (London) by 4 in the first round, when his highest break was 50 and his average 8, and F. Nichols (Leeds) by 71 in the second, when his highest break was 41 and his average 10, came through to the final, on the last day of which Earlam had runs of 247, 183 and 118 and a 30 average. Earlam averaged 20.8 for the match and Helyer, who did not make a century, 11.8.

Immediately following this, Earlam walked away with the first British Empire Championship at Thurston's, an event for which overseas nations had been pressing for some years but which the B.A. and C.C., with their customary foresight, had resisted. In September 1922, however, the event was approved in principle with Bonzoline balls (not ivory) to be used, with the winner's country staging again two years later.

Various delays occurred. A. Stanley Thorn, Secretary of the B.A. and C.C., said he was not really in favour of an Empire Championship as the Amateur Championship was quite sufficient. The B.A. and C.C. favoured a straight knockout but South Africa held out for a round robin and won the day. Scotland meanwhile decided to opt out of the Amateur Championship by running their own self-contained National Championship rather than an elimination event for the Championship itself. The B.A. and C.C. in turn decided that their Championship was not open to Scottish, Irish or colonial players but continued to accept entries from Wales. Australia sent an entry from George Shailer for the "Open Championship of English Billiards" but this was later transferred to the Empire Championship.

When this took place, it was a dire financial failure. Earlam outclassed the field with a 83 session average against Percy Rutledge (South Africa) and a string of big breaks. He beat Shailer 2,000 (29.4) – 1,394 (20.8) in the deciding match.

Earlam immediately turned professional but could not bridge the huge gulf in class that this represented. A few years previously, Fry had needed a start of half the game to narrowly beat Reece. Willie Smith, then at the height of his powers, gave Earlam 10,000 start in 20,000 and beat him 20,000–15,925, a hammering from which Earlam never recovered, for after two or three years on the professional fringes he dropped out of the game altogether.

Earlam's success in the amateur ranks also caused the adoption in 1927 of the 25 hazard rule which had been introduced to the Professional Championship the previous year. Red ball play was still the dominant factor, though, as Steeples beat Horace Coles 3,000 (18.9) – 2,449 (15.5) in the final.

Steeples made a break of 233 in the semi-final and 212 in the final.

With Arthur Walker again guaranteeing a South African entry, this time the six foot five inch policeman Allan Prior, to join one each from England, Scotland and Wales, the Empire Championship was repeated in London the following year when Prior, a slow, careful, accurate player, surprisingly won it by defeating both Coles (Wales) 2,000–1,438 and Steeples 2,000–1,563. Prior's 21.3 average against Steeples was the best of the tournament and Steeples's 236 break was a tournament record.

Steeples's father then died and he did not enter the 1928 English Championship. Neither did McLeod and Simpson's entry was not accepted. Bert Good, the red ball specialist, re-entered after an absence of thirteen years and compiled a 268 Championship record in reaching the final where he was beaten by Arthur Wardle (Manchester), who thus won the title at his first attempt, his semi-final win by 247 over Coles being the key.

The following year, Wardle failed to emerge from the Manchester qualifying area when he was beaten by Maurice Boggin – this being prior to the days when champions were given exemption until the competition proper – and had his entry rejected for the 1930 event on the grounds of professionalism, as McLeod's was in 1929. The irony here was that this was the first year that previous winners were excused the area qualifying rounds.

During the 1929 Championship, Coles equalled Earlam's session average record of 83 – though Coles's feat was performed under the new limitation – and made 6 centuries in 2,000 up against F.V. Stacey. Coles won the title though Boggin, starting with a fluke, increased the Championship break record to 349.

The third British Empire Championship at the Carlton Hotel, Johannesburg, in 1929 saw Coles, who had represented Wales in 1927, representing England, but victory went to a slow, deliberate red ball player, Les Hayes, an Australian schoolteacher who had acceded to the Australian Association's request to sign an agreement not to turn professional for at least three years afterwards. Not one 20 match average was recorded. Hayes beat Coles 2,000–1,676 and Prior 2,000–1,512 in the vital matches and Prior beat Coles 2,000–1,916 for second place. Prior's break of 266 was a new South African record.

Louis XIV playing Billiards at Versailles

The drawing room of William Dufton, a nineteenth century professional

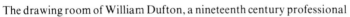

William Cook (in play) against John Roberts in their championship match on February 11, 1870 at St. James's Hall

**Facing page** Melbourne Inman

William Mitchell

Tom Reece

Edward Diggle

Charles Dawson

H.W. Stevenson

W.J. Peall

**Below** Tom Newman

# CHAPTER V

# The Twenties
## (Professional Billiards 1919–1929)

The war ended in 1918 but there was no truce between Inman and Reece, whose rivalry had become legendary. Each provided the perfect foil for the other. Reece was a temperamental, artistic touch player, Inman a supreme competitor, the master of frustrating safety tactics. Reece's taste was for close, delicately controlled play, Inman's for all round play with the balls kept at medium or even long distance. Inman was good at forcing shots while Reece's attitude to them was one almost of revulsion. Nothing ever upset Inman but anything could upset Reece. And if he was upset he would not talk to anyone for days on end.

They did not like each other but, almost like those marriages which remain on the point of disintegration for over fifty years, their constant mutual chipping satisfied some kind of emotional need. In their first match, in 1903, Inman gave 16 consecutive safety misses and Reece 15; a couple of days later, Inman gave 10 and Reece 9. Reece led until the last 400 points, but Inman won.

In 1921, Reece beat Inman by 334 in 18,000 in a match in Sydney and told a local newspaper: "Inman has always been on my shoulders. He has unnerved me, made me anxious and fretful and haunted me like a nightmare. Now I have thrown him off." He had not, for Inman was to win most of their matches until well into the 1930's.

Inman's open and sometimes forcing style of play tended to produce a few flukes – much to Reece's displeasure.

"How did you do that?" asked Reece acidly after one such.

"I believe you know my terms for tuition, Mr. Reece", replied Inman implacably.

On another occasion they were playing in a provincial hall when two urchins briefly put their heads round the door.

"Put it across him, Tommy", yelled one inelegantly.

"Would you mind telling your friends to be quiet, Mr. Reece", said Inman.

Either could flourish without the other as straight man. Inman, who was an erratic motorist, left a club one night after giving an exhibition, only to mow down a row of red lamps. As the night watchman emerged from his hut to remonstrate, Inman roared: "I've taken all the reds. Where are the bloody colours?" and disappeared into the night.

A local official irritated him at another exhibition by carrying the rest round with him as he alternately fielded out and stood stock still as a shot was played.

Inman endured it for a few minutes until he finally exploded: "For God's sake, put that away. You look like bloody Neptune stood there."

Reece was once playing an exhibition in a sergeants' mess when his opponent, playing downwards as the cue-ball lay near a cushion, mis-cued violently and tore the cloth. "The sergeant was attempting to play a cannon THROUGH the table", Reece explained helpfully.

His contempt for Snooker, which was gaining popularity in the halls, knew no bounds. "A game to be played in corduroys and clogs" and "an excellent game for navvies to play in their lunch hour" were two typically scathing verdicts.

One of Inman's successes was their semi-final in the 1919 Championship but Reece, nothing daunted, appeared on the final night of Inman's comfortable final win over Stevenson. Lord Alverston, then President of the Billiards Association, who had earlier that week sentenced the notorious Dr. Crippen to death, was just handing over the cup to Inman when Reece interjected: "Excuse me, my lord. But if you knew as much as I do about Inman, you would have given Crippen the cup and sentenced Inman to death."

Inman did not think it right that the champion should have to play through the event so did not enter the 1920 Championship in which Willie Smith recorded a record average of 51.4 in beating Claude Falkiner to win the title. Inman arrived at the last night of the match to deliver himself of a strange speech in which he referred to himself as undefeated champion.

"Of course you are", said Smith. "If you don't enter, you can't be beaten."

One thing led to another and the outcome was one of the great money matches of the age for which Thurston's took an amazing (at the time) £1,800. Inman started at 11–10 on and Smith allowed him to lead by 1,000, but once his backers had managed to place all the bets they wanted, Smith cut loose and won by over 4,000.

Smith had arrived, not just by winning the official Championship, but by becoming number one in the public eye by beating the champion who had decided not to enter. It reproduced the situation of the John Roberts era and anticipated the time when Smith himself and then Walter Lindrum stood out of the Championship at the respective times when each would have won it.

Monetary considerations were much involved. Smith and Inman both decided to scratch from the 1921 Championship, for which they both entered, because the Association's intention was to promote it at Thurston's, which seated only one hundred and seventy-two spectators, rather than a larger hall where not only could more money have been taken but cheaper seats could have been available for the "Working classes" or "average chap". Smith, who never forgot his days as a linotype operator, always regarded these enthusiasts as his best supporters though this was not only a question of background but of style, for Smith's pattern of play was not dissimilar from that of any useful amateur – only twenty times more consistent. He did not go in for long repetitive runs of specialist strokes (his contempt for "cushion crawlers" when nursery cannons virtually took over the professional game in the 1930's amounted almost to paranoia) so his all round common man type of game was always varied and interesting.

Smith never forgot, either, that, at fifteen, he had been declared a professional for accepting 10s.6d. expenses for playing at Middlesbrough Conservative Club. His lasting sense of resentment with governing bodies led him to become awkward, cussed and, at times, mulishly unwilling to do anything which he himself had not suggested.

Meanwhile, Smith's and Inman's defection from the 1921 Championship left six aspirants: Falkiner, Stevenson, Reece, Fred Lawrence, Tom Tothill and Tom Newman. Newman, in 1914, receiving 2,000, had won all his matches in the big professional handicap at Burroughes and Watts by double the points which had been conceded to him though he had twice been narrowly beaten by Smith in week-long matches. Nevertheless, it was apparent, even then, that Newman and Smith were two of the game's rising stars. Newman took longer to reach the top but his temperament was more uncertain than Smith's. He also had a suspect cue action with his cue arm pulled round his back, a defect which made him fallible at long range, at difficult opening shots and at potting.

There was, though, nothing wrong with his delicacy of touch and close control and, with Smith and Inman out of the way, he came through to win the 1921 Championship. He made a 467 break and averaged 54 in beating Tothill 8,000–3,267, breaks of 627, 531, 492, 401 and an average of 56.7 in beating Falkiner 8,000–6,627 in the semi-final and slaughtered Reece 16,000–10,744 in the final. To cap this, he recorded a 1,024 break against Lawrence at Burroughes which was the first thousand by non-specialised strokes under the then current rules.

Falkiner and Stevenson went off on tour to South Africa where a young New Zealander, Clark McConachy, beat the former by more than his start. Stevenson's tour was to last twenty-one months and fifty thousand miles (taking in South and East Africa, India, Burma, China, Japan, New Zealand and Australia) but his most significant meeting was with the young Walter Lindrum, a left-hander and then a red ball player. Young Lindrum made a break of 1,417 against the old champion in beating him 16,000–6,545 in Sydney, at one stage making 7,348 points out of 8,000 off the red. Stevenson, who was also on the end of a 713 red ball break in losing to Fred Lindrum, was loud in his scorn of the methods employed but there was no arguing with the scoreboard.

Lindrum and McConachy were obviously future Championship contenders and in this same year, 1921, another appeared in Joe Davis who made his debut in the St. Dunstan's professional handicap at Thurston's. Receiving 100 in 250 from Aiken, the old Scottish champion, Davis compiled a 147 break at his first visit and went on to lose in the semi-final to Lawrence where he crucially over-looked the relatively new rule forbidding two consecutive safety misses without an intervening score and saw his opponent run out in a close finish.

On his twentieth birthday, Davis was beaten 7,000–6,134 on his home table at the Victoria Billiard Hall, Chesterfield, by Lawrence for the Midland Professional Championship but then, remarkably, scored 2,740 in two sessions on the last day to beat Albert Raynor, the Sheffield man who had given him his first professional match, by a mere 123. He took second prize of £15 in the Second Division Championship behind Arthur Peall, beat Lawrence to win the Midland title at the second attempt and then, having been 500 behind going into the last day, beat Peall 7,000–6,857 to win the Second Division title and go into the Championship proper.

Smith and Inman again stood out of the 1922 Championship for the same reason as before, though Newman had murdered Inman in a fortnight's match 16,000 (609, 606, 582) – 11,759 (565) and Falkiner, who had returned from his tour much improved, beat Smith before losing a return. Newman lost to Smith by only 255 and then, against Falkiner, made a new world record of 1,274 terminated by a foul stroke when his cue grazed the object-white. The match between Newman and Smith to decide the round robin Burroughes and Watts tournament was virtually for the game's number one position but there was, strangely, hardly any safety play and Newman won 16,000 (57.1 average) – 15,697 (56.3).

In the Championship, Reece beat McConachy but then lost to Falkiner after being 1,441 in front after five sessions, Falkiner eventually running out with 371 to win by 711. Newman, at this stage, was much too good for Davis but then had a great battle in the final as Falkiner, trailing by 1,908 at halfway, compiled 562 and 312 in succession and actually got his nose in front both on the second Wednesday and Thursday.

On the latter occasion, Newman replied with 292 and 304 unfinished to lead by 242 at the end of the session and carried this break to 710 but there was still only 238 in it going into the last day before a final spurt saw Newman home by 833. The averages, 56.4 for Newman and 52.7 for Falkiner, were Championship records and in the first week Newman recorded session averages of 174, 221 and 133 in succession.

As in the previous year, having won the Championship, Newman again had yet to prove that he was number one and embarked on seven test matches against Smith round the country. Smith aggregated 110,266 to 109,334 but all matches were close and reporters commented on the regularity with which a player holding a substantial lead was caught.

At least in 1923 the Championship was a true test, for Smith and Newman played a tough final. Smith led by 975 after the first day but Newman, who had made a new Championship record of 850 in the semi-final, got in front on the twenty-first of the twenty-four sessions only for Smith to win by 820. Smith's top breaks of 451 and 446 were below Newman's best of 638, 629 and 575 but, as was generally the case in their matches, he was the more consistent.

Smith and Newman were clearly the two best players and set new record fortnight's averages of 89.9 and 86.9 respectively in a match at Burroughes and Watts, with whom Smith had just signed what was at that time an exceptionally attractive contract, but Smith's relationship with the governing body, always uneasy, took a turn for the worse when he submitted his entry for the 1924 Championship two hours late. It was also conditional on not playing before April 14 and the avoidance of any clash with a match he had arranged with Inman on dates officially set aside for the Championship. His entry was rejected.

He pushed up his personal best break to 922 and then 974 – and sat out Newman's third four figure break, 1,208, which started with a fluke. Davis, whose previous best had been 599, made a 980 in the Second Division Championship but did not take up his option to play in the Championship proper. £200 was the entry fee for the Championship and since £6-7 was considered a good fee for one-night exhibitions, and week's matches were uncertain financial propositions, this was considered steep. Even Newman and Smith were charging only £60 a week.

McConachy, again over from New Zealand (though looking back from his eightieth year he was to lament that every one of his trips to Britain left him worse off than before), lost by nearly half the game to Newman who, having played fifteen weeks with Smith (in one of which he averaged 98 to Smith's 102) was as match tight as anyone could be.

Newman recorded the first Championship thousand, 1,021, in the final against Reece, the only other entry, but the Oldham man gave him a rougher ride than anyone considered imaginable, leading 8,000–7,446 at halfway and by 236 on the second Tuesday. On the Friday afternoon, he scored 997 for a 99 average while Newman scored 668 for 60 but the champion proved good enough to get home by 1,155 points.

There was action in Australia where Falkiner played Walter Lindrum, then twenty-six, and substantially helped him develop the nursery cannon technique with which he was, a decade later, to dominate professional Billiards to such an extent that he and his closest rivals were to kill the game as a spectacle. Actually, it could not have been too spectacular to witness the Gray-like methods with which Lindrum compiled a break of 1,589 against Falkiner after losing the white at 292.

Even in 1924, breaks and averages were increasing to the point where various artificial curbs were actively discussed. Newman officially suggested placing the red on the pyramid spot after it had been potted from its own spot and that the D should be removed and only the three spots, on one of which the cue-ball would have to be placed when playing from hand, should remain. He played a match with Tothill in which, upon his reaching 200 in a break and Tothill 125, the balls were spotted and the game continued by playing at the red first.

Tothill himself lent his name to, of all things, a green billiard cue claimed to "positively improve anyone's game. This exciting invention relieves eye strain and sharpens the vision. The green tint of the shaft contrasts with the white ball, at the same time hiding the grain of the wood." In 1927, Inman made a break of 642 on a table with $3\frac{1}{4}''$ pockets but this attempt to make the game more difficult was not popular with the public.

Even allowing for the fact that the Australians were using Composition balls while professionals in Britain were still playing with ivories, Lindrum was already an exceptional player. He beat Falkiner in two out of three of their matches, averaging 108 for the fortnight in the last and making a break of 1,219 to Falkiner's best of 1,001; but the latter was unsuccessful in his attempts to persuade him to visit Britain where the British professionals were keen for the time being to preserve ivories as their chosen ball, as they felt confident of beating any colonial challengers, like Lindrum, with them.

In the new home season of 1924–5, Davis started to come through by beating Newman (receiving 6,000) and Reece, level, by 4,970 with a break of 702 and several 100 session averages but the Championship was in a shambles, Smith pulling out after signifying his intention to enter, to leave Newman and Reece as the only two entries, Reece having entered only because he thought Inman was going to. Reece put in breaks of 512, 335 and 335 on the first three days but Newman made 957 and 672 on the fourth day and won by almost 6,000 points.

Reece, incidentally, left the hall a few minutes from the end of his match with Davis, still in play, needing only a few more points to win. As he reached the street, he threw his hat in the air and cried: "Hurray, Davis has beaten Old Reece!"

Davis, receiving 3,000 in 9,000, beat Smith by 831 at Liverpool and receiving 2,500 in 7,500 beat him again at Preston by 621. Receiving 4,000 in 18,000 from

Newman he won by 3,136, but receiving 6,000 in 18,000 from Smith, lost the first match by 520 and won the second by 769, Smith making a 1,047 in their second match. Newman, who had made 60 centuries in a fortnight against Peall, then played Smith in a three Test series, for £50 each match, sponsored by *The News of the World*, with limitations of 25 consecutive hazards off the red and 25 consecutive cannons. Smith won the first two matches by 4,139 and 2,227, leaving Newman a consolation win by 881 in the third, Smith thus confirming in the public eye that he was still number one.

Smith declined to enter the 1926 Championship in which Newman beat Davis, the only other entry, out of sight. The next week, the Championship having served as a mere interlude between *The News of the World* series and this, the last week of the season, Smith made 6 breaks over 500 against Davis at Northampton. The last day of the match was the first of the General Strike and Davis had to buy his first car to get home to Chesterfield.

The conditions for the 1927 Championship made it impossible for Smith to compete without loss of face for the challenge system was resurrected to leave the champion clear until only one challenger remained. The entry fee, reduced to £100 the previous season, was reduced again to £50. Reece was again in the field, rumours having spread that he had discovered an amazing new scoring method. He duly produced it against Inman (who else?) when he made a break of 1,151 by means of the pendulum cannon. This break included 568 consecutive cannons. Gesturing towards his hapless opponent during this sequence, Reece asked "Has that man paid to come in? He's a spectator" – but Inman, as usual, had the last laugh in winning 8,000–5,527.

Reece, in fact, was so preoccupied with trying to obtain pendulum cannon position that he made only 11 centuries in the week while Inman made 28 with a top run of 459. The old champion also gave Davis some trouble in the semi-final, containing him and irritating him with some astute safety play in getting 1,000 in front before Davis cast all caution to the winds to win by 1,105.

The final, at the Orme Hall, Manchester, was the first ever to be held outside London and was also memorable for a break of 2,501 by Davis made by means of the pendulum, which took him from 1,589 behind to 630 in front. That very day Reece was in the midst of a 3,964 break against Arthur Peall at Thurston's and it was obvious that action had to be taken to prevent this stroke from unbalancing the game. Neither was Davis's break enough to prevent Newman from retaining the title, for Newman himself made a 1,012 pendulum break, following an orthodox 1,073 and ultimately clinched the match by playing through the second Saturday afternoon from 73 unfinished to 739 unfinished and in the evening to a completed 891. During the season's play Smith made 66 breaks over 500, Newman 41 and Davis 19. Davis also made his first thousand, 1,011.

Smith, more and more, cast himself in the role of the odd man out and played club exhibitions through most of the 1927–8 season. He would not enter the Championship and he proved such a prickly negotiator that attempts to match him with Newman also proved fruitless. The Championship thus ended in a third Newman/Davis final, though there was an early surprise when Tom Carpenter, the Welsh champion, who struggled valiantly but without real success for many years to break into the top class, beat Reece before losing to Davis.

In the final, Davis made 60 centuries and Newman 50. After the second evening, Davis won every session except two but Newman actually got his nose 24 in front on the second Tuesday before Davis won his first Championship by a margin of 1,126 points. It was the last to be played with ivories for the B.A. and C.C., who had adopted Crystalate balls for the Amateur Championship of 1926, decided to introduce them for the professional event of 1929 and to abolish the challenge principle by making the holder play through.

The introduction of Crystalate immediately saw breaks and averages increase, although in Australia, where ivories had never been used, Lindrum and McConachy were already recording bigger breaks and better averages than those of the Championship final. Lindrum made an 816 break in twenty-three minutes and became the first player to make thousand breaks in consecutive days with 1,380 and 1,415 at Wellington. McConachy was also topping the thousand regularly and occasionally beating Lindrum, but in the 1928-9 season it was Fred Lindrum who came to England to challenge British domination.

Through quotes in newspapers, there had been considerable verbal sparring between Walter Lindrum and Smith (still number one in the public eye) about the possibility of a summit match, but meanwhile Smith fell upon the lesser Lindrum like a hungry lion, averaging no less than 161.6 for the fortnight in beating him by a breathtaking 19,178 points.

Smith made breaks of 1,140, 1,108, 1,108, 1,041 and six more over 900 while Lindrum's highest was 468. It was a family insult which Walter was to wait his chance to avenge. Meanwhile, Fred was completely shattered, lost to Peall conceding him only 1,000 and was 10,000 behind at the end of the first week against Davis when he conceded the match through illness.

Playing with Crystalate, Smith looked as if he would never stop scoring. In the 1928-9 season, he made fifteen thousands and a hundred over 500 while, on the other side of the world, Walter was compiling four thousands in a week, including one of 1,953 against his young nephew Horace, who was confidently expected to become one of the greatest upholders of the Lindrum tradition - a task for which he had the ability but, despite much publicity on his behalf, much of it instigated by his extremely aggressive mother, not the temperament.

Top of Smith's feats was a break of 2,743 against Newman at Manchester on the day of the Manchester November Handicap. He met Jimmy Wilde and Jim Driscoll, two great boxers of the day, and Leo Oppenheimer, a professional backer, for tea. Wilde asked how he was getting on.

"Not bad, I'm 2,250 unfinished", came the reply. Oppenheimer immediately made out a cheque for £500 with which to back him against Lindrum.

"I put a match to it," said Smith. "They couldn't understand it. What was I doing? 'I'm saving your money', I said. 'I've no chance.' I couldn't make them fast enough. I could make a hundred in four or five minutes but if he got the nurseries on he could do it in less than half the time." His prognostications were to prove all too accurate.

Davis and Newman played six Tests with Newman aggregating 52,391 and Davis 50,829. The highest breaks were 925 by Newman and 900 by Davis and the averages 89 for Newman and 87 for his opponent. Davis lost to Smith by only 725 and then beat Newman for the 1929 Championship.

This was a fine match, not only statistically with Davis averaging 100 and Newman 96 with 63 centuries for the winner and 57 for the loser, but as a contest, for Davis, 782 in front at halfway, found himself 107 behind within ninety minutes of the resumption as Newman compiled consecutive breaks of 576 and 531.

Newman was 44 in front after eight of the twelve days' play but on the ninth evening Davis scored 1,055–106 with breaks of 588 and 358 unfinished and looked the winner from that point. Smith, meanwhile, had set sail for Canada and Australia to play Lindrum.

"Why are you going if you've no chance", he was asked.

"For the money", he said.

# CHAPTER VI

# The Age of Lindrum
## *(Professional Billiards 1930–1939)*

Willie Smith's 1929 tour of Australia and his matches with Walter Lindrum were to mark the start of a new and, in a sense, final phase in professional Billiards. Smith could play the all round game just about as fast and as well as it was possible to play it. Lindrum, a master of all phases, had nursery cannons as his supreme weapon. The only way to beat him, when he was really trying, was to play nurseries even better. No one could do that, but in the attempt Davis, McConachy and Newman were to play them to such an extent that the public concluded there was very little resemblance between the game they played and the cannon exhibitions of these Billiards giants. Billiards was to earn the unhappy distinction of becoming the only game ever to perish as a public spectacle because its leading exponents were too good.

However, in the opening skirmishes of the tour in which Smith beat Fred Lindrum, conceding him 10,000 in Sydney, and McConachy beat Walter in Melbourne, there was nothing to indicate anything but a close struggle. Walter won their first match in Melbourne 24,234–23,147, breaks of 991 by Walter and 1,058 by the Englishman being the highest. Lindrum also made a century in ninety-five seconds. Their second encounter in Sydney was one of the all time great matches which Smith won 23,446–22,317. Lindrum made a 1,434 but broke down at the first shot of the evening session for Smith to reply with 1,383. Lindrum also had 965 and 1,090, in which he reached 1,000 in thirty-six minutes, scoring exclusively with nurseries after 350. Smith's winning effort was a 1,028 which occupied sixty-seven minutes on the last day, Lindrum being in play with 701 unfinished at the close.

Smith then set a new Australian record break of 2,030 in beating McConachy, playing through a whole session from 485 to 2,001 (keeping going with a five cushion cannon with the red in baulk in the 1900's) and eventually breaking down at a long jenny. He afterwards lost a return to McConachy but in the interim he contested the rubber match with Lindrum for which a Sydney newspaper had put up a prize of a one hundred guinea silver tea service.

This unfinished, as it proved match proved highly significant for both. Some of the Sydney betting fraternity, wanting to ensure an Australian victory, broke the cue Smith had used all his life, his beloved "pit prop".

"How long did you take to get used to another one?" he was asked in his ninetieth year.

"I never did", he replied.

Tragic as this was in a sporting sense, a far greater tragedy befell Lindrum. His pregnant twenty year old wife had been knocked over by a bus and was in bed when the match started. Complications had set in but she had set her heart on the tea service and her husband was determined to win it for her. He was leading by 3,000 points when his wife's illness turned to pneumonia. She rallied and asked constantly about the tea service but, under the strain, his game started to deteriorate and Smith, on the second Thursday, got in front. His wife, who had suffered a severe relapse on the Wednesday, had again pulled round by Thursday teatime when she told him: "You've got to make a 2,000 break for me." He resumed Thursday evening at 144 unfinished and played through the whole session except for the last ten minutes to reach 2,002, only to discover when he returned to the dressing room that his wife had had a final relapse and there was no hope for her. She died within a few hours. The match was abandoned with Lindrum leading 21,431–19,308 with the respective averages 114.6 and 102.7 . . .

Made as it was under such severe emotional pressure, Lindrum always regarded that break as his greatest, but the whole traumatic experience created an emotionally tender area which made him more and more obsessive about Billiards, harder to deal with in contracts and personal arrangements and, except when he was actually playing before the public, prone to depression and lethargy.

The immediate step he took to help him towards recovery from his grief was to sign a contract with Burroughes and Watts and return to Britain with Smith, but yet another wrangle prevented the 1930 Championship being truly representative. The Billiards Association who governed, through their Chairman, John Bisset, with an Olympian hand, had as usual allotted the final and some heats to Thurston's. Thurston's offered to give the final away but Bisset would not have the Association's authority questioned. Burroughes and Watts, who had Lindrum, Smith and McConachy under contract, stated strongly that the Championship should be played on "nameless" tables. The upshot was that the entry list consisted only of Davis, Newman, Falkiner and the veteran Inman.

There were a number of Championship records. Newman, in the course of submerging Inman 24,001–10,104, made a break of 1,567 and another of 1,047 during which a Graf Zeppelin was heard hovering overhead. Anxious not to miss seeing this new phenomenon, Inman rose from his seat, with the words: "Keep it up, Tom," and stepped out into Leicester Square.

Davis was given an unexpectedly hard fight by Falkiner, to whom he had been successfully conceding 3,000 start, when his lead of 2,204 dwindled to only 304 with three days to go. Falkiner, presaging the future potency of nursery cannons as a scoring force, had a record 230 in succession in a break of 499 and then got in front but Davis had the better of the run and scored off two double baulks in running out the winner 21,975–19,815.

The final saw Davis shatter Newman's record break with 2,052, losing the white at the end. He made, in all, nine breaks over 500 and 51 centuries while Newman made twelve 500's. Davis led by 516 going into the last session and put himself out of reach with 352 and 161 to win 20,918–20,117. The averages of 113.3 and 109.9 were records too. It was the first Championship to be played over sessions of a fixed time duration rather than to a target number of points.

No one, of course, was under any illusions about where the real number one position was being decided. Lindrum, not too pleased to discover that his first playing venue was a cellar in Glasgow, nevertheless made a 910 break during his first session there and a 1,083 in his second. He beat Smith by a modest enough margin, 22,694–21,200. More or less the same happened at Newcastle when, in another cellar not to his liking, he made breaks of 1,110, 1,271 and 999 to Smith's best of 991 and 924 in winning 23,400–22,039. Lindrum then made six thousands in a week, including three in consecutive sessions, and won by 7,983; and reaching London, beat him 28,003–21,962 at the Farringdon Hall with the aid of his first triple thousand, 3,262, and five other thousands. Smith, who made a 1,490 break and averaged 147, was thus beaten out of sight.

Smith, who had persuaded Lindrum to come to Britain, began to express resentment that he was being used as a punchbag, for Lindrum was so fast, so fluent, so magically in control of the balls that there was no stopping him. In the London match he reached 1,000 in only thirty-nine minutes and the whole break of 1,116 took only forty-three. His fastest ever thousand, in Johannesburg in 1933, was to take only twenty-six minutes and his fastest hundred only twenty-nine seconds.

Amazing to relate, it was only in Smith's matches that the progress of each break was called. The accepted practice was to call the progress of the match and announce the total of a break at its conclusion. And there were an awful lot of breaks to call. Lindrum, after being 4,101 in front and making five thousands in a week, was just beaten by Smith (by 378) who made four. Smith's wounds were also soothed by another narrow win over the Australian, and Lindrum, after beating Davis 29,056–26,172 in a match which eclipsed the record aggregate for a fortnight by 5,500, then cast all restraint aside and, after hammering Smith 30,817–19,334 with ten thousands, avenged family honour in full measure by beating him 36,256–14,971. Lindrum made eleven thousands and a 998 and averaged 262. Smith averaged 109 and lost by 21,285.

McConachy, who beat Davis three times out of four this season, and Newman and Smith, was arguably the world's second or third best player at this time but on the whole received fewer opportunities. Lindrum that season took £2,193.17s.3d. as his share of gate receipts and, from all sources – it was well known that he would put his name to anything from a set of cushions to a block of chalk for £100 – grossed £3,000. He left for home muttering resentfully about a "small profit" but was back for the 1930–1 season for an international tournament promoted by Bill Camkin, a lively Birmingham billiard trader, at seven points between Bradford and Plymouth.

It was to prove the greatest tournament ever seen. Davis, Newman and McConachy played level and Lindrum conceded each of them 7,000 start. It ended in a triple tie with Davis, Newman and Lindrum winning four matches each and McConachy none. Davis and Newman, in opposition, had personal averages of 175 and 142. Lindrum made thousands in five consecutive sessions against McConachy at Southampton and then, meeting him again at Thurston's, averaged 195–313 for the second week – including a new record break of 3,905 in which, resuming at 3 unfinished, he played through the afternoon session to 2,378, another sessional record, and for eighty minutes of the evening before he lost the object-white and left a double baulk.

Davis could nevertheless have taken first prize if he had beaten Newman in their last match at Plymouth. Starting the last day 581 behind, Davis got in front with a 1,001 break but after the lead had changed hands several times Newman clinched the match with a break of 871.

The tournament thus went to a play-off. Newman, averaging 122.3, beat Davis for the third time in succession and then averaged 169.3 against Lindrum but, even with his 7,000 start, this was not good enough. Lindrum averaged 248.1 and won 25,807 – 17,436. He made breaks of 2,835 and 2,583 and scored half his points from nursery cannons. Newman, who had been no less than 8,439 in front at halfway, scored one-third of his points by this method.

A new rule was introduced during the season. If a player ran a coup and his opponent then made 25 hazards off the red, the object-white was placed on the centre spot of the D and the break could be continued with a cannon. On the second occasion this rule came into operation, Lindrum made his 75 off the red, played a red to white cannon and compiled a break of 1,201. There was, incidentally, no official directive to warn the player that he was reaching the hazard limit, but Charlie Chambers, the resident referee at Thurston's, started to do so after 10 hazards had been played and this became the accepted practice.

The Championship in that 1931 season was, literally, a non-event. Davis, Lindrum, McConachy and Newman, after considerable debate, all refused to enter, partly because, for commercial reasons, they wanted to play on the new Janus cloth, and Smith, who had said several times that he would not enter, did so on the last possible day, after the other four had decided not to, apparently because he was afraid that McConachy might be declared champion unopposed. Ironically, as he was putting his entry in the post, the B.A. and C.C. extended the closing date by another three weeks. This infuriated Smith and he was in no way placated when, though he remained the only entry, the B.A. and C.C. failed to declare him champion.

Lindrum and Newman then went to Australia, where the former immediately set a new Australian record of 2,608. Newman almost immediately had to be operated upon for appendicitis but had his convalescence aided when Lindrum returned from several weeks on tour to throw the cash proceeds on his bed and insist upon splitting them fifty-fifty.

Smith and Davis were meanwhile at daggers drawn.

Davis was champion all right but he wanted to prove it to the public – and earn some money by playing Smith. He threw out many challenges but Smith bobbed and weaved by imposing totally unacceptable conditions including, once, that the match be played on twenty-four different club tables. Smith, living comfortably off his Burroughes and Watts contract, could pick and choose his engagements. He refused to meet Davis "for personal reasons on a private matter" and, eccentrically, challenged Lindrum to play him with ivories. Davis eventually challenged him for £1,000 a side: Smith replied that not only could he not accept because of his Burroughes and Watts contract, but that Davis himself had a contract that precluded such a meeting. Davis's solicitor made both Smith and the newspaper apologise.

Though he was still rolling out his thousand breaks and three figure averages, Smith was unquestionably nervous of the nursery cannon specialists; but eventually *The Sporting Life* brought them together for a three match series at the Dorland Hall, London, Manchester and Leeds, one match each on a table of the players' choice, the other on a neutral table. Three lengths of cloth and six sets of balls were selected, sealed by a neutral party and kept in a strong box in a bank vault. All this took until January 1933.

In the meantime in 1932, Smith had again objected to the Championship conditions, this time because an entrant could only offer suggestions on tables, venues, etc., after payment of a £50 deposit. He did not enter. After prolonged discussion, it was decided that the Janus cloth, a cotton, napless product much inferior to West of England woollen cloth (save that its manufacturers, W.F. Reddaway's, were prepared to pay the leading players handsomely to play on it), would be used for the event, for which Davis and McConachy were the only entries.

McConachy won two of the three warm-up matches and seemed to have a slight edge in the nursery cannon department which now tended to be the key to most big matches. The runs of close cannons were growing longer and longer with McConachy, in a break of 1,130, beating, in February 1932, Lindrum's sequence of 284 with one of 297 in which, instead of taking the balls round the corner, he was able to turn them no less than nine times along and back across the top cushion. The standard of play in this match was amazing, McConachy making consecutive breaks of 509 and 661 unfinished in one session and in another twice scoring off double baulks to initiate breaks of 389 and 656, Davis replying to the latter with 828. Next day, Davis took an unfinished 120 to 1,486 and McConachy played out time with 600 unfinished, only one shot being missed in the whole one and three quarter hour session. In the closing stages, McConachy had breaks of 990 and 902 and Davis one of 923 before McConachy won by 473.

But McConachy failed to reach these heights in the Championship, which Davis retained by a margin of nearly 6,000 points. Davis, who was 4,000 in front after four days, made breaks of 1,058, 844 and 774 and scored over 11,000 of his 25,161 points by close cannon sequences. Davis averaged 112 for the match and McConachy 98.

Lindrum had preferred to leave a little earlier for a tour of the United States and Canada with Newman rather than compete in the Championship, a preference which Davis wryly admitted in his autobiography he did not much regret, for in January 1932 at Thurston's, Lindrum had compiled against him a new world record break of 4,137 to supersede his own 3,905.

Lindrum played through most of Tuesday afternoon and all Tuesday evening to leave himself in play with 3,151 at the close. Thurston's was bursting at the seams on Wednesday afternoon to see the Australian, after making a short speech when he passed the record, go on to 4,137 before missing a cushion cannon with the rest. Davis, to his eternal credit, replied with 1,247, the first time opponents had ever made consecutive thousand breaks.

That season, in a much lower key, two future Snooker greats were continuing to ease their way in: Fred Davis, who had made a break of 187 in beating Lewis Bateman to win the Junior Professional Championship in 1931, ten years after his illustrious brother had done so, retained it in 1932 (and again in 1934); and Walter Donaldson in this year retained the Scottish Professional title with a top break of 307 and an average of 28.5 which now looks very useful but then hardly rated a mention.

The start of the 1932-3 season was notable for the introduction of the 100 point baulk line rule which, in an attempt to curb the excessive runs of nursery cannons which were dominating the professional game, insisted that the cue-ball should cross the baulk line at least once in every hundred points in breaks of 100 points or more. Mere playing from hand did not satisfy this condition for it would then have been a simple matter to play in-off the red and then pot it to regain position at the top of the table. Even so, the leading players adapted very quickly, most of them soon favouring leaving a thin cut red into the top pocket so that the cue-ball could be brought round the table off three or four cushions to regain top of the table position.

In the first match played under these rules, McConachy made breaks of 850, 616 and 553 and Newman one of 515. Nevertheless, Lindrum expressed his disapproval of it and he and Newman, when the promoters of *The News of the World* tournament gave the five invited entrants the option of playing under this or a 75 consecutive cannon limitation (after which a pot or in-off had to be played) opted for the latter. Davis and McConachy said that they did not mind either way but Smith, after failing to reply to the official questionnaire, withdrew from the tournament and went once more into the professional wilderness.

The promoters – in deference to Lindrum, whom they naturally wanted to appear, and as three of the other four, as close cannon artists, were also quite happy with any variation of the rules which gave more scope to their speciality – chose to depart from the governing body's experimental rule, sure proof that players and commercial interests were far more powerful.

McConachy, despite inadvertently coming away from a weekend with Thelma Carpenter (then Women's Amateur and later Women's Professional Champion) at the Solent Cliffs Hotel which her family kept at Bournemouth, without his cue, compiled a 1,321 in winning a close match with Davis, but Lindrum failed to make a 1,000 break against Newman and Davis. Newman, who later that month made a 1,062 in losing narrowly to McConachy, beat Lindrum when receiving 3,000, much less than usual, in a week's match and Lindrum, quite unjustifiably, thought the rule a threat to his supremacy.

The B.A. and C.C. bowed to pressure and the baulk line rule was modified so that the cue-ball needed to "cross the line" only once every 200 instead of 100 points, an alteration which meant that, if the line stroke was accomplished early in the break, the best part of 400 could be scored before it needed to be played again. Lindrum did not like even this modification though he had ridiculed it by taking the balls two and a half times round the table in a run of 529 nursery cannons, so pacing his break to cross the baulk line when he was supposed to. He also made four thousands and a 996 in a week against McConachy.

*The News of the World* tournament nevertheless went ahead under this new rule and Newman won it undefeated. Lindrum, conceding 6,000 in each match, failed to record a win. Newman made a break of 1,544, McConachy one of 1,402 and Davis of 1,263. Still later, the rule was tightened by a stipulation that the baulk line had to be crossed between 180 and 200 in every 200 but even this restriction proved not only artificial but ineffective.

When the long awaited clash between Smith and Davis finally came to pass at the Dorland Hall in January 1933, the match was played under the 100 point baulk line rule, Smith arguing that the contract had been signed when this was in force. Many punters backed him but his absence from the main stream had blunted his competitive edge and Davis slaughtered him 17,335–12,706. Smith pulled his game together to win a desperately close finish in Manchester but

Davis again won comfortably in Leeds to leave no doubt who was boss – of the British scene at any rate.

There remained, though, the 1933 Championship which saw Davis defending against Newman, McConachy and, for the first time, Lindrum. Naturally enough, Lindrum was expected to walk away with it, but then so had Gray, the in-off specialist, been expected to when he failed even to reach the final. In fact, there was almost another surprise, for Lindrum (after beating Newman with the aid of what remains a World Championship record break of 1,578) beat Davis by a mere 694 points after a tremendous struggle.

In the semi-finals, the referee, the undisputed one-armed professional champion Arthur Goundrill, officiated at the Dorland Hall for eight hours a day as these matches were played concurrently. 77,968 were scored in this fortnight and he called all of them. He also called breaks in the final of 1,492, 1,272 and 1,013 by Lindrum and 792 by Davis. Lindrum averaged 92 and Davis 89. Goundrill, who had lost an arm in the 1914–18 war, possessed a formidable array of trick shots and in May 1921 had become the first professional ever to play before the King at Buckingham Palace.

It was the last time the Big Four all played in the same tournament. Lindrum, everyone acknowledged, was in a class of his own. It appeared, for most of the time, that he was also in a world of his own. "His head was so full of Billiards there was no room for anything else" was one contemporary opinion. He was, in a personal sense, unreliable in that his grasp of appointments and times was at best intermittent. Joe Davis has told the tale of going to his hotel room one day when he was due at Thurston's in a few minutes to continue a big unfinished break – with a large crowd assured – only to find the Australian slumped and unshaven, apparently quite unable and unwilling to bestir himself. After cajoling him into shaving and virtually pressing him into his dress suit, Davis was given the doubtful pleasure of watching Lindrum carry his unfinished break to over a thousand and add another of nearly a thousand later in the session.

Sydney Lee recalls walking back with Lindrum to his hotel after one afternoon session in which his tip had almost come off. Lindrum voted for a cup of tea and a few minutes "watching the girls go by" before re-tipping his cu but the number of minutes grew and grew until it was time to depart for the evening session. With his tip still only half secured to his cue, Lindrum made a four figure break. Much later, when Sir Robert Menzies, who became Australia's Prime Minister, took Lindrum along to the Governor-General's residence, he threw the billiard balls haphazardly on the table and invited the champion to show his host how to make a thousand. He did not require a second attempt.

Lindrum was, simply, a genius who conquered his sport more thoroughly than any other player has ever conquered any other. Obsession is perhaps a constituent of genius and obsessed he was. He could never be bothered with business negotiations and in his attitude to money it was not so much its reality that interested him but the satisfaction it provided as an index of his worth.*
He left England owing large enough sums for goods purchased within the

---

*He was constantly befriended by Camkin but once, after staying with him for a fortnight, he went literally down the road to sign a contract for Camkin's arch local rivals, Padmore's.

English billiards trade for these debts to be advanced as an important reason why he never returned. He was not very discriminating in his relationships with women and one's ultimate impression of him is of a lonely man, to some extent isolated by his genius but even more by a wall of his own construction. Perhaps a clinching example of his inability to give was a reluctance, so repeated that it became a refusal, to pass on any of his knowledge of the game, particularly to such amateurs as Tom Cleary, later World Amateur champion, who managed many of his exhibition tours in the 1940's. Cleary was one of many who testified to an extremely likeable side to Lindrum, but Lindrum's inner self was buried so deep that no one could reach it.

Though McConachy was also an obsessive about Billiards he was a genius only in his infinite capacity to take pains. He was such a slow player that the others often found him torture to play. As a boy he practised hour upon hour in his father's Billiard hall and made a 1,093 break off the red with Composition balls when he was seventeen. New Zealand professional champion since beating W.H. Stevenson in 1915, he became first a top of the table artist and then a nursery cannon specialist, making 466 consecutive cannons in 1932, taking the balls nine times back and along the top cushion. He became the first player ever to make two thousands in consecutive visits and he recorded breaks of 1,943 against Davis and 1,927 against Lindrum.

His fetish for physical fitness was sometimes playfully exploited by his contemporaries.

"How are you?" one would say.

"Fit as a buck rat", McConachy would reply, eyes ablaze, shoulders back, stomach braced flat and hard as a spade.

Once, he picked up a chair one-handed and when the possibility was mooted that he could even pick up another chair in which Lindrum, in a typical half-asleep pose, was sprawled, he responded eagerly to the challenge. Pulses racing, veins throbbing, he lifted the chair but was, of course, in no fit state to play Billiards a few minutes later. On another occasion, he walked round the table on his hands.

For all his eccentricity, he was a man of uncompromising honesty and integrity. Alone among the Big Four, he did not win the Championship in the great days of Billiards but his devotion to the game was absolute and it was fitting that the title should come his way in the twilight of his career after the war.

Newman was a man who never had an unkind word said about him. Born at Barton-on-Humber, Lincolnshire, he came South with his father, who owned Billiard halls in Nottingham and then London, making his first century when he was eleven and his first 500 when he was fifteen. He signed a three year contract to play John Roberts Junior after beating him with 5,000 start in 18,000 and developed into one of the game's greatest players, particularly in cannon play and all close quarter work.

He lacked Lindrum's genius – as everybody did – and his match temperament, particularly in opposition to such a forceful character as Davis, was perhaps suspect to some degree. But it does appear tragically inappropriate that fate dealt out to this nicest of men a particularly unpleasant and lingering death from cancer of the throat in 1943.

Davis, second only to Lindrum at Billiards and undisputed King of Snooker – though the latter was not to be worth much until just before the war – was, even in the early 30's, becoming the dominant figure in the professional game, not only though his prodigious ability on the table but his acumen and organisational qualities away from it. In marginal matches, the force of his personality was often to prove the determining factor, so much so that some players literally became afraid to beat him – with or without a handicap – even when they had the chance.

His inner eye, as clear as the left eye on which he had to rely almost totally in playing, was always focused on his personal progress, status and profit – it had to be – but he did also have some sense of vision for the game as a whole which his contemporaries, who just got on with playing, lacked. He was, of course, to become completely identified with the rise of Snooker, the possibilities of which he was just beginning to explore concurrently with playing some of the best Billiards that has ever been played.

Meanwhile, having won the Championship and taken the cup back to Australia with him, Lindrum not only declined to return it but insisted upon the next Championship being played in Australia. The B.A. and C.C. were angry but could do little about it for Lindrum's ultimatum had again illustrated how, once a player gained possession of the title, he could manipulate circumstances in favour of retaining it while the so-called governing body stood impotently by.

The B.A. and C.C. thus granted the 1934 Championship to Australia, the first time it had gone abroad, and instituted a United Kingdom Championship which was won by Davis who, starting the last day 229 behind, beat Newman 18,745–18,301 in a titanic battle in which Newman recorded six consecutive session averages of 111, 113, 197, 105, 99 and 151 in the middle of the match and made the four highest breaks, 809, 693, 603 and 547, before Davis, whose best were 537 and 504, won through on his supreme competitive qualities.

In May, Davis set sail for Australia only to find that Lindrum, in his vague way, had done nothing whatever about promoting the Championship or any exhibitions to enable Davis to keep body and soul together. Davis was forced to do almost all the organising himself, including one exhibition at which he and Lindrum shared the princely profit of £1.

McConachy, the third entrant for the 1934 Championship, twice beat Lindrum in Australia in July, making a break of 1,927 in an hour and fifty minutes, and Davis also beat Lindrum twice out of three. But when it came to the Championship itself, at the Railway Institute, Melbourne, Lindrum beat McConachy 21,903–20,795 (Lindrum 1,065, 807; McConachy 892, 829) and then Davis 23,533–22,678 (Lindrum 1,474, 1,353 [reaching 1,000 in thirty-four minutes]; Davis 824, 728).

But for Professional Billiards as a whole the danger signals were unmistakably out. Dwindling attendances, long matches, the preponderance of close cannon play and of course the perennial internecine strife within the game were leading – too late – to all sorts of proposed remedies. The baulk line rule had been the most notable but it hardly bothered the top players and 500 breaks were made by both Smith and Newman when they played an experimental game in which all shots from hand had to be played from one of the spots on the baulk line. A week of separate thousand or 800 up matches instead of a single continuous match merely made results even more insignificant.

But possibly worst of all was that Lindrum, having retained the

Championship after a struggle, was disinclined to put it at risk again. He never returned to Britain and Davis, having taken over six months to earn enough to get home, never returned to Australia. Davis was keen to play him and both could have made a great deal of money but Lindrum grew more irrational as the years wore on and serious negotiation with him was impossible. There was no gainsaying his skill – in 1940 he made a break of 3,361 under baulk line rules when he was conceding Fred Lindrum 7,000 and only counting breaks over 700 – or his efforts for charity during the war, for which he received the OBE in 1951, but he simply would not put his title or, in later years, even his status on the line. He compiled breaks of 3,737 and 3,752 in consecutive visits to Melbourne in 1944 and thousands whenever he liked. When he toured, though, he fitted his own set of cushions to whatever table he played on and in his latter years, before his death in 1960 at the age of 61, refused even to have any kind of opponent in his exhibitions. He played a few games with McConachy in the 40's but would not play him for the title, though there was a short period when McConachy might possibly have beaten him, particularly as Lindrum was, it appeared, nervous of matches which really mattered.

Meanwhile, Davis returned home to find that *The Daily Mail* had partially halted the slide in Billiards as a public spectacle with a successful American tournament on sealed handicap lines at Thurston's. The sealed handicaps were kept in the safe of the Arundel Hotel, whose owner, John C. Bisset, was still Chairman of the B.A. and C.C. Davis made a break of 2,002, a new record under the baulk line rule, and Smith made a break of 1,022 but it was Newman, receiving 1,000 from Davis and conceding Smith 500, Inman 7,000 and Reece 9,000, who won all his matches to take the trophy.

Davis, with a 1,022 break in thirty-five minutes including 224 nurseries, beat Smith easily and then Newman, easing up, to retain the United Kingdom title. Davis made breaks of 1,264 and 1,002 and on the ninth evening Newman averaged 272 to Davis's 127.

It was at this point that the B.A. and C.C. tightened the 200 baulk line rule to stipulate that the crossing should occur between 180 and 200 though the rule did not apply to amateur play.

The well-handicapped veteran, Inman, won the 1936 *Daily Mail* Gold Cup tournament but it was the mixture as before for the United Kingdom Championship in which Davis and Newman averaged 125 and 114 respectively in the final. Davis made a break of 1,784, a new world record under the revised rules, and in presenting the cup Sir Emsley Carr of *The News of the World* suggested that after thirty-five ball to ball cannons the next cannon should involve the cue-ball striking not less than two cushions.

Davis and Newman met annually in the next three United Kingdom finals though Newman was to remark as early as 1937 that playing so much Snooker was beginning to affect the capacity of the top Billiards players to "stay in" on the rare occasions they played Billiards. Three weeks' Billiards was all Newman had in 1937, his first season in twenty years that he did not record a single thousand break. He did, in 1938, pluck out one amazing session, a lifetime best aggregate of 1,595 for an average of 266 with breaks of 484, 403 and 630 but he could not seriously challenge Davis's supremacy.

The World Championship, though, remained a dead issue until Lindrum, whose total of 711 thousand breaks, 29 over 2,000, 17 over 3,000 and one of 4,137, has never been even remotely challenged, relinquished it in 1950.

# CHAPTER VII

# The Rise of Amateur Standards
## (Amateur Billiards 1930–1940)

The 1930's saw a great leap forward in amateur standards. England had outstanding amateur champions, like Laurie Steeples and Sydney Lee, at the start of this period, and Kingsley Kennerley and Joe Thompson at its close, but it was, in the long run, more significant that the game in other countries should develop strongly enough not only to produce a player of such supreme quality as the Australian Bob Marshall but many more players of good quality than hitherto. Britannia ruled the waves for a while longer but once these waves had broken and recoiled, the tides of the game began to flow in an altogether less predictable manner.

The 1930 English Championship produced the first significant showing from Lee, who at his first attempt had won the London section at the age of fifteen in 1927, though he was swamped 2,000–623 by Steeples in the semi-final when the Yorkshireman made a break of 354 in averaging 62 in the second session and averaged 83 in the third to equal Cole's record. The final, between Steeples and Coles, was of excellent quality with both finalists making 2 double centuries before Steeples regained the title.

Bigger breaks meant shorter sessions and even with hazards limited to 25 there was rather too much repetitive play. Therefore, the 1931 Championship saw the hazard limit reduced to 15 and matches altered to a time limit basis.

A week before his twenty-first birthday, Lee clinched the first of his four successive Championships by beating Steeples and Boggin the last two rounds. His 2,814–2,332 win over Steeples was built on a 955–271 first session lead and despite a 346 break by Steeples, who made a desperate effort against the clock in the last session with runs of 40 and 64 close cannons. Lee's winning margin of 3,793–3,134 over Boggin concealed the fact that he was only 160 in front with half an hour to go before he added a 213 break.

Steeples had already been nominated to carry England's colours in the 1931 Empire Championship at Pitt Street Y.M.C.A., Sydney but, following his success, Lee's entry was hastily added. It never looked anything but England first and second. Steeples made a 461 unfinished in twenty-eight minutes with a 111 session average and 50 match average in beating Bill Hackett (New Zealand) and one of 421 in twenty-two minutes with a 83.3 session average in beating W.L. Goldsmith (Australia). Lee made a 433 break in beating Hayes but the play-off for first place did not produce these sort of fireworks. Steeples won 2,000–1,126 but averaged only 26.7 to Lee's 15.2. Tragically, Steeples shortly afterwards had to retire from the game on doctor's advice.

Lee won the 1932 and 1933 National Championships without undue difficulty though Coles made a new Championship record of 363 in the 1933 semi-final. He was such a good player and so devoted to the game that professionalism beckoned and he announced that the 1934 Championship would, whatever happened, be his last before he played his first professional engagements against the veteran ex-champion, Inman. As it happened, though, he was given an unexpectedly tough tussle by Frank Edwards, a Stourbridge builder, whose first time striking of the cue-ball, with no preliminary address, contributed to a highly individual and fast style of play. Edwards was actually 8 points in front after two days but Lee, the sounder player, outpointed him by 485 on the third afternoon and won by 420.

Lee went on to win the 1933 Empire title at Thurston's though he had a scare in his first match when he trailed the Welsh champion, Tom Jones, by 300 points at the end of the first day before winning by 390. He equalled his own amateur record of 4 centuries in a session in the last match against Prior and was unbeaten.

Outstanding as he was as an amateur, he was never able to break into the top flight professionally, first because the top professional standards set by Lindrum, Davis, Newman and McConachy were so superhumanly good, second because there was no demand to see second best, and third because Billiards was fading fast as a public entertainment. The traditions of the event ensured a fair amount of continuing interest for the Amateur Championship but professionally there was nothing for it but to give lessons and obtain what club exhibitions one could. Lee became adept at both and in the next forty odd years coached players of both sexes and all standards, including several celebrities.

In this period, he also played exhibitions in several thousand clubs, and late in his career added another string to his bow by refereeing the popular BBC 2 Snooker series, "Pot Black"; but for all the good professional tournaments were to do him, they might as well not have been invented.

It was in the early 1930's that three players who were all to win the Amateur Championship at least three times were making their first impressions upon it. Edwards first reached the final in 1932; Herbert Beetham (Derby) had lost only by 237 to Edwards in the 1933 Birmingham area final; and Leslie Driffield (Leeds), with a 205 break near the end, beat Edwards on the post in the first round of the 1935 Championship, the year in which Alf Gover, the Surrey and England fast bowler, competed.

With Lee out of the way, Coles beat Boggin to win the 1935 title and, this time playing for England, won the Empire title with new records against the first Indian to compete, P.K. Deb, of 1,243 (session aggregate), 2,164 (day aggregate) and 4,155 (two day aggregate). Coles then retired and two new men contested a desperately hard fought 1936 final: Beetham and Joe Thompson (Millom).

Thompson led by 407 halfway through the third session before Beetham made a break of 266, a record under the new 15 hazard limit. From then on, there was not much in it, and had Beetham not missed a long in-off into the top left-hand pocket, the only one this amazingly consistent hazard striker did miss in the entire match, with only three minutes to go, he would probably have won. As it was, Thompson got home by a mere 30 and Beetham had to wait until 1960 to win the title.

Good player that he was, Thompson could only finish third out of four competitors to Bob Marshall, who was to win the Australian title nineteen times, and Prior in the Empire Championship in Johannesburg. Marshall, whose four Empire/World titles (the title was to be changed in 1950) started this amazing sequence in incredibly inauspicious surroundings. With the afternoon sessions taking place in daylight and workmen walking about on and hammering on the iron roof, all sorts of shots were missed, but as daylight faded and the workmen went home the standard improvèd.

Marshall was held until half an hour from time by Prior, when late efforts of 77, 197 and 91 took him home by 365, and was pressed all the way by Thompson, who made a 245 and was in the match until forty minutes from the end. Earlier, when the scores were level at 324, Marshall had made a new South African record of 248 off a double baulk. He won eventually, 2,852–2,468, an aggregate of 5,230 for three two and a quarter hour sessions.

With 5 centuries in a session against the second South African, Gus Bowlly, in clinching the title, it was clear that Marshall was an amateur of exceptional quality. A short man, who played quickly and got very low on his cue, Marshall and his great compatriot, Tom Cleary, were perhaps the two greatest amateur top of the table exponents of all time, Marshall perfecting the postman's knock sequence with the object-white pinned tight on the top cushion behind the red spot, while Cleary preferred the greater variety of the "floating white", always keeping the object-white near and behind the red spot but using an area of as much as 18 inches either side of it.

Though the best English amateurs knew most of the top of the table moves and employed them up to a point, the main emphasis in the English amateur game was on hazard play, partly because the speed of the tables, particularly those with steel block cushions, made in-off sequences easier to compile. Australian tables, however, with Walter Lindrum from his eminent position advocating cushions as slow as possible to assist his nursery cannon play, tended to be very much slower, making top of the table easier – if one had the skill – and in-off sequences harder work. Strip rubber tended to be used for Australian cushions, another factor which made them not only slower than British but more responsive to spin.

Marshall's success, matching Lindrum's in the professional sphere, was of such a quality that it could not be written off as the infliction of a merely temporary reverse on the English, who still liked to think of themselves as the masters.

As it happened, the next English champion was a player of more than ordinary quality and a top of the table specialist to boot – Kingsley Kennerley who had got his nose inside the Congleton Brass Band Club by joining as an eleven year old apprentice cornet player. He made little progress with this instrument but his membership did enable him to witness an exhibition by Jim Harris, a visiting professional, which so fascinated him that he played truant from school next day, went to the club, picked up a cue and started to play. Within three or four months, he was making 50 breaks, exceptional in itself but the more so since he attempted from the start to play top of the table. This was how Harris had played and Kennerly had concluded that this was the idea of the game.

Soon, his father was to leave instructions that he was to be thrown out of the local Billiard hall whenever he appeared, but the Billiards bug had well and truly bitten. By the age of fourteen, he was making double centuries and had gone through a season of local league Billiards undefeated. When only twenty-three, he lost narrowly in a quarter-final of the Amateur Championship and the following year he not only won it but the Amateur Snooker title also, the only player apart from Sidney Fry and Laurie Steeples to perform the double in the same year. To make 1937 a year of even rarer vintage, Kennerley set a new amateur four sessions aggregate record of 3,760 and made a total of 47 centuries in the tournament. His new world amateur record break of 549 stood as the English Amateur record, despite rule revisions which made breaks easier to compile, until 1978.

Kennerley successfully defended his title in 1938, when he set a new record of 5 centuries in a session and when the combined aggregate in the final (Kennerley 4,714 Thompson 3,925) was the highest ever. Kennerley averaged 29.8 in this final but when it came to the deciding match against Marshall in the 1938 Empire Championship in Melbourne he averaged 35 and was hammered 6,639–4,705, Marshall averaging 49. In the circumstances, he did well, for less than a week after the long sea voyage he beat Cleary, playing in his home city on strip rubber cushions of which the Englishman had had no experience, 1,685–1,211. It was apparent, though, even at this stage, that the title lay between Marshall and Kennerley.

First, Marshall set a new world amateur match average record of 52; then Kennerley made a new record break for the event, 472. The play-off, though, was largely decided in the first two sessions. Marshall led 1,048–538 after the first and set a new world amateur record average of 115 in taking the second 1,864–250 with breaks of 384, 230, 335, 270, 230 unfinished. Marshall averaged 56 to Kennerley's 55 in the third session and 80 in the fourth. He was played out but with two sessions to go his lead was impregnable.

Kennerley retained his domestic title in 1939, setting a new two day aggregate record with 4,324 which included a new session aggregate record of 1,218 at an average of 50.8, though this was exceeded by Arthur Spencer, a twenty year old left-hander from Doncaster, with 1,266 (52.8). Both players were over the top when it came to the final when the averages were 22 for Kennerley and 16 for Spencer. Kennerley also beat Spencer, though much more narrowly, in the 1940 event, which was at the time designated a wartime Championship but which seems to have acquired full Championship status with the passing of the years. All matches but the semi-finals and final (which were staged at Thurston's) were played at the Kennington Temperance Billiard Hall in a special five hundred seat match arena.

There was to be no return meeting between Marshall and Kennerley for the latter, after the war, turned professional. His degree of professional success, though, was hardly more substantial than that of Lee, even though he was much the better Snooker player. He had reached an impasse; he had gone as far as he could go as an amateur but could make no money out of it and there was no public for professional Billiards.

Curiously enough, the decline of the professional game coincided with a rise in amateur standards. The top amateurs were still nowhere near so good as the top professionals had been, but they played, with the large exception of nursery cannons, a more professional type of game. With disuse, professional standards were to slip much further to the amazing point in the late 1970's when only a couple of professionals, who were primarily Snooker players anyway, could match the top amateurs at the three ball game.

One promising avenue for developing the game opened – and then closed. In April 1937 the B.A. and C.C. and the International Union of Amateur Billiard Federations, the governing body for the continental pocketless game, held a joint conference in London which led to a visit to Beaulieu-sur-Mer in the South of France for a tournament, the English Billiards and Snooker sections of which were dominated by Thompson and H.F. Smith. The tournament was repeated the following year and in 1939, when the B.A. and C.C. were formally affiliated to the continental body, the association was trying to secure a venue for the union's AGM in London when the outbreak of war brought this joint venture to a close. The English body has never seriously sought to reactivate the matter, respond to approaches from the continent or even consider the implications and possible benefits of closer and more regular contact between the two codes.

The B.A. and C.C. Chairman John Bisset, first elected in 1925, was in his time considered autocratic but, in retrospect, he appears possibly the best Chairman the body has had. In 1938 a vote of no confidence was proposed because the council was elected at the AGM, which favoured the London faction, instead of being formed democratically by regional associations nominating their representatives. A compromise was reached whereby the provincial element on the council became more numerous but it was not until the advent of proportional representation (based on one council member per hundred affiliated clubs) which came into effect in 1970 that the B.A. and C.C. could be said to have become – and even then with some reservations – a democratic body.

Ironically, this seemed to make the quality of council member and the quality of administration worse rather than better. In retrospect, Bisset can be forgiven his faults because of his energy and love of the game. A link with Europe, a serious investigation of the possibilities of organising tournaments on undersized tables, basic administrative efficiency and respect (even if agreement was sometimes lacking) were all to prove beyond either the vision or capacity of subsequent administrations. It was even to take until 1972 for the body's title to recognise Snooker's standing when the B.A. and C.C. became the Billiards and Snooker Control Council.

# CHAPTER VIII

# Birth and Growth
*(Snooker 1875–1940)*

In 1875 Colonel Sir Neville Chamberlain was a young subaltern with the Devonshire Regiment stationed at Jubbulpore. During the rainy season the officers' long afternoons were spent at the mess Billiards table where the parent game was less popular than various round games which were more suitable for more than two players and to which it was easier to add a modest gambling element.

Pyramids, perhaps Snooker's most obvious forerunner, was a game played with fifteen reds, initially placed in a triangle, with the apex red on what is now the pink spot but which was then known as the pyramid spot. Each time a player potted a red, all his opponents paid across the agreed stake money per ball.

In Life Pool, each player was given a cue-ball and an object-ball (e.g. white on red, red on yellow) so, for the second player, his object-ball was the first player's cue-ball and so on. The object was to pot one's specified object-ball three times. Each time a player's ball was potted, he lost a life and had to pay an agreed stake. When he had lost three "lives" he paid an extra sum for a "star" (or extra life) and when that was gone he was "dead". When only one player remained he scooped the kitty.

Black Pool was a development of Pool in that a black ball was added. When a player had potted his allocated ball, he could attempt the black. If he was successful, each of his opponents paid across an additional sum and he could then attempt the nearest ball. Joe Davis spent many of his youthful hours playing a similar game, Pink Pool.

Black Pool was the preferred game among the Devonshire officers but it was Chamberlain's inspiration gradually to add other coloured balls so that Snooker came to be played with fifteen reds, yellow, green, pink and black. Blue and brown were added some years later.

These new colours produced a game whose variety (and variety of monetary forfeits) immediately caught on. The concept of break building was much in the future and even the point values of the balls were not established until a little later; but it was in these casual and almost chance beginnings that the game undoubtedly had its origin.

When Compton Mackenzie, the novelist, interviewed him in 1938, Chamberlain recalled that the Devons one afternoon received a visit from a young subaltern who had been trained at the Royal Military Academy, Woolwich. In the course of conversation, the latter happened to remark that a first year cadet at Woolwich was referred to as a "snooker" with the implication that this was the status of the lowest of the low. The original word for a cadet had been the French "neux" which had been corrupted to "snooker".

Chamberlain said: "The term was a new one to me but I soon had the opportunity of exploiting it when one of our party failed to hole a coloured ball which was close to a corner pocket. I called out to him: 'Why, you're a regular snooker!'

"I had to explain to the company the definition of the word and to soothe the feelings of the culprit I added that we were all, so to speak, snookers at the game so it would be very appropriate to call the game Snooker. The suggestion was adopted with enthusiasm and the game has been called Snooker ever since."

In 1876, when Chamberlain left the Devons to join the Central India Horse, he took the game with him. After being wounded in the Afghan War, he served with the Commander-in-Chief of the Madras Army and was with him every summer when he moved to the hill station at Ootacamund. Snooker came to be recognised as the speciality of the Ooty Club and the rules of the game were drawn up and posted in the Billiards Room.

During the 1880's rumours of this new game reached England and when John Roberts went out to India on one of his tours he had it in his mind to find out the rules. One evening in 1885 in Calcutta, Chamberlain was dining with the Maharajah of Cooch Behar when Roberts was introduced to him. Roberts duly brought the game back to England.

It was many a long day before Snooker became widely played. Not every hall nor every club could afford a Snooker set of twenty-two balls though it was not long before the manufacturers appreciated Snooker's superior commercial possibilities. Even so Billiards remained such a popular game to play that not until the Second World War could a Billiard hall risk carrying fewer sets of Billiard balls than they had tables.

By 1910 a measure of breakbuilding had come into the game as one F.H. Garside received a certificate for a break of 99 against Sir Charles Kirkpatrick at his home and Tom Aiken, the Scottish Professional Billiards champion, was reported to have made one 102 at Snooker and Cecil Harverson two. Phil Morris, a Tottenham marker, made a 103 at the Eagle Hotel, Tottenham.

In 1912 the official record, that is, on tables with standard pockets, was 73, jointly by John Roberts and James Harris. In 1915 George Hargest, the manager of the Lucania Hall, made a break of 112, a total clearance, with Durolite balls, at Blackwood, Monmouthshire. In the same year, William Murray made a 103 at the Collingwood Billiard Hall, Newcastle, of which he was manager. Tom Newman made an official break of 89 in 1919.

As far as competition was concerned there was nothing until 1916 when Harry Hardy, owner of Hoprend, Hopsack and other winners of the Waterloo Cup, suggested an Amateur Snooker Championship in aid of the British Sportsmen's Motor Ambulance Fund. The standard was poor and in 1918, in fact, an American, H.H. Lukens, won the Championship after only a few weeks' practice at the Palmerston Restaurant, which he immortalised by playing in the tournament under the pseudonym of T.N. Palmer. (J. Howard Shoemaker came over from the New York Athletic Club in 1923 with the intention of emulating his compatriot but was prevented from playing by an untimely attack of appendicitis.)

The rules of Snooker, which had been subject to many local variations, were codified when the Billiards Association and Billiards Control Club amalgamated in 1919. The drawn game was abolished when provision was made for the black to be re-spotted at the end of a frame if the scores were equal. The free ball was introduced to supersede the B.C.C. rule that if a player was snookered after a foul he could have the snookering ball(s) taken up so that he could play onto the "nearest ball playable", though, when in hand, a player was judged to be snookered or not from the brown spot only and not any part of the D. The penalty for going in-off a red was still only one, the four point minimum penalty still being a few years away.

Low as the standard was in the Amateur Championship, it was not long before the provincial players, nurtured in money games, elbowed the more "gentlemanly" type of entrant to one side, though not before Sidney Fry, in 1919, had become the first to accomplish the Billiards/Snooker Amateur Championship double, a feat he was within a ball of repeating in 1921 when he had a shot at the black in the final before losing to M.J. Vaughan (Coventry).

The seven frame final was decided then, as it was until 1927, the year in which area qualifying was also introduced, on aggregate score. The change to a decision on the basis of frames was precipitated, after several years' rumbling, by the 1926 final in which W. Nash beat F.T.W. Morley, who entered under the name of his step-father, Leaphard, 383–356, though Morley won four of the seven frames.

Jack McGlynn, at different times of both Birmingham and Nottingham, won the title twice around this time, as did Walter Coupe (Leicester). Play was largely of a tactical nature, a red, a colour and safety being the order of the day. Breaks of 27 by McGlynn and W.E. Foster (Kettering) were the best up to 1925 when the record shot up dramatically to 62 through W.L. Crompton (Blackpool).

In 1927, the year the touching ball rule was introduced, Ollie Jackson (Birmingham), a safety expert whose top break in the Championship was 38, won the title but did not defend in 1928 when Pat Matthews, a twenty-three year old watchmaker who attributed his success to a fruit diet, principally prunes, beat Frank Whittall (Birmingham) 5–4, on the final black, to record the first of his four titles.

There were a few professional matches in the 1920's: Fred Lawrence beat Albert Cope 31–27 for the Midland Professional Championship in 1921; J.S. Nicholls beat W. Davies 1,032–777 (the aggregate score of eighteen frames) for the Welsh Professional Championship in 1922; and R.S. Williams made a break of 81 in South Africa, where Snooker was reported to be very popular.

The first week's Snooker match at a major London venue was staged as a season curtain raiser at Burroughes and Watts, Soho Square, in September 1922 when Arthur Peall beat Joe Brady 34–14. On January 29, 1923, Con Stanbury, a burly Canadian, who spent the last thirty years of his life in London, largely as a coach, until his death in 1975, potted the last 14 reds, 14 blacks, yellow and green in a break of 125 in a game at the Palace Billiard Hall, Winnipeg, albeit on a table with $3\frac{5}{8}$" pockets.

Snooker was chiefly a gambling game or a respite from Billiards, but the Billiards Professionals Association, an organisation for markers and professionals attached to clubs rather than the big names of the day, organised a Snooker tournament in 1923 in which Tom Dennis, who owned a Billiard hall in Nottingham, made a 76 break. On August 24, 1924 Dennis wrote to the B.A. and C.C. asking the governing body to promote an Open Professional Snooker Championship but A. Stanley Thorn, the Secretary, replied: "The suggestion will receive consideration at an early date but it seems a little doubtful whether Snooker as a spectacular game is sufficiently popular to warrant the successful promotion of such a competition."

George Nelson, a Leeds professional deeply involved in the promotion and trade aspects of the game, was publicly urging the B.A. and C.C. to wake up to Snooker's potentialities and the indefatigable Bill Camkin produced a book of rules. The Midland Counties Billiards Association, with whom Camkin was closely associated, imposed a minimum penalty of 4 points for a foul stroke, contrary to the then official rules.

Camkin was also very much involved in instituting the Professional Snooker Championship. As a proprietor of Billiard halls, he knew full well how popular Snooker was; and a conversation with Joe Davis, who had played Snooker since his youthful days of managing Billiard halls around Chesterfield, led to Davis's writing to the B.A. and C.C., drafting the conditions under which such an event could take place. The Association gave their consent and issued these conditions. The players arranged their own venues with the final at Camkin's in Birmingham. There was a five guinea entry fee, a five guinea side stake and fifty per cent of the entry fees were to be divided sixty-forty between winner and runner-up with the other fifty per cent going to the B.A. and C.C. Gate receipts were to be divided equally between the players after expenses.

Davis, whose break of 96 with Vitalite balls against Newman on February 4, 1925 had superseded Newman's professional record of 89 set in December 1919, predictably won the tournament and pocketed £6.10s. from the gate receipts, though the Billiards Association used the players' half of the entry fees to buy a trophy. Camkin himself refereed the final in which Davis made a break of 57 and in one frame recorded runs of 32, 34 and 35 in consecutive visits. This was thought to be an exceptional sequence at the time. (It was in this year, incidentally, that the present "touching ball" rule was adopted.)

The 1928 Championship was played on a challenge basis with Davis exempt until the other contenders had been reduced to one. This turned out to be Fred Lawrence who, in the challenge round at Camkin's, Birmingham, extended Davis to 16–13. It was during this season that Davis made his first Snooker century, 100, against Fred Pugh at Manchester when he took on local aspirants between sessions of a Billiards match. Newman, in October 1927, had made a 97 against Davis at Thurston's, while in Sydney Frank Smith junior had made a break of 116 in a 141–0 frame but this kind of feat only rated a paragraph at the time. Davis potted the first 14 reds, in a break of 95, before snookering himself on the last red against George Nelson at Otley, and Alec Mann made breaks of 99 and 106 at the Central Restaurant, Birmingham.

Though chiefly preoccupied with Billiards, Davis introduced Snooker as a supporting attraction whenever he could – there was, after all, some mileage in being the Snooker champion – and was successfully conceding 14 start to Newman.

The 1929 Championship attracted only five entries with Davis making a break of 61 in beating Dennis 19–14 in the final and there was an increase of only one for the 1930 event in which Davis displayed his finest Championship form to date, making breaks of 58, 44, 48 and 50 in the first three frames in beating Lawrence 13–2 and one of 79, a Championship record, in his 25–12 win over Dennis in the final.

There was some good Snooker being played in the Antipodes, notably by Murt O'Donoghue, who became the first player to clear the table from the opening stroke with a 134 in Auckland, in 1928, followed shortly afterwards with 136 and 138, and by Frank Smith junior with 127 (14 reds, 10 blacks, 3 pinks, 1 blue, yellow to pink) at the Hotel Australia in 1931. O'Donoghue hustled throughout the 1920's in his native New Zealand and Australia prior to building up a chain of twenty-seven Billiard clubs. He became a wealthy man and has never, he says, regretted his decision not to pursue the game competitively. His knowledge and skill are beyond dispute for even in his seventies, with defective eyesight, he could give striking demonstrations of his skill at close quarters – especially at nursery cannons – and was much respected as a coach. How he would have fared in matches against the top professionals, however, must remain a matter for conjecture.

The 1931 Professional Championship was a narrower affair than ever with only two entries, and Davis defeated Dennis 25–21 in the latter's own room at Nottingham. This, though, was the toughest match Dennis ever gave the champion for he led 6–4, 14–10, 17–15 and 19–16 before Davis took the next five frames to go in front 21–19. Davis made breaks of 72, 58 and 53.

Century breaks were still uncommon and even the relatively few who made them did not always go on to establish further claims to fame. J.G. Thompson, a Sunderland amateur, who made an unofficial break of 108 in Sloan's Rooms, Sunderland, was a case in point. In match play, the Billiards players of quality seemed to have the craft to overcome those who relied more heavily on their potting. Laurie Steeples, for instance, retained in 1930 the Snooker title he won in 1929 to become the second player to record the Billiards and Snooker double, though he was precluded from attempting a Snooker hat-trick (only to be accomplished by Jonathan Barron in 1970–2) by his journey to Australia for the 1931 Empire Billiards Championship. In his absence, Matthews recorded the second of his four wins by beating Harry Kingsley (Nottingham) 5–4 in the final.

From 1932–6, amateur Snooker consolidated its popularity without its leading exponents noticeably improving their skill. There was an important rule change in 1934 when the so called crawl stroke, rolling the cue-ball up behind a nominated free ball, was outlawed, first as a six months' experiment but then permanently.

The same period, though, saw quite spectacular advances in break making by professionals. Horace Lindrum (né Morell) made an unofficial 139 break in Melbourne in March 1933; Alec Mann of Birmingham, in late 1932, took the first 12 reds, 11 blacks and a pink in a break of 95, the first time anyone in Britain had come within striking distance of the 147 maximum; Walter Lindrum made a South African record of 113 at Bulawayo in September 1933; and O'Donoghue, on September 26, 1934, playing in his own club at Griffith, New South Wales, against Maurie O'Reilly, actually achieved the 147, not on a standard table but the first maximum nevertheless. A special certificate, signed by one hundred and thirty-five spectactors, was later presented to him.

Davis, who recorded only the centuries he made in public, still held the official record of 114 and in 1933 increased the World Championship record to 72 in beating Willie Smith in the final of an event which still attracted only five entries. The previous year, when he defeated McConachy, and the following year, when he defeated Newman in a match spread over three days at Nottingham and two at Kettering, saw Davis confronted by only one challenger but the Championship started to widen out in 1935 when Stanbury became Canada's first entrant. As a player without any grounding in the gentler game of Billiards, Stanbury constituted almost a new breed, revelling in the power shots which the Billiards/Snooker players tended to avoid automatically on aesthetic grounds. His own career, in retrospect, seems to have hinged on missing a simple middle pocket pink which cost him a 13–12 loss to Willie Smith, who went on, very comfortably, to reach the final. A win for Stanbury here would have established him but, as it turned out, despite many subsequent efforts and near misses, he could never quite make it.

It was this 1935 Championship, however, in which Davis set a new Championship record break of 110, which established the event as a paying proposition. The following season saw the first week long Snooker matches at Thurston's (albeit in the first two weeks of September) where previously the game had been seen only in a supporting role to Billiards or in the Snooker Championship itself.

Horace Lindrum, aged twenty-three, made a break of 71 at Thurston's against Newman in his first public frame in England and became the first Australian to enter the Championship in 1936. Clare O'Donnell, an even harder hitting Canadian than Stanbury, who eccentrically kept his chalk under his bridge hand when striking, made Canadian representation up to two, beating Sydney Lee but failing to appear for the final session when trailing Lindrum 19–6. He did not enter again. Stanbury lost by the odd frame for the second time, 16–15 to Alec Brown, a former Speedway rider, who thus reached the semi-final at his first attempt. It seems to be unrecorded how Stanley Newman, a younger brother of Tom, came through to the semi-final but at this stage Lindrum, with a break of 101, beat him 29–2. Davis beat Brown 21–10 in the other semi-final.

The final was certainly the greatest Snooker match there had yet been. Lindrum led 3–2, 6–4 and 11–9 before Davis, with breaks of 75 and 78, won four out of five on the third afternoon to lead 13–12.

Lindrum levelled at 15–15; led 21–19 and 26–24 and, with the aid of a lucky snooker, won the first frame on the last day to lead 27–24. But this was as far as he got for Davis won ten in a row, achieving a winning lead at 31–27 and completing the sequence at 34–27. Thurston's was packed and it was abundantly clear that Snooker had become the major game, a conclusion which was underlined when *The Daily Mail* switched their Gold Cup tournament from Billiards to Snooker. In October 1936 *The Billiard Player* changed its name to *Billiards and Snooker*. (Apparently aghast at its own daring, it changed back after the war.)

In December, Davis and Lindrum (receiving 7) played the first ever week long non-Championship match in the provinces at Nottingham. Davis, off scratch, won *The Daily Mail* Gold Cup tournament with five wins out of five (making 5 centuries) but the great feature of the event was a new world record of 133 by Sidney Smith, the first ever "official" total clearance. "Thurston's Doors Locked" was one headline which eloquently stated Snooker's new crowd pulling status.

Lindrum (receiving 7) made breaks of 141 and 135 in beating Davis 39–36 in Manchester though his failure to apply for record recognition suggests the pockets may have been more generous than standard. Lindrum (receiving 7) also beat Davis 74–69 in Snooker's first ever fortnight's match at Thurston's and regained the world break record with 135, only for Davis to equal it.

Though century breaks lower down the scale were still rare – Willie Smith's personal best, for instance, was still only 94 – Davis, Lindrum and Sidney Smith were giving clear indications of the potentialities of modern break-building Snooker. Breaks were rising too on the amateur side. Kennerley held the official record with 100, though on December 3, 1935 George Hardman had made a 104 at Blackburn on a Riley standard table. Hardman, ignorant of the correct procedure, failed to apply for official recognition.

In the Amateur Championship, W.H. Dennis, son of Tom Dennis, made a 52 break in 1937, the year he lost to Kennerley in the final, though Kennerley himself was unquestionably the most accomplished breakmaker. He made a 101 break when in Australia for the Empire Billiards Championship in 1938 and created a new Amateur Championship record in 1939 with a break of 69, though Percy Bendon beat him 6–4 in a close five and a half hour final just as Pat Matthews had edged him out 6–5 in the 1938 final. Kennerley, who reached four consecutive amateur finals, won his second title in 1940 by beating Albert Brown, who, like him, adopted professional methods and later turned professional. Bendon and Matthews, steady and tactically tough, battled more in the old amateur tradition though Bendon made 2 and Matthews 1 break over 40 in the 1939 Championship. Bendon, incidentally, was barred from the 1940 Championship for professionalism though he never played as a professional, while Tommy Gordon, who was to win three Amateur Championships after the war, was trying unsuccessfully to break into the professional scene and kept body and soul together by refereeing all-in wrestling.

A new challenger for the Professional Championship in fact emerged in the last few years before the war – Fred Davis – though his Championship debut in 1937 could hardly have been less auspicious. Unknown to anyone save himself, he was starting to suffer from myopia, so it was hardly surprising that the promise he had shown in three times winning the Junior Professional Billiards Championship was not being fulfilled. Very much overshadowed by his elder brother Joe, from whom the only advice Fred ever received was to stop grinning while he was practising, Fred was quietly helping out in the family Billiard hall in Chesterfield, unable even to tell the time accurately from the hall's large clock in order to book patrons on and off tables unless he stood directly beneath it. Self-conscious as he was, though, he told no-one of his affliction, even when the balls started to look like balls of wool or even when he lost 17–14 in the Championship to W.A. Withers, a Welshman whom Joe immediately hammered 30–1. Belatedly, Fred consulted an optician and was fitted with a then revolutionary design of swivel lens spectacles, which has proved the saviour of many a spectacle wearing player since. Immediately he began to play very much better, beating Herbert Holt and Alec Brown in the 1938 Championship before losing honourably to Sidney Smith, then ranked only behind Joe and Lindrum.

On November 14, 1938, incidentally, Brown was the central figure in an incident which led the B.A. and C.C. to stipulate that a cue "must be at least three feet in length and conform to the accepted shape and design." With the cue-ball marooned in the middle of a pack of reds, Brown produced from his pocket a tiny ebony cue, complete with tip, one of the few that his father, who ran the Billiard room at the Piccadilly Hotel, had made. He duly chalked the tip and played his shot. His opponent protested. Brown argued that he was within the rules. But Thurston's great resident referee, Charlie Chambers, a permanent feature since 1915 (he died in 1941) awarded a foul, sensing no doubt that the use of this implement was outside the spirit if not the letter of the law. Another rule had been cleared up in September 1938 when players had been allowed not to have to audibly nominate colours unless their choice was not obvious.

Joe, of course, was still winning the Championship with plenty to spare and had also made the first of his many trips to South Africa in 1937 where he made a 141 break, the year in which the South African Amateur Snooker Championship was instituted. In 1938 he pushed the official break record up to 138 in *The Daily Mail* Gold Cup. Conceding large starts (40 to Newman for instance) he yet won the tournament with four wins out of five. He also made a break of 134 from the opening stroke in an exhibition in Jersey.

The 1939 Championship provided Joe with the strongest challenge he had yet encountered when Fred made a new Championship record break of 113 and was beaten only 17-14 in their semi-final. In 1940 it was even closer. Fred beat Sidney Smith 17-14 in one semi-final while Joe was beating Walter Donaldson 22-9 in the other and pushed his elder brother all the way in the final before Joe clinched it with a century break, 37-35. It was to be the last time they ever met in the Championship.

# CHAPTER IX

# Prosperity and Desperation
*(Snooker 1946–1963)*

The end of the war left the public with a huge appetite for entertainment. During it, Joe Davis had raised over £125,000 for war charities and had also made a considerable name for himself on variety stops from the Palladium downwards with an act composed of trick shots played in front of a huge angled mirror. His brother Fred and Walter Donaldson were both in the army but both were demobbed in good time to participate in the first post-war World Professional Championship in 1945–6.

Joe and Fred each made a Snooker century in the same session in a match at the Houldsworth Hall, Manchester, and in Birmingham Fred made 133 and Joe 134 in consecutive frames. But it was not to be a Joe v Fred World final for the latter was eliminated in the semi-final at Oldham by Horace Lindrum.

The final was over a new marathon distance of one hundred and forty-five frames, a fortnight's match, and instead of being played in the intimacy of Thurston's, which had been bombed during the war, it was played at London's Royal Horticultural Hall. Several broadcasts added to the interest and the crowds of twelve hundred per session, at prices ranging from 5s. to £3, poured £12,000 into the box office. Entertainment tax was reduced from forty-eight per cent to thirty-three and a third per cent the day before the match began and the players came away with the unheard of sum of £1,500 each for their trouble. Joe never looked like losing and his 78–67 victory was assisted by 6 century breaks, the two highest of which, 133 and 136, were both, in their turn, new Championship records.

This was Joe's cue to retire from World Championship play as twenty years' undefeated champion. He was nevertheless to dominate Snooker for another fifteen years. He was elected Chairman of the resurrected Professional Billiard Players Association in September 1946; he, Bob Jelks, the Billiards trader who had staged the 1946 final, and Sidney Smith were the partners in Leicester Square Hall, which opened on the old Thurston's site in Leicester Square; and most of all, he remained far and away Snooker's leading personality, so much so that, like John Roberts before him, he could rule as a king in exile. He was beaten three times on level terms by Fred before he retired, but lost to no-one else level and to very few even when he was conceding 7 or 10. As the best player, the chairman of the players' body and the one with the biggest say in who played at Leicester Square, the game's showcase, he virtually ran professional Snooker. When television came along in the 50's, it was with Joe

**Above** George Gray

**Right** John Roberts junior

**Below** Thurston's: Tom Newman in play against Joe Davis

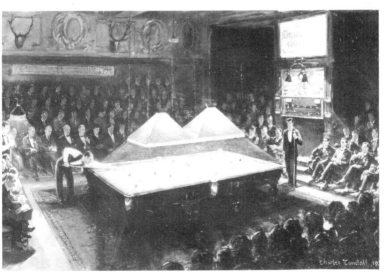

Blackpool Tower Circus: Walter Donaldson and Fred Davis await the start of a session in one of their great World Professional Snooker Championship finals.

Walter Lindrum

Willie Smith

Walter Lindrum (left), Joe Davis, Tom Newman and Clark McConachy with promoter Bill Camkin on one of their Big Four tours

Clark McConachy

the BBC negotiated; when a player wished to become a professional he needed Joe's approval or he was frozen out. In a word, he had it all tied up. It was even more remarkable that, however busy he was, however many deals or conversations he might have been involved in only minutes before, his concentration was absolute once he went to the table.

That Joe had the interests of the game at heart there is no doubt. With professional players squabbling and an ineffectual governing body there was a desperate need for a strong man to take charge as he did. Neither did anyone begrudge him his legitimate commercial pickings. But his retirement from Championship play was soon to devalue the Championship itself – just as Roberts' withdrawal had devalued it. In less than ten years, professional Snooker was to decline from that peak of the 1946 final almost to the point of extinction.

The 1947 Championship was the first to take place without Joe and was also the first in which John Pulman, a future world champion, competed. Pulman had won the 1946 English Amateur Championship as an unknown from Exeter by beating Albert Brown (who also turned professional immediately) 5–3. Pulman, it was agreed, was an outstanding prospect though his highest break in that final was only 25. Incredible as it would seem today, Pulman did not make a century break until he had been a professional for several months.

Pulman went out to Brown, who also beat John Barrie and Kennerley to win the qualifying section before losing to Lindrum, in some eyes the obvious heir apparent, in the quarter-final. However, when Donaldson defeated him in the semi it was confidently predicted, not least by Joe, that Fred would keep the title in the Davis family. The final, over two weeks, proved a tremendous first attraction for Leicester Square Hall when it opened in September 1947 and Donaldson, who had singlemindedly locked himself away practising in an obscure loft, confounded the pundits by winning 82–63. Davis made the only 3 centuries, 103, 107 and 135, but Donaldson, with a mixture of deadly long potting, relentless safety and absolutely no risks, inexorably ground out a victory.

It was effective, but it was not artistic, exciting or fluent. Donaldson's reluctance to use side for positional reasons – or indeed to do anything which might compromise the all important objective of potting the next ball – gave his game a stark appearance which complemented his dour, thrust out, determined Scottish chin. He was a literal kind of man and he played a literal, point-by-point type of game. He made few concessions to the public who came to watch and, though well enough liked by his fellow players, a sense of humour and gracefulness in defeat were not his strongest attributes. Once, when Fred won the last six frames to beat him in Newcastle, a mutual friend, seeking the right word of consolation, said: "Walter, I don't know what to say."

"Then don't bloody well say anything!" Donaldson exploded.

Nevertheless, Donaldson was champion. But was he number one? In a match for the "real" Championship, that is, the one which the informed public identified as being for the number one position, Donaldson held Joe to only two frames at halfway before being beaten 42–29. Joe again beat Donaldson at the Kelvin Hall, Glasgow, where eighteen hundred saw one session and ten thousand attended during the week. He made a new world record break of 140 and shortly afterwards one of 112 in which he took blacks with the first 14 reds.

He could easily have left himself on the blue from the last red and gone on to make 145 but elected to play the red very slowly to stay on the black. It just failed to drop and he had to wait until 1955 before he achieved the game's first maximum under standard conditions.

Pulman, beating Willie Leigh on the final black, won the qualifying section in 1948 and Brown, who had taken six wickets for Warwickshire against the Indian tourists before the war, pulled off a surprise by beating Sidney Smith 36–35 to reach the semi-final. The final, only some six months after the 1947 final, saw Fred depose Donaldson by the ample margin of 84–61. The match failed to produce a century (Fred 96, Donaldson 88) partly because, from the outset, Fred was determined to give nothing away in the safety exchanges whereas, the previous year, he had taken risks and paid the penalty.

That autumn the *Empire News* sponsored a professional handicap tournament which ran throughout the 1948–9 season. In addition to the announced handicaps, there was also, for the first and last time, a sealed handicap, for Joe won the first prize of £450 only by virtue of receiving two frames under sealed handicap from Fred. The brothers played on level terms but everyone expected Joe, who until this match had never lost to anyone, to be conceding a couple of frames. Therefore, when Fred won 36–35, having taken a winning lead at 36–33, it was a bizarre anti-climax when the contents of the sealed envelope were revealed.

The handicapping had been done by Harold Mayes, sports editor of the *Empire News*, for whom Fred was writing a column in opposition to Joe's in *The News of the World*, so it was, in a sense, one up to the *Empire News* to have "their man" conceding start to Joe. This partially obscured the significance of Fred's victory in which he had inflicted two consecutive whitewashes, 138–0 and 129–0, the former with a 138 break. Joe himself had played well and had made a break of 123 which had almost become a new record of 141, but somehow Fred's victory never achieved a sense of reality with the public.

Many judges within the game felt that in the late 40's and early 50's Fred was at times playing marginally better than his brother but the media, of which Joe was a shrewd manipulator, surrounded the undefeated champion with an aura of invincibility which nothing could shake. The relationship between Joe and Fred cooled for a while until Fred accepted the situation. It was, in a sense, his greatest misfortune, as far as recognition was concerned, that his name should be Davis.

It was also tough in those days for a professional who was attempting to break in. Pulman had a generous and enthusiastic patron, Bill Lampard, who built a billiard room for him to practise in at his Bristol home. Pulman reached the world semi-final for the first time in 1949 by beating his old amateur adversary, Albert Brown, but two other hopefuls were not so successful.

Conrad Stanbury, who had been entering since 1935, was in some strange fashion involved in all three matches in the qualifying section – and won them all 18–17. The second of these was against Jack Rea, Northern Ireland amateur champion in 1947, who in the 60's and 70's developed a uniquely entertaining vaudeville style for his exhibitions, a sphere in which he became highly popular and successful, but who at that time was in charge of the Snooker and Racing Room at the East India Sports Club, the nearest he could get to earning a living as a professional. After receiving an almost papal audience from Joe Davis, he was admitted to the legitimate professional ranks and actually led Stanbury 12–3 before losing 18–17, a defeat which condemned him almost automatically to another period of obscurity before another chance came his way. For Stanbury too it was a Pyrrhic victory: Donaldson slaughtered him 58–13 in the quarters.

Donaldson also hammered Pulman 49–22 and led Fred 45–39 in the final but Fred levelled with a 6–0 session and eventually, from 60–57, romped away to a winning lead at 73–58 by winning all but one of the next fourteen frames. Again, caution was the watchword and several sessions took over three hours. There was only one century, 102 by Fred.

Fred then beat Joe for a second time on level terms, 37–34, but the public and indeed *The Billiard Player* attributed the result to Joe's recent trip to Bermuda where he had beaten the Canadian champion, George Chenier, 41–30, a result which impressed the maestro sufficiently for him to invite Chenier to Britain for the 1949–50 season. Another visitor was the South African professional champion, Peter Mans, who had made a 137 break in 1946 and whose son, Perrie, was to reach the semi-final of the World Championship in 1976 and the final in 1978.

The *Empire News* switched its sponsorship from its own tournament to the World Championship, offering £450 to the winner and £150 to the runner-up in addition to any gate percentages which might be agreed with individual promoters. Leicester Square Hall was meanwhile taken over by a new £1,500 professional handicap tournament sponsored by *The News of the World* in which the daring step was taken of reducing matches from six to three days' duration. Fred declined to play as he thought that three day matches were an insufficient test.

One match created a sensation when Sidney Smith, who won 19–18, was awarded one frame on the grounds that Mans had played a deliberate miss. Joe Davis, from –7, remarkably won the tournament with Sidney Smith (+14), Albert Brown (+19), Lindrum (+13), Mans (+13), Pulman (+14), Donaldson (scratch) and Chenier (+13) finishing in that order. Lindrum, Mans and Chenier, as professional champions of their respective countries, quaintly conceded one point per frame to Smith and Pulman.

Chenier partially atoned for that disappointing showing when he beat Mans (to whom he had lost 23–14 on level terms in *The News of the World* tournament) 37–34 in the World quarter-final at Scunthorpe. He lost 43–28 to Fred Davis in the semi-final at Oldham but became the new World record break holder with 144 against Donaldson at Leicester Square (15 reds, 12 blacks, 3 pinks and the colours), the last shot a miraculous cut black with the cue-ball almost on the pink spot. During this visit Chenier also brought home to other professionals the possibilities of "plants" and "sets", for these "combination" shots were much used in Pool, Snooker's American sister game, played on smaller tables with larger pockets, at which Chenier was a player of high standard.

This record stood for only five weeks, however, for Joe Davis, playing Chenier at the Houldsworth Hall, Manchester, then compiled a 146 taking a pink after his sixth red. He also potted the brown, with a stroke in which luck was a necessary adjunct to skill, by playing off the opposite side cushion when snookered by the blue.

The surprise of the season, though, was reserved for the World final at the

Tower Circus, Blackpool, when Donaldson beat Fred Davis 51–46, gaining a winning lead at 49–42. The Scot had experienced a disappointing season but Fred, by his decision to stand out of *The News of the World* tournament, had had little match play. The latter led 17–13 but was well below his best while Donaldson was at his most determined. There was an inordinate amount of safety. One frame took an hour. Several sessions took four hours, but once Donaldson had levelled at 18–18 he was never again in arrears. The highest breaks were 79 by Davis and 80 by Donaldson.

The new *Sporting Record* tournament started inauspiciously when Lindrum withdrew. A very fluent and attractive player who had grown less and less fond of the nervous strain and tension of cut throat match play, Lindrum had been accustoming himself to wearing contact lenses and for most of the season had displayed form inferior to that which he had shown on previous visits to England. Nevertheless, when the handicaps for the tournament were announced, he took them as a personal affront. The Davises were on scratch and the handicaps ranged down to Sidney Smith (receive 21) and Lindrum (receive 23). The absurdity of one professional conceding another two points per frames was self-evident. So too was Lindrum's chance to take advantage of the handicapping to win first prize. As it was, he stood on his dignity and refused to play, thus initiating a breach with Joe which was to last until shortly before his death in 1975. Joe, incidentally, won the tournament and reaffirmed his ascendancy over Fred by beating him not only in this but 82–63 in a fortnight's match.

Storm clouds also began to gather in the relationship between the professionals and the B.A. and C.C. when the P.B.P.A., in October 1950, applied to the B.A. and C.C. for permission to introduce the "play again" rule in *The News of the World* tournament. This eminently sensible rule simply gave a player the option of requiring his opponent to play again after he had committed a foul, a rule which has now become so completely an accepted part of Snooker that it seems remarkable that there was any opposition to it. But the B.A. and C.C., composed of amateur enthusiasts, either thought they knew better than the best players in the world or, more to the point, discerned a threat to their authority. They agreed to the rule only on condition that any records set while it was in operation could not be eligible for official ratification.

While Fred Davis regained the world title in 1951 and Alec Brown, receiving 30 start from Joe and lesser starts from everyone, won *The News of the World* tournament with an unbeaten record, discontent simmered. In the summer of 1951, Joe made breaks of 103, 128 and 134 in consecutive frames, the first time there had been such a hat-trick, but while he was making this tour of South Africa the professionals' disenchantment led to a break with the B.A. and C.C. which was never completely healed.

The B.A. and C.C. high-mindedly declared that the World Championship was primarily an affair of honour and led to players deriving more prestige and more engagements. They published figures which revealed that Fred and Donaldson had shared £966 and £500 from the 1950 and 1951 finals when the B.A.'s and C.C.'s shares were £100 and £58 respectively but the argument was less about the ratio than the total, not to mention the negligible returns from the pre-final heats.

The professionals decided to boycott the World Championship organised annually under the auspices of the B.A. and C.C. and institute their own event, the World Professional Matchplay Championship, in opposition to it. This immediately became, in the public eye, the World Championship because all the leading players, except Joe, played in it. The B.A. and C.C. stubbornly organised their own event in which Lindrum, who was not by now in the best mood to co-operate with his brother professionals, and McConachy, who felt he had to support the official body because they had given him the chance at the Billiards Championship, were the only entries. Lindrum won a farcical match 94–49, though, shortly afterwards, McConachy made a 147 break on a non-standard table at London's Beaufort Club against a well known referee, Patrick Kitchen.

Fred beat Donaldson 38–35 to win the "real thing" and also beat Joe 20–17 level in *The News of the World* tournament in which Sidney Smith won the £500 first prize. The Championship also featured a first appearance by a seventeen year old confidently tipped as a future champion, Rex Williams, who only once in the 1951 Amateur Championship had conceded two frames and lost only five in all. Playing like a professional both in design and execution, Williams made a break of 74 and a string of 30's and 40's, quite a contrast to the run of amateur champions for the previous few years who, good players though they were, had obvious limitations judged by professional standards.

The Amateur Championship was expanding: Vic Oliver, the comedian, and Henry Hall, the band leader, were among the record entry of one hundred and eighty-nine in 1947 and in 1948 there was a unique finalist from the new record entry of one hundred and ninety-nine in Tommy Postlethwaite (Wolver-hampton) who, due to an accident when he was twenty which severed the tendons of his thumb, bridged between his first and middle fingers, the only player of any great ability ever to have done so. Tommy Gordon (London), a supreme tactician, recorded the first of his three wins in 1949 and Kennerley's break record of 69 was eclipsed in 1950 by James Longden, a very attractive and promising young player from Sheffield who mysteriously faded out of the game as quickly as he had entered it.

Longden was beaten in the semi-final of this Championship by Alf Nolan, a shrewd, calculating left-hander from Newcastle, primarily a Billiards player, whose suspect cue action and lack of cue power limited his range of shots. There was nothing lacking, though, in his tactical or competitive qualities, as he had shown when recovering from 3–5 to beat Gary Owen, born in Llanelli but then living in Great Yarmouth, 6–5 in the final. Owen, who had been reinstated as an amateur in 1947 – his father ran a billiard hall – was to spend years in the wilderness as a result of this traumatic defeat when success might have led to a professional opportunity. He continued to play but domestic responsibilities and lack of money kept him out of the Amateur Championship for a decade till he triumphantly returned in 1963.

Williams, then, was the first professional recruit since Pulman and Albert Brown in 1946 and he was, incredibly, to be the last until 1967, but his professional baptism showed just how wide the amateur/professional gap still was: he was hammered 39–22 in the Championship by Alec Brown. He was also beaten into third place by Rea and Kennerley in the qualifying round of *The News of the World* tournament, played on level terms, in which Rea, with some spectacular long potting and some generous starts, eventually finished second to Joe. Perhaps worst of all he was to have only a few seasons of professional competition until, at a vital stage of his development, the professional game collapsed. This was to leave him first in the frustrating situation of playing brilliant Snooker in practice day after day, including three 147 maximum breaks, with no regular opportunity of testing himself against (or establishing himself as) the best. He became sidetracked into business interests in the game, some of them very successful, but with this diversification his play suffered and he never reached the number one position which had been so confidently predicted for him. Ironically, it was at his "second" game, Billiards, in which he had also been an outstanding Boys and Junior champion, that he was to become World champion, albeit in a depressed era of professional Billiards.

Fred beat Donaldson twice more, in the 1953 and 1954 World finals, and also beat Joe level 21–16 in the 1954 *News of the World* tournament in a year in which Joe was for much of the time at his peak, making centuries in three consecutive frames both against Willie Smith and his brother. As an afterthought, he also made an 829 Billiards break against Smith, the highest there had been since the war. Fred did not then carry out his stated intention of retiring from Championship play but, as Donaldson did so, the Professional Championship continued to lose credibility. Donaldson acted out his disillusion with the game by turning his billiard room at his Buckinghamshire home into a cowshed and breaking up the slates of his table to pave a path.

The advent of television was making Snooker a tough market in which to make a living and the imminent closure of Leicester Square Hall, in one way or another the home of the professional game for fifty-four years, because of the termination of its lease from the Automobile Association, made prospects even bleaker. But the hall was at least to close in a blaze of glory for Joe, having made his second 146 in *The News of the World* tournament, in which he was second to Rea, brought his career to a climax by compiling the game's first official 147 against Willie Smith on January 22, 1955.

It was, of course, an amazing achievement, Snooker's equivalent of Sir Roger Bannister's epoch making, sub four minute mile. Breaks of 147 – authenticated by witnesses – had been made before but never in a match in which the public had paid for admission, when there was a properly appointed referee officiating and, most important of all, when the pockets of the table had been tested with the official templates and found to be standard. All these conditions, of course, were fulfilled in Davis's break, the key shot to which was the fourteenth red (see diagram). Davis had, of course, in playing the thirteenth black, intended to leave the cue-ball behind the red in order to take it into the top pocket but missed his position so grossly that the only possibility was to pot it along almost ten feet of side cushion into the baulk pocket. To have potted this ball under such extreme mental pressure made it stand out in his mind as one of the most memorable shots of his career.

Pettily and short-sightedly, the B.A. and C.C. refused to recognise the break on the grounds that professionals were still playing under the "play again" rule (though this had not, of course, cropped up in this particular frame). The rancour which followed was eventually glossed over when this body recognised the break in April 1957. The rule itself was adopted by the B.A. and C.C. on January 8, 1958.

In Donaldson's absence, Fred's opponent in the 1955 and 1956 World finals

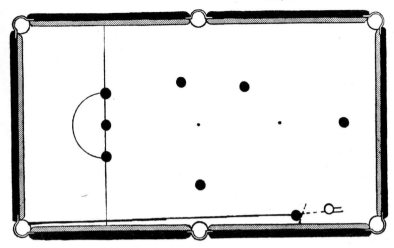

was Pulman, to whom Joe, in *The News of the World* tournament, which went out into the provinces for the 1955–6 season, was still giving 14 start. Both finals were close and Pulman had a great chance to win in 1956, when he led 31–29 starting the last day before dropping the afternoon session 5–1.

Pulman, never one to conceal his feelings at the table, was Fred's direct antithesis in temperament. Great competitor though he was, Fred was always smiling and joking even when the going was rough whereas Pulman tended to explode at even quite insignificant mishaps or imperfections. Typifying this clash of temperament was an incident at Leicester Square Hall when Pulman, missing a pot which left Davis in perfect position for a big break, stormed angrily from the room. A bell underneath the scoreboard which the resident referee could press had long been available for this sort of contingency. When Pulman, simmering in the manager's office, heard the bell ring his spirits revived at the implication that all was not lost and he returned eagerly to the fray. What he did not know was that Davis had drifted out of position and, instead of taking a risk to keep the break going, had trickled the cue-ball up behind the green to leave Pulman impossibly snookered.

"Fasten your seat belts", said Fred impishly as the crowd waited for Pulman's entrance, a jest which was amply justified by his reaction.

Pulman became champion in Jersey in 1957, but, with Fred not competing and only three other entries, victory had a distinctly hollow ring. He lost to Fred level in the 1958 *News of the World* tournament but, receiving 10, beat Joe. From having six players in 1957, the tournament was reduced to four in 1959 when, in one day matches on level terms, Fred beat Joe three out of three, Donaldson three out of three and lost to Pulman twice out of three to take the top prize of £625.

In a newspaper article Williams alleged that a closed shop was operating in favour of the older professionals. Joe replied with some chilling figures to illustrate the hazards of promotion: Fred and Williams had played for £9 each in an unsuccessful three day match at Langley the previous season. The desperation in the air was epitomised by Joe's attempt to launch another game,

Snooker Plus, with two additional colours, mauve and orange. *The News of the World* switched its sponsorship to a three man Snooker Plus tournament but the public rejected the game for the gimmick it was. The plain fact was that, good as the Davises, Pulman and, just behind them, Rea and Williams, were, only very few permutations could be made from such a limited cast of players. The contests between them were devoid of bite, variety, surprise or any sense of occasion or importance.

Joe continued to play – and play well – until 1964. He appeared regularly on television – the formula for television Snooker was generally Joe v A.N. Other – played as many exhibitions as he chose and took his total of Snooker centuries in public to 682.

But the professional game was dying of anaemia. From 1957–1964, Pulman held the Championship unchallenged and talk and interest within the game was confined almost exclusively to amateurs.

After Williams had won the Championship in 1951, Gordon, champion in 1949, completed a hat-trick in 1953, when George Humphries missed a pink with the rest which would have given him a 6–5 victory, and in 1956, when he beat Ray Reardon, who was to win the World Professional Championship six times between 1969 and 1978, 11–9. Reardon, in fact, led 7–3 but his tip flew off with his first shot on the second day and, playing with a borrowed cue, he lost all five frames in that afternoon session. Even in those days Reardon was an outstanding potter, if at times an inclination to overplay his hand led to his losing to shrewder competitors with a more limited range of shots. Reardon's youthful rivalry, in Tredegar, had been with an even more remarkable talent, Cliff Wilson. Their matches, whether in the Welsh Championship (when Reardon invariably won), the Welsh qualifying section of the English Championship (when Wilson invariably won) or for money, with hundreds of supporters for each man, were modern Snooker's nearest equivalent to a bare knuckle prize fight. When Reardon left Tredegar to live in Stoke, first as a miner then as a policeman, the edge went from Wilson's game. His father, who had been his greatest supporter, died and he also had trouble with his eyesight. He retired, except for a few games in 1960, from 1957–1972 but returned triumphantly in the mid 70's to recapture in 1977, in storybook fashion, the Welsh Championship he had previously won in 1956.

Had professional Snooker not been so dead, had the media been alive to the wonders he was performing, Wilson could have achieved in the 50's what Alex "Hurricane" Higgins was to achieve in the 70's. So confident and aggressive that often, if there was no pot on, he would just bang the balls round hopefully rather than play a safety shot; such a fast, deadly, first-time potter that, from baulk, he would take a long pink from its spot in preference to yellow, green or brown, so nonchalant that he would pot a ball four feet along a cushion in just the same way that he would pot one over a pocket, Wilson destroyed player after player at Burroughes Hall, where his Amateur Championship matches always attracted capacity houses.

On his first appearance as a seventeen year old in 1952 he demolished Gary Owen 5–2, having lost the first two frames, before losing in the semi-final to the ultimate winner, the Irishman Charles Downey, an artist at the slow drag shot and an extremely sound match player. In 1953, when Gordon won the title, young Wilson had him on the ropes needing a snooker in the last frame, which Gordon eventually got to win 5–4, before the 1954 Championship saw him reach the final. He beat Reardon only 5–4 on the final black to get to London and played some astonishing Snooker in beating Norman Buck (Romford) 5–3 with successive frame wins of 102–7 and 134–5, the latter with successive breaks of 62 and 68. Geoffrey Thompson (Leicester), not a great potter, but an extremely polished player round the pink and black spots, came through the other half of the draw and the final was to prove fully worthy of the new two-day twenty-one frame status it had been given.

Thompson won the first frame 111–0 and led 4–1 at the first interval. Wilson recovered to 3–4 and led 61–1 in the next, only for Thompson to win it with a 65 clearance. Wilson made it 6–6 but recklessly lost an early lead in the next to go behind again. He had a chance to lead 8–7 before valour once more outweighed discretion. From 7–9, Wilson recovered to 9–9 but Thompson clinched the match 11–9 with a far from easy pink.

It was marvellous entertainment and it now seems incredible not merely that no-one should have encouraged these players to make their careers in the game but should actually have done the opposite. Thompson, in fact, turned professional in 1969, on a rather half-hearted part-time basis, when he was nowhere near such a good player as he had been in his Championship year and thereabouts.

The 1955 champion, Maurice Parkin (Sheffield), also turned professional in 1969 and he was also much too late. Sound rather than brilliant, he beat Nolan, who also reached the English Billiards final that year, 11–8, after Nolan, in a match which produced an extreme clash of styles, had beaten Wilson 6–5 in the semi.

Pat Houlihan (Deptford), another fast, talented, exciting player who had dominated the London section since 1954, Ron Gross (Greenford), who won the first of his three English titles in 1957, and Marcus Owen (Walthamstow), who won the first of his four titles at his first attempt in 1958, were other players who turned professional very belatedly and achieved infinitely less than they might have done had they turned at the right moment.

The great weakness of the professional game was that there was no standard channel through which a leading amateur could pass in order to earn a legitimate living at the game. It was held against Houlihan – and to a certain extent against some of the others – that he spent his time playing for money in billiard halls, a few of which were frequented by the criminal fringe. The determination of Joe Davis and his colleagues to uplift Snooker's status – which indeed they had – was wholly admirable but, in retrospect, their lack of forethought in failing to bring new professionals into the fold (a failing in which they were no worse than generations of their predecessors) was certainly not in Snooker's long term interests. The bottom was dropping out of the professional market but interest in Snooker could have been revived if exciting players like Wilson, Houlihan and to a lesser extent some of the other leading amateurs of the time had been properly handled instead of simply discouraged as "not the right type". As it was, resentment against an apparent professional closed shop built up at a time when a blind eye was more regularly being turned, not only in Snooker but in other sports, to amateurs receiving a few pound notes for exhibition appearances.

More and more competitors in the Amateur Championship were playing on professional lines. Centuries in practice games by amateurs were by now quite common and there were more good breaks in the Championship itself. In 1957, for instance, there was an 88 by Austin Whiteside in the Manchester area, a 79 by Harry Holroyd in the Yorkshire area and in 1958, 85 by Albert Chew and 80 by both Jim Heaton and Roy Lomas, the latter ratified as a new Championship record – all in Manchester. None of the break makers prospered though, and Gross, who in his prime very rarely missed a shot he should have got and also had the knack of knowing exactly what his limitations were and playing to them, not only beat Stan Haslam for the 1957 title but won again in 1960 and 1962.

Marcus Owen, younger brother of Gary and the more complete player, won at his first attempt in 1958 when his quarter-final victim was Reardon, who perhaps never forgot this and subsequent defeats by Owen in his amateur days. In fact, in the 1974 Professional Championship, when Reardon was indisputedly the professional number one and Owen had only just turned professional after a too lengthy retirement, Owen turned the clock back to give Reardon his only difficult match of the tournament.

Owen's semi-final opponent that year was another future professional, John Dunning (Morley), whose best Amateur Championship showing this was. Owen was leading 5–4 when his tip came off. Dunning sportingly lent him his cue, then Houlihan and Gross both offered theirs in turn and Owen struggled home 6–4 prior to beating Jack Fitzmaurice, the most consistent Midland player of the era, 11–8 for the title. He retained the title in 1959 with an 11–5 final victory over Alan Barnett (Wolverhampton) which included an eight frame winning streak.

Dead as the professional scene was, the amateur game was on the verge of a take-off. In 1958, a British Team Championship, with the Leicester Square Hall match table as first prize, attracted one thousand one hundred and nine five-man teams when it was organised by *The News Chronicle* and won by Abertillery Central Club. Why that take-off failed to eventuate is hinted at by the entry of only one hundred and eighty-two when the B.A. and C.C. ran a similar tournament in 1959. It failed to catch the popular imagination and was not repeated.

In July 1958, the B.A. and C.C. rightly barred the jump shot and foolishly gave official recognition – clearly not with very much thought – to a World Open Snooker Championship which was played in Australia in 1960. The field was not at all representative and Fred Davis, the only British player, was in a class of his own in winning all six matches, a 5–4 defeat of the South African professional, Fred van Rensburg, being his only moment of difficulty.

Not for the first or the last time, the game's potential was wasted through inefficient and unimaginative government. In 1961, pleading poverty, the B.A. and C.C. suspended the reimbursement of train fares for competitors in the Competition Proper but, almost paradoxically, that year provided one of the most genuinely amateur champions of modern times, Alan Barnett, who at that time was working all hours to build up a business at his two newsagent shops in Wednesbury.

Barnett, a sharp, confident potter, not a particularly good positional or safety player but blessed with an excellent match temperament, eliminated Gross and Fitzmaurice before facing a new entrant, Ray Edmonds (Cleethorpes), who was later to win two world amateur titles.

Edmonds had beaten Owen, the favourite, 6–5 and led Barnett 6–4 at close of play on the first day of the final. Barnett, who had risen at six o'clock in the morning to start the day at his shops before taking the train to London, then travelled back on the midnight train, snatched a few hours' sleep, rose at six to get the day's business under way at his shops and again made the train journey to London ready to play at three. It was just about the worst preparation he could have had but amazingly it was Edmonds who appeared to run out of steam at 9–9 as Barnett won the next two frames relatively comfortably for the title.

A glimpse of just how far the gap had narrowed between amateurs and professionals was afforded by the first ITV tournament in October 1961 when four professionals played four amateurs. Gross (receiving 18) beat Fred Davis 3–0; John Price (Tredegar), losing English Amateur finalist in 1960, (receiving 21) beat Jack Rea (receiving 10) 3–2; Thompson (receiving 21) beat Rex Williams (receiving 10) 3–0 and Jonathan Barron (Mevagissey) (receiving 21) beat Kingsley Kennerley (receiving 10) 3–1. With all four professionals out first round, it was obvious – even allowing for the fact that the matches were very short – that lack of competition was taking the edge from the professionals' games.

The effects of this were to become even more acute as the professional situation failed to improve. Barron, incidentally, beat Gross 4–3 in the final and the professionals were dropped from the tournament the following year. Television Snooker in the early 60's then dropped into the pattern of Joe Davis playing another professional on BBC with a variety of amateur events on ITV. The latter eventually led to the B.A. and C.C. disgracefully helping to prearrange certain matches in order to ensure that the fifth frame would be the decider. The B.A. and C.C. was, as usual, in dire financial straits and pleaded that it needed television fees to ensure its survival and that these fees would cease if matches were not exciting enough.

By now there were only six active professionals: Joe, Fred, Pulman, Rea, Williams and Kennerley. Joe had no financial worries. Fred was comfortable, first at his hotel in Llandudno, then at his farm in Liss. Williams had a family printing business to fall back on. The others relied on exhibitions, many of them in aid of national charities. Rea, naturally an attractive player, began to stress repartee, imitations and jokes more and more as he realised the market for "straight" Snooker exhibitions was very limited. Williams, the youngest and most ambitious, revived the Professional Championship in 1964 on a challenge basis. He obtained the B.A. and C.C.'s approval and recognition, and the support of Burroughes and Watts, where the first match of this kind between Pulman and Fred was played, and also took the lead in re-forming the professional association. He also promoted a four man, week long professional tournament at Blackheath, Staffordshire, which was won by Pulman. All this was much better than nothing for it did at least keep the professional game alive but the vital element of new faces was still missing.

Pulman beat Fred 19–16 for the revived professional title, Davis leading 13–11 but then losing a frame through not nominating a free ball, even though it was obvious. This anomaly in the rules – at that time and until 1976 all free balls had to be audibly nominated, however obvious – seemed to turn the match and Pulman was to retain his title through six more challenges, one of them comprising a six week tour of South Africa with Williams, which concluded with a defence against Van Rensburg in a week's match. The finest of these matches was the one in 1965 when he beat Davis only in the last of their

73 frames, Pulman making a break of 112 and Davis one of 105.

In the South African series Williams set a World Championship record break of 142, superseding his own previous record of 141 against Fred Davis at Birmingham in 1956, and after the series made a 147 against Mannie Francisco in an exhibition match which was officially recognised as a joint world record with Joe Davis's 147 in 1955.

Meanwhile the amateur game progressed. Roland Foxley (Canterbury) made a new English Championship record of 85 in the Home Counties section in 1962, Jim Heaton (Bolton) made an 86 on a non-standard table in the Manchester area and then Thompson abruptly broke the century barrier with 115 in the Competition proper, a new world amateur record, before going out 5–1 to Barron.

Barron looked certain to take the title when he led Gross 5–0 at the first interval in the final and 7–3 overnight but from 3–8 Gross won seven frames in succession in winning 11–9.

Momentously, the 1963 Championship was divided into Northern and Southern sections and reimbursement of travelling expenses was resumed. Gross won the Southern at Burroughes and Watts and Gary Owen, returning for the first time since 1952, won the Northern at Leeds. Owen then won nine frames in succession from 2–3 to beat Gross 11–3 in the final at Blackpool Tower Circus, a success which gave him the right to represent England in the first World Amateur Snooker Championship in Calcutta.

# CHAPTER X

# The Amateur Climax
*(Billiards 1946–1963)*

The history of professional Billiards since the war needs lamentably little telling. There were a few professional matches in the post-war years and there was a match for the World Professional Billiards Championship in September 1951 but by the time the next title match was played in August 1968 the B.A. and C.C. had come to take so dim a view of the future of professional Billiards that, in one of their lowest financial moments, they actually had the Championship cup melted down. Since then, the Championship has at least been regularly contested on the challenge principle; but professional Billiards, despite a few flickers of interest, has remained Snooker's infinitely poorer relation.

In contrast, the amateur game thrived for a while in that top amateur standards rose to a level equal to all but the very best pre-war professionals. The more advanced breakbuilding techniques reached a greater number of countries and from 1951, when the Empire Amateur Championship was re-named the World Amateur Championship, more nations competed and good players began to appear in countries which had no previous Billiards tradition of any great substance.

Unfortunately the growing popularity of Snooker in Britain blinded the B.A. and C.C. to its responsibility to safeguard the future of Billiards. After ignoring the danger signals, they accepted disgracefully easily that Billiards was a dying game and then, in the late 1960's, in a pathetic attempt to induce some Snooker players to play it, altered the rules in such a way that its distinctive charm and character was largely destroyed. In the mid 1970's there was a modest revival when Billiards was virtually dragged along on the coat tails of Snooker's progress but a great deal of hard work is still required to undo the effects of the shameful years of neglect.

For some five years after the war, the modest level of interest there had been in professional Billiards just before it was maintained. The survivors from the Golden Age rolled out their thousands when they had the opportunity (McConachy 1,426 and 1,001 unfinished in Scotland in December 1947) but for the most part an hour's (or less) Billiards served as a curtain raiser to Snooker, the main business of the evening, an ironic reversal of the position in the 1920's when Snooker padded out the session when the sessional Billiards points were scored too quickly.

John Barrie of Wisbech, winner of the Boys Championship in 1940, recorded a 790 break in February 1948 which contained only one in-off and with his polished top of the table game looked a first class prospect in beating Willie Leigh and Kingsley Kennerley before losing to Sidney Smith in the 1948 United Kingdom Championship. Smith had not, in fact, played a serious game of Billiards since 1939 so he was not the player he had been when making 3 breaks over 1,000 (highest 1,292) or when Willie Smith, his great friend and mentor, averaged 261 for a fortnight against him, he himself had averaged 136 and made 13 breaks over 500. His experience of big time Billiards told in the end but Barrie had his nose in front at half way and went down only 7,002–6,428. Smith averaged 40 and Barrie 36, nothing to write home about judged by Davis/Lindrum/McConachy/Newman standards but still double what the best amateurs were generally managing in their Championship.

Smith, in fact, was a fine player of both Billiards and Snooker who never fully emerged, psychologically, from his early years in the business. As a young professional, times were hard and this always seemed to be at the back of his mind in later life. He often waited on a cold station most of the night to catch an early train rather than book into a hotel and when he was given access to a practice table at Burroughes and Watts to give lessons he would often do so between the afternoon and evening sessions of a match he was playing at Leicester Square. He was educated enough to write his own newspaper articles and he was the earliest television commentator but his obsessional hard work and economies, together with a tendency to tinker with the mechanics of his game, ultimately seriously undermined his public performances.

On a lighter though no less arduous note, Norman Thomas, a Coleford, Gloucestershire amateur, completed forty-four hours fifty minutes' continuous play against a relay of opponents to beat by two hours the time established by John Roberts Senior in 1846. Dickie Flicker of Hackney then played Snooker for forty-five hours twenty-seven minutes at Leicester Square Hall, playing one hundred and thirty-seven frames, potting 1,668 balls and walking twenty-four miles, four hundred yards round the table.

Willie Smith and Claude Falkiner brought good crowds to Leicester Square for a week's Billiards which showed that the charm, quality and design of their games was undiminished by the years. They missed when they never would have missed in their prime but this seemed to make the exchanges more rather than less interesting. Smith also played Joe Davis in an annual week's match of Billiards and Snooker at Leicester Square but any talk of a real professional Billiards revival inevitably foundered on the question: who could Davis realistically play?

In one session, Davis performed the amazing all round feat of 639 at Billiards, 2 centuries at Snooker and a 64 which looked like being a third. In the previous session, he had made 667 at Billiards and 130 at Snooker, missing a difficult pink with a possible new world record of 143 on.

The play took place in an atmosphere quite free of the bitterness there had been between the two in the 1930's, the only reference to which was Smith's remark in some by-play, when Davis had snookered him and was offering manifestly the wrong advice to escape from the snooker: "I don't agree with your advice, Joe. In fact", he said, smiling as he thought about it, "I've never agreed with anybody."

The following year (1949) Davis (top break 527) did not play quite so well but Smith, then sixty-four, actually played better with 2 breaks over 300 and started favourite for the 1950 U.K. Professional Championship. This was not such a shambles as the 1949 "no contest" when both entries, John Barrie and Sydney Lee, withdrew, though the draw was rendered radically uneven by the late withdrawal of Sidney Smith on somewhat flimsy grounds. Barrie therefore had to play three matches to win the title and duly did so by beating Kennerley, whose bye to the final carried the penalty of depriving him of matchplay on the Burroughes and Watts match table. Barrie made breaks of 454 (versus Lee), 428, 402, 401 (versus Smith) and 714, 363, and 393 (versus Kennerley) who made a 473. In the last one and three-quarter hour session against Lee, Barrie scored 1,089 for an average of 136 with breaks of 454, 292, 114 and 270 unfinished.

Occasionally there was talk of Joe Davis going to Australia to play Walter Lindrum for the title or of Lindrum coming to Britain but when, in 1950, McConachy challenged Lindrum for the Championship, the latter promptly announced his retirement. The B.A. and C.C. decided that McConachy would play the winner of the 1950-1 U.K. Championship for the world title.

It proved to be Fred Davis who won it by beating Willie Smith and Kennerley but, with Leicester Square Hall heavily booked for the season's Snooker events, the date set for the Blue Riband of Billiards was the first week of September 1951. Davis considered this far too early and refused to play and Barrie was nominated to take his place.

McConachy, having recorded 21 breaks over 1,000 in the previous eighteen months, won comfortably 9,294–6,691 with a match average of 60 to Barrie's 44.9. In the fourth session, McConachy scored 1,100 for an average of 137 and made breaks of 481, 423 and 438 to Barrie's best of 367 and 336. It was good Billiards but not a patch on what his best had been. He returned to New Zealand and the Championship went into cold storage for no less than seventeen years.

Most of the leading amateurs were also of pre-war vintage. Marshall and Cleary were outstanding and between them dominated the Australian Championship. From 1936 to 1970, Marshall won nineteen titles, Cleary five and another very good top of the table player, Jim Long, the other five.

Cleary won his first Australian title in 1947, when Arthur Bull was second and Marshall third, setting a new Australian amateur break record of 435 in the process. Marshall increased the break record to 500 and then 540 in 1948 (when he also had a record session average of 73) and won both this year and in 1949 when Cleary missed a simple drop cannon when only 39 behind with seven minutes to go. The winner of the 1950 Australian Championship was assured of a trip to London for the 1951 World Amateur Championship and Cleary effectively booked his ticket by beating Marshall easily 2085–1272, the latter incredibly making only 2 centuries in the match. Earlier in the event, Cleary set a four hour aggregate record of 3,185 and also made a 432 break in thirty-three minutes.

Marshall, as the Empire title holder, was, though, quite rightly invited to compete in London as well and the other main title contenders appeared to be Wilson Jones, the young Indian champion, and Frank Edwards, who had won the English title in 1949, 1950 and 1951, each time defeating in the final the Welshman Joe Tregoning. Tregoning did not compete in the world event as Wales nominated their current champion, Willie Pierce.

Jones had started principally as a Snooker player, winning the Indian title in

1948, but a tour by Kennerley had interested him in top of the table play and a visit by Marshall in 1949, when the Australian made an Indian record break of 405 in twenty-eight minutes and an aggregate of 1,379 in two hours, also substantially furthered his Billiards education. Jones was beaten by T.A. Selvaraj, a redoubtable red ball player, in the 1949 Indian Championship but won it in 1950 when he beat Edwards, who was making a tour, 1,498–1,431 prior to beating Selvaraj by 72 in the final to earn his London trip. Jones also beat another notable visitor, Cleary, by some 600 in the 1951 Indian semi-final prior to beating Selvaraj easily in the final.

Edwards was unquestionably the most attractive English player of the period. Though he had been competing in the Amateur Championship since 1926, he did not show to any great advantage in the first three post-war Championships. Mendel Showman, a left-handed Mancunian, won a dour final against Herbert Beetham in 1946 and Joe Thompson won in 1947 and 1948 after Beetham, in the quarters, had led him by 347 going into the last session only to lose by 122.

That the 1949 Championship was to prove the start of the Edwards/Tregoning era was on the cards even as early as the area qualifying rounds when Tregoning, on his first appearance in the Bristol area, amassed a four hour aggregate of 2,256 with breaks of 236 and 229 in the third session, the first time two double centuries had been made in the same session in the event. Edwards, in the Birmingham area, made a 242 (fifteen minutes) and a 234 (fourteen minutes) in the same session in aggregating 2,171 for the four hours. These two duly reached the final and Tregoning was 53 in front at halfway before Edwards ran riot by scoring 1,071 with breaks of 285 and 286 in the fourth session and 1,268 (eclipsing Arthur Spencer's 1,266) in the fifth session for an average of 55, equalling Kennerley's record of 5 centuries in a session plus a sixth completed from 63.

Edwards beat Tregoning more easily in the 1950 final and also won comfortably in 1951 when both players recorded their highest averages and highest aggregates of their three finals, Edwards making 14 centuries and averaging 25.8. Every session was full and spectators were turned away at two but the unpalatable fact underlying some great entertainment was that the Australians were making bigger breaks and were much more consistent. Edwards was fluent, spontaneous, at times unbelievably fast, a first time striker of the cue-ball no matter how difficult or easy the shot might be. It was not sustained precision Billiards but its positional lapses, retrieved with a jenny, a cushion cannon or a screw shot, made it a more interesting spectacle. There was more excitement in an Edwards hundred than a Lindrum thousand.

Edwards, in fact, was to achieve a creditable second place in the World Amateur, beating Cleary but losing to Marshall in the last match of the tournament 3,429 (35.8) – 2,719 (28.3). Edwards made a personal best break in Championship play of 345 in the second session but Marshall went into the fourth and last session 765 ahead. The Australian made breaks of 228, 291, 225 and 325 while the Englishman's best, apart from his triple century, were 186 and 190. It should also be said that Marshall's victory was achieved in highly unfamiliar table conditions, the superfine, superfast cloth of Burroughes Hall being foreign both to his style of play and the usual run of Australian tables. Cleary, by his standards, was inconsistent and Jones, partly through inexperience, could not settle to the conditions at all, losing his first match to

Walter Ramage, a highly competent Scottish red ball player, and his last to Pierce, who scrambled a pot and a cannon in the last two shots of the match to win by 4. Marshall, with breaks of 417, 380 and 423, set British all comers aggregate records of 1,336 for a session (beating Edwards's 1,268) and 2,580 for two sessions (beating Coles's 2,164) and averaging 67.9.

There was absolutely no doubt about Marshall's supremacy. Shortly before coming to London, he had won the 1951 Australian Amateur (Cleary not entering for strategic reasons) by beating Jack Harris 4,873–1,681 in the final and recording a 110.8 world record session average with the aid of a 589 unfinished. When he retained his domestic crown in 1952 with another stunning set of statistics which included breaks of 498, 418 and nine more over 300 and match averages of 52.6 and 51.4 it was difficult to envisage him losing in the 1952 World Amateur in Calcutta.

But the title was to return to English keeping through Leslie Driffield, who had earned his trip to Calcutta by beating Beetham in one of the most thrilling finals on record. Beetham led most of the way but Driffield kept fighting back, notably with a 322 when Beetham was 443 in front. An 83 unfinished enabled Beetham to lead by 37 going into the final session, an effort which he carried to 212, but Driffield eventually got 44 in front with ten minutes to go and held on to win by 101.

Driffield, who had been entering the English Championship since 1935, was to win the title for six of the next eight years and eight times in all with a style which had been clearly influenced by Willie Smith, with whom he had played a great deal in his native Leeds. Consistency, concentration and tenacity were the hallmarks of Driffield's success. The top of the table game hardly figured in his play but his hazards were struck with relentless efficiency and he seemed never to miss a shot which was within his ordinary range. Rarely one to play a slightly risky shot to obtain perfect two-ball position when he could obtain one-ball position with complete certainty, Driffield played the all round percentage game probably better than any other amateur ever played it. His cue action, which tended to end with the tip of the cue pointing at some distant corner of the hall, was not one for the purists, some of whom also shuddered at his habit of playing in carpet slippers and a short-sleeved shirt. His wildly flowing grey locks made this aspect of his appearance resemble that of a demented orchestral conductor but by the ultimate test of any player – what he has won – his place is unquestionably among the great amateurs of all time.

Marshall began his attempt to retain the world title by beating Ramage comfortably but the applecart was well and truly upset by the gifted but inconsistent Indian number two, Chandra Hirjee, who defeated him 1,644 (27.3) – 1,539 (25.5) after the Australian had been 243 in front at the interval. Hirjee had earlier led Driffield by 43 with twenty minutes to go before the Yorkshireman got home with 123 and 54 unfinished and Ramage surprisingly repeated his London win over Jones who, completely demoralised, offered little resistance to Driffield and also lost to Hirjee who, with his inspired mood ebbing away, then lost to Ramage. Marshall thus needed to beat Driffield in the last match to force a play-off but never looked like doing so. Driffield led 363–68 after forty-five minutes, 757–457 at the interval and put himself out of reach with 127, 150 and 146 in the first hour at night to lead by 730 with only an hour to go.

After the disappointment of losing the world title, Marshall bounced back by increasing the world amateur break record to 702 in beating Cleary in the 1953 Australian final, an effort which began with a fluke from a Cleary double baulk when he was 400 behind with less than an hour to go. Jones also rebuilt his confidence by beating Hirjee, albeit by only 61, to win his fourth Indian title in 1954 and Driffield ground down all opposition to win the English Championships of 1953 and 1954.

Driffield, though, could not spare the time to defend his world title in Sydney in 1954 and Edwards, whom he had defeated by over 1,000 in the 1954 English final, was nominated to replace him. In 1953, Edwards had set a new English record with 6 centuries in a session against J.A.P. Holmes (Southampton) who was lucklessly on the receiving end of 5 in a session in 1954.

Edwards was playing well but when he reached Sydney he found great difficulty in adjusting to the four-length table with strip rubber cushions and lost his first match to Cleary by 861, the contests being of six rather than four hours (unlike Calcutta) because there were only five competitors.

Marshall then beat Jones by 809, though his highest break was only 161 and Jones's 153, so it was not altogether surprising that Cleary should then beat Marshall by 605 (Cleary 243, Marshall 258). In his elation at clearing this vital hurdle, Cleary compiled a new Championship record break of 682 (thirty-two minutes) in beating the South African, Taffy Rees, and then beat Jones comfortably to clinch the title.

The tournament had a beneficial effect both on Edwards, who was third behind Marshall, and Jones, who was fourth. Jones made a 440 break and a new eight hour aggregate record of 3,775 in beating Hirjee in the 1955 Indian final and Edwards, in 1955, regained the English Championship in an event notable in its early stages for a new English session average record of 103.3 by Alf Nolan, a left-hander from Newcastle. Alf Nolan was later to win both the English Billiards and Snooker titles, against the ever luckless J.A.P. Holmes. Nolan's eleven visits for 1,137 comprised 309 (from 63 unfinished), 55, 6, 159, 461 (second only to Kennerley's 549 in 1937), 116, 13, 6, 6, 68, 47. He went on to beat Driffield by 61 in the quarter-final, and Beetham, and held Edwards for two days before the latter made two 237's in the fifth session and averaged 50.5 in the last.

Edwards, who made a new four-hour record of 2,339 against Clem Hay (Rochdale) in the quarter-final, retained the English title in 1956 with his only Championship win over Driffield after the latter had led by 403 starting the last day. This melted to 145 going into the final session and from then on it was touch and go until a 72, mostly in-offs, clinched the title for Edwards in the last five minutes by a mere 58 points.

Driffield amply avenged himself in 1957 when he buried Nolan in the semi-final by 1,505 (with a fourth session average of 86.1) and Edwards by 1,570 in the final. 1958 was also a Driffield landslide for, after beating Beetham by only 128 in the semi-final, he swamped Jack Wright, the younger of two talented brothers from Earl Shilton, Leicestershire, who were both to reach the English final but who never consistently summoned the ability to produce their considerable best when it mattered most. Wright had beaten Edwards in the first round, when the latter had failed to compile a single century, but he was overwhelmed by 1,896 in a final distinguished by Driffield's consecutive breaks of 365 and 277 which helped him average 85.3 for the fifth session.

There was no world event to play in between 1954 and 1958 because the Championship scheduled for Johannesburg in September 1957 was called off in May "owing to many insurmountable difficulties in concluding arrangements", a polite phrase which embraced the escalating tension between the governments of South Africa and India and which was to foreshadow some stumbling blocks in future Championships.

Like Driffield in England, Marshall remained supreme in Australia, beating Cleary to win in 1955, not entering in 1956 (when Long beat Cleary in the Victoria Championship and went on to win the national title), and reaching new heights in 1957 when he broke the world four hour record against J. Harris with 3,364, making breaks of 278, 323, 193 and 336 in the first session and 380, 342, 289 and 224 in the second in which he averaged 90.3. He averaged 70.1 for the match. In the whole event, he made eight 300's, three 400's (including one of 462 in twenty-four minutes) and a 596. He beat Cleary, who averaged a respectable 32, by 1,518 in the deciding match. However, he did not defend in 1958, when Cleary equalled his record of 7 centuries in a session and made two 446 breaks in winning the title easily. So when Calcutta's offer to stage the World Championship in late 1958 was accepted, Marshall was neither Australian nor defending world champion. Consequently, the Championship took place without him and the eagerly anticipated Driffield v Marshall return match never materialised.

But what a tournament it nevertheless was! Jones had lost the Indian title to Hirjee in 1956 and regained it in 1957, the year, incidentally, in which McConachy, now the only professional working seriously on his Billiards, miscued on a massé at 999 in Dunedin. In 1958, though, Hirjee again beat Jones in the Indian final so the host nation, as was its right, fielded two first class competitors.

Driffield started like a machine with a 79.7 match average against Maung Hman (Burma) which superseded Marshall's previous best World Championship mark of 67.9 in 1951 and which included a 306 break and three more over 200 in a second session average of 109.9, a figure which exceeded Marshall's 109.6 in 1938 but fell short of the 112 by Steeples in 1931.

Throughout the tournament, the standard of play, in terms of breaks and averages, was to remain extraordinarily high. Cleary had a 431 in beating Wilfred Asciak (Malta) but the first significant result was a win for Jones over Cleary by 1,069 which included a break of 501 by the Indian.

The matches between the big four – Driffield, Cleary, Jones and Hirjee – were played over four sessions. The order of play was that the last two matches would be Driffield v Cleary and Driffield v Hirjee but it was the Driffield/Jones match which was to decide the Championship. It was one which was to produce an outstanding reversal of fortune.

Driffield, sound and methodical as ever, outpointed his opponent in each of the first three sessions to lead by 529. Jones scored only 14 in his first seven visits and Driffield took his advantage to 660 with only ninety minutes to go. Abruptly, Jones came to life with 170 and 232 to narrow the gap to 262. Driffield made 124 but Jones with 113 and 117 got to within 170. Some poor leaves for Driffield, some of them from Jones's astute safety, brought the Englishman almost to a standstill and Jones, with 147 and 106, went 68 in front and held on to win 2,865 (36.7) – 2,729 (34.9). Cleary then beat Hirjee to leave Jones the only undefeated player and Jones, starting with 3 double centuries and 3 single centuries in the first session, beat Hirjee by 1,768 to win the title.

Driffield recovered from the trauma of his amazing final session against Jones to take second place, beating Cleary 3,311 (61.3) – 2,844 (53.6) in the last match, aided by breaks of 396 and 470 in the last session in which he averaged 102.1. He also made a break of 499 against Hirjee in his last match. At the other end of the scale, the standard of play may be judged from the fact that Hman, who finished last, made a 215 break against Asciak and 4 centuries and a 97 in one session against Cleary.

All this took place without Marshall, who nevertheless returned to the fray to beat Cleary in the 1959 Australian Championship by 438, an event in which he set a new world session record of 1,876 and a new four-hour record of 3,391. In this match he had breaks of 619 (twenty-six minutes), 536 (twenty-two minutes) and 395 for the match average of 82.7. He scored 1,686 in six visits and 2,662 in nine in setting a new world record session average of 115.

Driffield hammered Beetham (whose 481 unfinished in an earlier round remained until 1978 the second highest in the English Championship) in the 1959 English final. In 1960, the allowance of consecutive hazards was raised from 15 to 25 and Driffield, averaging 102.2 in one early session, looked as though he would score for ever. Surprisingly, though, he made a semi-final exit to Reg Wright, who could then hardly raise the proverbial gallop against Beetham in the final. Beetham won by over 1,000, needing to average only 21, ironically much inferior to many averages he had recorded on the losing side. This gave him his passport to Edinburgh for the 1960 World Championship.

With Hirjee having retired because of a mysterious skin complaint, Jones, who had compiled a world record 8 centuries in a session in the 1959 Bombay State Championship, had little difficulty in winning the 1960 Indian title and was India's representative. Marshall did not compete in the 1960 Australian Championship, but Cleary was beaten by 354 by Long in the Victorian final and it was Long who came to Edinburgh.

The increase of the hazard limit was much in Beetham's favour, and the cool climate and the lack of atmosphere which the generally poor attendances at Collins Music Hall engendered, affected Jones, accustomed to warmth and large excited crowds, and to some extent Long, much more than the phlegmatic Englishman.

Beetham had some difficulty with the promising twenty-five year old South African, Mannie Francisco, who was to finish fourth and later figure prominently in succeeding Championships, but overcame his first test against Long 1,364 (32) – 1,013 (23), leading by 550 early on. Jones led him 403–95 but, flogging the red ball, Beetham won 1,291 (26) – 1,053 (21), a stark contrast to the sort of statistics which had been recorded in Calcutta in 1958.

Jones consoled himself with a 589 break against Asciak but Beetham had only to beat the Irishman, Bill Dennison, to take the title. As it happened, this was not so easy. "We'd been practising together", said Beetham. "So he wasn't frightened of me." Dennison, in fact, led by 100 with only seventy minutes left, but Beetham rallied with 184, 103 and 90 to win 1,173 (28) – 845 (20).

Full of confidence, Beetham retained the English title in 1961 though the Championship was more notable for the arrival on the scene of a few new faces. Mark Wildman, then twenty-five, hitherto thought of as a Snooker player (he had made a 108 break on television just previously), made a 375 break in the London section and one of 367 when 272 behind with forty-five minutes to go against another newcomer, Clive Everton, before losing by only 237 to Beetham. More dramatic still, though, was the debut of Norman Dagley, who was to dominate the Championship a little later, who snatched victory by only 3 points over the London champion, Jack Karnehm, with two quick cannons in the last few seconds. Dagley also stayed with Beetham until the champion pulled away in the last forty-five minutes of their quarter-final with a 297.

But for giantkilling there was nothing to surpass the 1,145–815 defeat of Driffield by the Ashington red ball specialist, John Sinclair. One break of 141 by Sinclair contained only two cannons and in the whole four hours he missed only one top pocket in-off and one in the middle. In its single-mindedness it was worthy of George Gray and Driffield, frustrated and kept out for long periods, could average only 15 with only one century. Sinclair also produced a 339 break against Reg Wright in the semi-final but by then Wright, who made a break of 361, had the match won. Wright had played so well that he appeared to have every chance in the final but he was rarely able to get out of first gear and Beetham, with three session averages over 60 and a break of 399, drubbed him by 2,017.

Marshall beat Cleary in both the 1961 and 1962 Australian Championships and on a tour of India scored 1,781 in fifteen visits against A. Sinha for a new world record average of 118.7 to beat the 115 he had set in the 1958 Australian Championship. With the 1962 World Championship in his home city of Perth, he was obviously favourite but Jones beat him 1,656–1,488. Cleary who had twice beaten Long since Edinburgh to recapture his position as Australian number two, surprisingly lost to India's number two, Banerjee, 1,893–1,303, but then beat Jones 1,808–1,421 to put Marshall back in with a chance.

Beetham had started with three wins but the relatively slow tables did not help his game and he was beaten, not badly but nevertheless with conviction, by Cleary, Jones and Marshall. If Cleary had not slipped up against Banerjee it would have been a triple tie but, as it was, it came to a play-off over eight hours between Marshall and Jones.

Jones made an early 489 but Marshall, in a fabulous third session, out-pointed him by no fewer than 1,200 in setting a new world record average of 128.4 in winning 3,623 (53.7) – 2,891 (30.6). It was his fourth and last title. In 1963 he faced Cleary for the last time and beat him by 1,277 for the Australian title. He retired with no intention of playing again though he was to make a brief comeback – though as a much reduced force – when he won the 1969 and 1970 Australian title and competed, with little success, in the 1969 World Championship in London.

Beetham came within one match of a hat trick of English Championship wins in 1962, reducing Driffield's lead of 1,167 after four sessions to only 215 with half an hour to go before Driffield played out time with 186. Driffield, with three breaks over 300 and a shoal of high session averages – with 81.8 as the best – looked as if he might again settle in to dominate the English scene, but in 1963 he was sensationally removed by Dagley who, with a 158 which occupied the last twelve minutes, beat him by 43.

Dagley's semi-final win over Nolan was even more sensational, as Nolan won each of the first three sessions to lead by 668 only for Dagley to make breaks of 142, 124 and 150 in the final period as Nolan, averaging only 6.7, seized up altogether. A 42 unfinished gave Dagley victory by 41 but he faded as the three-day final passed the halfway mark and Beetham administered the knockout with breaks of 314 and 311 in the fifth session, the first time two triple centuries had ever been recorded in the same session in the event. Dagley's lengthy innings as champion was not, however, to be long delayed.

# CHAPTER XI

# The New Dawn
*(Snooker 1963–1970)*

Sid Gillett, a director of Thurston's until he settled in South Africa as managing director of Thurston's (South Africa), had asked the B.A. and C.C. in 1952 to consider a World Amateur Snooker Championship and Australia had made a similar request shortly afterwards only to have it "deferred until some improvement in the B.A. and C.C.'s finances takes place." In 1958, the B.A. and C.C. announced its intention of inaugurating the event in London in 1959 but both India and Australia felt that London should not be the venue and persuaded two other countries likewise, so the event fell through until M.M. Begg, the Indian Chairman, donated a cup and concluded arrangements for a tournament in Calcutta in 1963 to which the B.A. and C.C. and other interested nations agreed.

As it had been for the World (then Empire) Amateur Billiards in its infancy in the 1920's and 1930's, the entry was small and restricted to those national associations who could afford to send a representative, a situation which was to change when government grants to sports bodies were to become the norm. Gary Owen was sent by means of an appeal fund and proved to be in a different class to the other four competitors. Playing with the technique of a professional, he won his four matches without being unduly extended.

The general standard might have been improved by the presence of a South African representative. Gerry Povall had established a new world amateur record break of 106 in the South African Championship in 1956 and Mannie Francisco, who had taken fourth place in the 1960 World Amateur Billiards in Edinburgh, was rated an equally good Snooker player. Just as surely as South Africa was prevented from competing because of differences between its government and governments in the Asian bloc, countries like Wales counted their financial assets or liabilities in petty cash and could not even contemplate sending a player to the other side of the world.

On his return Owen was beaten 4–0 by Barron (who created a sensation this season with a 107 break on television) in the English Championship in which Reardon returned to win the Southern area and John Spencer, playing his first full competitive season since making a break of 115 as a fifteen-year-old prodigy and giving the game up completely for ten years, won the Northern.

The national final started in bright April sunlight, the huge windows of the Central Hall, Birmingham, having escaped the attention of officials who had inspected the venue on a dark winter night. Nevertheless, the standard of play was high enough to foreshadow the epic battles which Reardon and Spencer were to contest as professionals. Reardon made a 74 break to lead 8–7 going into the final session and won 11–8 to establish a psychological ascendancy which was to become important later.

The following year Reardon looked set to retain his title when he led 5–1 in the Southern final only for Houlihan to recover marvellously to win 6–5. Spencer retained the Northern title, beating Edmonds 6–4 in the final, but Houlihan beat him easily, 11–3, at Blackpool Tower Circus to become English champion, a title which carried with it a place in the World Amateur in Karachi in November 1965.

However, hostilities between India and Pakistan not only caused the postponement of the Championship the following year but meant that England's second representative (in addition to Gary Owen as defending champion) was not Houlihan but the 1966 English champion, Spencer.

After two defeats in the English final, Spencer had been generally expected to suffer a third when Marcus Owen played brilliantly to beat Reardon 6–3 in the Southern final with breaks of 74 and 90. (His elder brother, incidentally, had lost 4–0 to Graham Miles, later a professional, who then lost 6–0 to Reardon in the semi-final.) Spencer beat Edmonds 6–4 for the Northern title and trailed Marcus 2–3 in the national final at Huddersfield Town Hall but then transformed the position by winning the evening session 5–0 (breaks of 58 and 59) and going on to win 11–5 with breaks of 53 and 101, the first century ever made in the amateur final.

It was Spencer who therefore accompanied Gary to Karachi where the Championship was confidently expected to lie between them. Spencer had an early scare when he had to win the last three frames to beat the Australian Bill Barrie (who had set a new Championship record of 73 in his first match) 6–5, but Owen always looked favourite. At 2–2 against Scotland's Bert Demarco, he compiled a new Championship record of 106, missing the last red; beat Spencer comfortably 6–2 with breaks of 73 and 52; from 1–2 beat Mohammed Lafir (Ceylon) 6–2 with the aid of a 118 clearance; and completed the round robin undefeated with a 6–0 win over Barrie. Spencer, who made a 101 against Demarco, was second.

India, for political reasons, was not represented, though a young Indian, Ratan Bader, had superseded Thompson's world amateur break record with a 122, a total clearance but for pink and black, in the West Bengal State Championship on December 8, 1964. Bader's previous best had been 82 in practice and 50 in a match and he never again made a century. Extraordinarily at a time when amateur centuries were becoming common, his record remained intact until 1977. Two of these centuries were in the 1966 Australian Championship, 108 by Barrie and 118 by Max Williams, the new champion.

Shortly after his return, Spencer expressed his dissatisfaction with the way the amateur game was run and said he would either turn professional or give up altogether. The National Spastics Society had several professionals playing shows on their behalf but called on Spencer to help out in the North, an offer which caused his professional career to mushroom. When Pontin's asked him to tour some of their Northern camps in the summer he was launched as a full time, if still struggling, professional.

Like Spencer, Owen, who was awarded the MBE on his return, withdrew from the Amateur Championship but did not turn professional until

September 1967 when he was offered a small advertising contract by Riley Burwat – Riley's had taken over Burroughes and Watts. Brother Marcus regained the Championship by beating Sid Hood 11–4 at Liverpool after destroying Barron 6–1 in the Southern final. Reardon, after a sensational 96 (the first 13 reds, 12 blacks) against George Jackson in his first match, fell 4–2 to Barron but these two were then invited to represent England in a three Test series in South Africa, winning the first and third 3–1 and 4–0 and losing the second 4–0 to Mannie Francisco and Jimmy van Rensburg.

South Africa had been unable to compete in either the 1963 or 1966 World Championships and, anxious not to be left behind internationally, particularly at a time when their domestic interest was high, financed this tour. During it, Ken Shaw of Union Billiards, around whom most professional activity revolved in South Africa, offered to arrange a professional tour for Reardon. It was this which enabled Reardon's professional career to get under way in December 1967 though after twelve months as a professional he had only £8 in the bank and Spencer, when the Professional Championship was revived in 1968–9, had to see his bank manager in order to raise the £100 entry fee.

For a combination of almost random reasons, there were now three new professionals. There was also some activity in Australia, where Eddie Charlton, a former miner and all round sportsman with competitive experience of Soccer, Cricket, Athletics, Boxing, Tennis, Surfing and speed Roller Skating, had turned professional in 1963, winning the Australian Professional Championship in 1964 and retaining it every year apart from a loss to Warren Simpson in 1968.

Horace Lindrum played regularly in public until 1967 – with a 147 on a non-standard table at the Penrith School of Arts in 1941 and some 750 century breaks in all – but never used his status to activate the competitive scene in Australia. Like many professionals in the game's history, his interest in the game tended to be limited to making a comfortable living from it with minimum risk to his reputation.

It was obvious from the outset, though, that Charlton was a competitive animal through and through and, though he was to attract plenty of criticism, some of it justified, from less lively fellow professionals, he was to transform the Australian professional scene through his chairmanship of the Australian Professional Players Association, through his promotional activities, and through his sales directorship of Heiron and Smith, the largest Australian billiard traders.

As a player, Charlton recalled Walter Donaldson: the same methodical, gun-barrel, straight cue action, the same competitiveness, the same consistency, the same disinclination to take risks, the same distrust of side and reluctance to use it – not an immediately exciting combination but one which made him terribly hard to beat. In 1967, at the Kempsey Crescent Head Country Club, he made total clearances of 137 and 135 in consecutive frames without his opponent having a shot and his form was such that Jack Chown, a wealthy Sydney enthusiast, sponsored his challenge for Pulman's world professional title, the last time this was defended on a challenge basis, at the Co-op Hall, Bolton.

Pulman was at that time playing a great many club exhibitions under an agreement with Players No 6, who were trying to reach the large market which clubs represented. The tobacco company also sponsored a national three-aside Amateur Team Championship which unfortunately lasted only two years, a fate which was to be shared by many sponsored events which the B.A. and C.C. played any part in organising, and most important the Pulman/Charlton match itself, a close one until Pulman won nine of the twelve Thursday frames, and which was successful enough with the public for the sponsors to offer support to a fully fledged World Championship in 1968–9.

Snooker was not to become a popular television sport until the advent of colour and the first "Pot Black" series in 1969, but it had nevertheless gained a foothold in the rapidly expanding field of sponsorship. It was to lose it because the sport's administration was poor, its press coverage virtually non-existent (it was to take Fleet Street sports editors almost ten more years before they could be convinced that Snooker was not dead), but most of all because of the incessant internal bickering, particularly between the B.A. and C.C. and the professionals. Though a Billiards issue was to provoke the final rupture, the relationship between the two sides went from bad to worse until the professionals finally dissociated themselves in 1971, reconstituted the P.B.P.A. (renamed, in April 1969, the World Professional Billiards and Snooker Association) and assumed complete autonomy for the professional game. It was to be the best decision they ever made.

The involvement of Players No 6 meant that the 1968–9 Championship was contested by eight players, four from the Leicester Square Hall generation, Pulman, Fred Davis, Williams and Rea, and four newcomers: Owen, Spencer, Reardon and a player of much lesser standard, Bernard Bennett, who had recently opened in Southampton the earliest of the new style Snooker centres which were to replace the dingy, disreputable Billiard halls of old. Jim Williamson, another great enthusiast, though not himself a player, promoted at the Queens Hall, Leeds, in January 1968, a round robin tournament won by Owen which was to preface his deepening involvement in the game, focused round his splendid Northern Snooker Centre, which opened, complete with match arena, in Leeds in 1974.

In no time at all it was obvious that the established professionals, without competition for so long, had lost their edge and that the newcomers, sharp from regular match play in the ever improving amateur world, were ready to take over. Spencer, on his Championship debut, beat Pulman 25–18 at Bolton, and Owen, still a Birmingham fireman, beat Rea 25–17, shortly after compiling his first 147 maximum. Williams and Davis, however, both won. Williams outclassed Bennett 25–4 and Davis, with a consummate display of safety tactics, beat Reardon 25–24 after a five hour three minutes final session which finished at one thirty-three a.m.

Owen then beat Davis 37–24 and Spencer crushed Williams 37–12 to ensure that a new name would appear on the Championship cup. This was generally expected to be Owen, who had generally had the better of his duels with Spencer, but the latter won the opening session 4–2 and was never behind. His 37–24 win was achieved, strangely enough, with the aid of only two 70's and three 60's, Owen's 80 being the highest break of the match, but in every other respect the new champion's play was a revelation. His long potting, his prodigious screw shots, even when cue-ball and object-ball were seven or eight feet apart, his uninhibited use of side, his bright attacking style, even the mere fact that here was a bright new face, made Spencer's win a memorable one. He took £1,780 as first prize.

Owen, now forty years old, never reached another world final while Spencer went on to establish himself as one of the great players of the 1970's. In 1971, Owen emigrated to Australia as attached professional to the Western Suburbs Leagues Club and enjoyed prosperity to a degree he was never able to achieve in Britain. In 1963, his English and first World Amateur Championship year, he had played deadly Snooker, potting brilliantly, playing watertight safety and competing with the aggressive, hungry keenness of a man who has identified an opportunity of securing a more comfortable way of life. Ironically, success blunted the very approach to the game which had enabled him to overcome such relatively weak points in his technique as a tendency to snatch on forcing shots and consequent limitations in his screw shots.

After the impact of Spencer and Owen contesting the 1969 final, the pendulum swung partially back to the longer established professionals when Pulman reached the final of the 1970 Championship, which was sponsored by John Player for the second and last time, by beating Owen comfortably in their semi-final. Adapting himself the better to an inappropriately difficult table at Bolton, Reardon eliminated Spencer in the other and looked as if he would canter away with the final at the Victoria Halls, London, when he led 27–14. Pulman, one of the game's grittiest fighters, recovered to 33–34, but Reardon then won the next three frames for his first world title.

Reardon held the Championship less than six months, for, in November that year, the event was staged again at various venues in Australia with nine competitors from six countries, the most internationally representative field there had yet been. The complex organisation involved the players in much travel, often by air, from match to match, and a makeshift system, not really satisfactory, halfway between straight knockout and a complete round robin, produced four semi-finalists, Reardon, Spencer, Charlton and a second Australian, Warren Simpson.

Simpson, a genial, talkative man and another Sydney-domiciled though New Zealand-born player, Norman Squire, who made over 2,000 century breaks, including a maximum, played exhibitions and tournaments when they came up but spent most of their lives playing for money, particularly in City Tattersalls Club, Sydney. Squire, in fact, died in 1976 during a game there. As well as straightforward wagers both were fond– say with 7 or 8 reds left in a frame – of taking bets all round the room as to whether they would clear the table.

Talented and quick but easygoing and tending to be imprecise in his positional play, Simpson (and even more so Squire) rarely had the hardness, the patience or the sheer consistency to beat Charlton, indisputably Australia's number one.

Charlton – drawn against Simpson – started an overwhelming favourite to reach the final but was involved in a minor car accident on his way to the match and started badly, losing the first three frames. During the tournament, Simpson's confidence had risen steadily for, after losing his first match to Paddy Morgan who had left Belfast and turned professional under the guidance of Murt O'Donoghue, he had beaten Pulman, Owen and Perrie Mans, who had succeeded his father as South African professional champion. A flying start to his semi-final was all he needed and he was never in arrears. The other semi-final was strangely one-sided for Spencer got right on top of Reardon and played better and better. When it came to the final, he was in unstoppable form, not merely with his potting – exceptional as this was – but with his use of screw and extreme side.

Diagram 1 illustrates the enormous amount of side he was able to generate and control, running through the blue with so much right-hand (check) side that the cue-ball checked back from the cushion at the same angle it had struck it and rebounded not only to the opposite side cushion but away from it into the middle of the table.

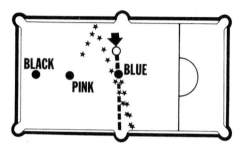

Diagram 2 reproduces a shot from the final which earned from Simpson the response "that was impossible" and from the audience a three minute ovation. With eight feet between cue-ball and object-ball, Spencer hoped to screw back some three feet for the blue or one of the baulk colours, but tremendous cue power and perfect timing, combined with unintentionally striking the cue-ball not only very low but fractionally to the right of centre, caused the cue-ball to recoil some twelve feet, as shown.

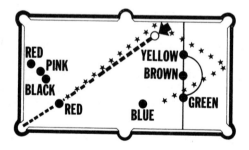

Spencer played a couple of slack sessions in the final, losing one 6–0, but the outcome was never in doubt. On the second day, he made breaks of 105, 126 and 107 in the space of four frames, the first time there had ever been consecutive centuries in the Championship. Casting statistics aside, it was not Snooker in the Joe Davis mould or that of the professionals who learned their craft in the Davis era. The keynote of Davis's style was super accurate control of the cue-ball whereas the style of Spencer and the best of the other new-comers of the 70's leaned more heavily on sheer potting ability, greater cue-power and more spectacular use of screw and side. Greater emphasis on potting (or at least attempting) long balls rather than trying to force openings with long bouts of safety play also characterised this apparently new approach though, as the sport expanded and the pressures on the players increased, fewer risks tended to be taken and frames grew longer.

Spencer, Reardon and Owen had conclusively proved there was no impenetrable mystique about being a professional, but the amateurs who followed them were not so successful.

David Taylor, who had come from nowhere to win the English Amateur title in 1968, went on to win the World Amateur title in Sydney in October that year by beating Max Williams (Australia) 8–7 after trailing almost throughout the final. Taylor's 96 was the highest break of the tournament and the ten competitors from seven countries, both records, were divided into two round robin groups, New Zealand, South Africa and the Republic of Ireland (who supplied a semi-finalist in Paddy Morgan) competing for the first time. Taylor, at the age of twenty-four, turned professional immediately but was unable to achieve any significant progress and after a couple of years lost his confidence.

Thompson, disillusioned with the amateur game, and another former amateur champion, Parkin, both failed to make much impact as professionals and this was also true of Gross and Houlihan, who turned in 1970. Graham Miles, the Midland amateur champion, turned in May 1969 with a slimmer record but improved steadily to reach the top class. Meanwhile the most amazing natural talent Snooker has ever seen had started to lay the foundation of his reputation. Alex Higgins, who had learnt to play in a Belfast Billiard hall called the Jampot, living off Coca Cola and Mars bars, scattered the opposition to win the Northern Ireland and All Ireland amateur titles in March 1968 at the age of nineteen and turned professional briefly before being reinstated in time to win, virtually single handed, the Players No 6 British Team Championship for Belfast YMCA at Bolton in 1969, when in two frames he turned a 154 deficit against Penygraig Labour into a 17 point lead, winning the first of these frames in only eight minutes.

A few months later, he was back in Lancashire. Carrying one small suitcase and his cue, he threw out, like a gunfighter in the Old West, his challenge: "I'm a Snooker player. I play for money. Who'll play me?" Virtually overnight, Lancashire was buzzing with talk of this incredible twenty year old Irishman who hardly seemed to aim and yet never seemed to miss. Receiving 14, he beat Spencer, the champion, 23–18 at Bolton and turned professional again under the wing of John McLaughlin, a Blackburn Bingo tycoon, who smartened up his appearance but soon found, as many others were to find, that Hurricane Higgins was ultimately unmanageable, though Dennis Broderick, the most durable of those who tried, did contribute to his crest of a wave capture of the world title in 1972.

# CHAPTER XII

# Downturn and Revival
*(Billiards 1964–1978)*

Once Snooker had overtaken Billiards in popularity, as it had shortly after the war, Billiards faced a long battle for its very survival. There was no professional activity at all between 1951 and 1968 and for much of the later part of the 1960's and early 1970's it seemed as if amateur Billiards might peter out similarly. With no professionals setting ultimate standards to strive for and great amateurs like Marshall, Cleary, Wilson Jones, Driffield and Beetham either retiring or passing their peaks, the Billiards tradition declined. Billiards remained healthiest not in the British Isles but in other parts of the Commonwealth where the pace of life was slower or where sophisticated professional techniques had been mastered by fewer players.

Particularly in Britain, cueists seeking cash or glory turned almost inevitably to Snooker rather than Billiards and with this decline Billiards skills tended to be passed on – in folk art or folk sport tradition – less than they had been. An official coaching scheme might well have halted the slide and in fact, a few years after one was introduced in England in 1969 – largely financed by the Billiards and Snooker Foundation, a joint B & S.C.C./Trade body funded by a voluntary levy on home sales – Billiards did start to make a modest recovery among the young. In general, however, the decline of Billiards was a sad story of neglect, maladministration and lack of imagination.

The picture was not one of unrelieved gloom, for the period contained players like Norman Dagley, Mohammed Lafir of Sri Lanka, the first player from a junior and unsophisticated Billiards nation to win a world title, and Satish Mohan and Michael Ferreira, the two Indians who stood at the head of what had arguably become, in depth, the leading Billiards nation, who would have been outstanding in any era. More nations competed in World Amateur Championships and players of world class became proportionately more widely spread. The Professional Championship was again contested, a few minor tournaments sprang up and the general outlook in the late 70's was certainly much more hopeful than it had been in the early 60's.

Alf Nolan's English Billiards title success in 1964 was to separate two eras rather neatly. From 1949–1963, the Championship had been won by either Edwards, Driffield or Beetham. Between 1965 and 1978 it was to be won nine times by Dagley. Nolan, once in the final before 1964 and five times afterwards, straddled both periods though he was probably a better player in the former than the latter. An excellent losing hazard exponent, Nolan never played the top of the table game to any significant degree and, as the years went by, an increasingly pronounced jerk in his action limited his range of shots. He possessed, nevertheless, a good all round game with tactical acumen second to none and a gift for putting certain opponents out of their stride. He developed, at one time, a habit of sitting with his back to the table when his opponent was in play; at another he used a different cue just for screw shots; and he had the ability, without putting himself off, of playing very fast or very slow as the situation demanded.

In his Championship year he beat Sinclair, who had removed Reg Wright and Beetham, and in the final, by a wide margin, Driffield who had made 3 double centuries on the last day to beat Dagley from behind but who then appeared burnt out, aggregating only 443 on the first day and 576 on the second.

Nolan, as English champion, went to New Zealand for the 1964 World Amateur where Frank Holz, one of the most energetic and capable organisers the game has known since the war, staged the event in his own small country town of Pukekohe. Driffield and Beetham were both invited to go too but the second English place was eventually offered to Karnehm. Wilson Jones, who had just won his ninth Indian title and a newcomer, Michael Ferreira, who had compiled a 353 break in his National Championship, represented India. Cleary, who was having difficulties both with his health and his game, was Australia's representative; Francisco, who had made a new South African record of 389 in his 1964 Domestic Championship (and an 88 at Snooker), three New Zealanders and a Pakistani, Minoo Mavalwala, completed the field.

Shortly before the event, on September 1, 1964, the B.A. and C.C., with an incredible lack of foresight and without consulting any other nations (in some of which Billiards was flourishing to a much greater degree than it was in Britain) had drastically altered the rules. By stipulating that the red was always to be replaced on its own spot when potted (except when the spot was occupied) and by reducing the permitted number of consecutive hazards from 25 to 15 the B.A. and C.C. not only restored a limited version of the spot stroke but removed the incentive for players to master the demandingly skilful top of the table technique based on alternating a cannon with no more than two pots. By making it easier to run up a break with the dull, repetitious and simple spot stroke method – as long as a cannon was played every fifteenth shot a break could continue indefinitely just by potting the red – the players who had mastered the pure top of the table technique were either penalised or forced, to give themselves a better chance of winning, to adopt the spot stroke. Even those who could not bring themselves to exploit it systematically employed it on occasion.

It did take a few months for the implications of the new rule to sink in in all their enormity and, as it happened, the Pukekohe event was won by Jones, a player who used it hardly at all. The Indian Association never actually accepted the rule for domestic competition though they did accept its later modification to five consecutive pots from the spot.

Jones was undefeated but he beat young Ferreira by only 144 and was given a struggle by Karnehm, who did splendidly to finish runner-up. In the latter match, Jones led by only 113 at the interval before 3 centuries in his first five visits on the resumption gave him a virtually unassailable lead.

Karnehm, who made a break of 390 in eighteen minutes against Mavalwala, survived a close finish against Ferreira, who was in play only six behind at the bell, and creditably recovered from an interval deficit of 213 to beat Nolan. Francisco, the only player to exploit the spot stroke as a policy, made a break of 518. Jones made 7 centuries in a session against Tom Yesberg, one of the New Zealanders, and in retaining his Indian title in 1965, just prior to his retirement, made a new world record of 8 in a session.

On his return to England, Karnehm fell to Nolan in the English semi-final but the Geordie was then deprived of his English title by Dagley, who had played out time with 90 unfinished to beat Everton by 11 in the first round before eliminating Driffield in the semi.

It is always dramatic when a player wins a major title for the first time, but the way in which Dagley retained the title in 1966 provided one of the most amazing stories in the history of the Championship. Groggy after two days in bed with flu, Dagley was outpointed by Nolan by nearly 1,000 points on the first day of the final. Feeling better when he resumed next day, Dagley over-turned these arrears to lead by 49 after five sessions and clinched the match with a 219 unfinished to win by 463, Nolan failing to make a century in the last four sessions. Driffield, who had stated for some years, even in those that he had won, that the bed of the table at Burroughes was too fast for Championship Billiards, did not enter for this reason.

In 1967, the Championship was split into Northern and Southern sections with the Northern at Priory House Social Club, Middlesbrough, and the Southern at Burroughes and Watts, whose takeover by E.J. Riley of Accrington involved the sale of their Soho Square property to the Hurst Park Syndicate and thus the closure of this richly historic match hall, which had been to Billiards what Wimbledon's Centre Court is to Lawn Tennis. It was also to mark the end of the tradition of leading trade firms providing match halls of elegance and distinction. Henceforth, England's leading Billiards and Snooker events were to be decided in much earthier surroundings.

Dagley looked a good thing for the Southern title but, as had always seemed possible since the partial restoration of the spot stroke, this Billiards artist was undone by the concentrated spot stroke assault of Geoffrey Thompson, primarily a Snooker player. A break of 368 was the centre piece of Thompson's semi-final win but he was hardly the same player in the final and Everton, who had beaten Karnehm in the other semi, disposed of him quite comfortably.

In the North, Driffield needed a 124 unfinished in the last seven minutes to beat a local hero, Bob Close, by 56 and beat Nolan by a mere 43 in the final. He then proved too consistent and experienced for Everton in the national final at the Albert Hotel, Liverpool, the permanent matchroom of the Liverpool Association, which was the kernel of the Lancashire Association, a body which in a few years was to exert a dominant influence on the B.A. and C.C.

This entitled Driffield to compete in the 1967 World Amateur at the Hotel Samudra, Colombo. It was fiercely hot and so humid that Driffield and Long both wore cotton gloves on their bridge hands. This was the only way they could make their cues travel smoothly through their bridges. In his third match, Driffield faced defeat when Francisco, exploiting the spot stroke to the full, made a 301 break to lead by 500 with an hour to go. Driffield rallied with 74 and 127 and, crucially, with a thirty-five minute 351, and won by 162. After this he was never in danger, beating Ferreira (who had made a personal best

Joe Davis

Leicester Square Hall

Walter Donaldson

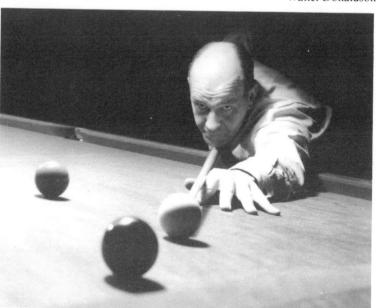

John Pulman

Rex Williams

Norman Dagley

Fred Davis

break of 507, the highest of the event, in beating Long) with the two best session averages 50.9 and 52.9, and the Ceylon champion, Mohammed Lafir, at that stage the only other undefeated player, 1,489–726. Lafir, who became a national hero through his exploits, was second, which was good going, even with a partial spot stroke in operation, for someone who had regarded himself as a Snooker player until his first significant Billiards success, beating Ferreira to reach the All India final in 1965.

Driffield last entered the English Championship in 1968 when he was beaten by 141 by Nolan in the Northern semi-final at the Black Swan, Sheffield. Nolan in turn fell to Wildman, who concentrated on the spot stroke so heavily that he potted the red from its spot 107 times in the first two sessions alone. It also loomed large in the 426 break on the second day which was the crucial element in Wildman's 75 point win.

Wildman went on to beat Everton by a mere 112 in a low scoring national final at Almondbury W.MC., Huddersfield, the loser's path to retaining the Southern title having been smoothed by a car breakdown which caused Dagley to default in the first round. The Southern event was accommodated both in this and the following two years in a basement room in Great Windmill Street, London, which could comfortably hold less than forty spectators. It was a period when it seemed doubtful whether either the Billiards Association or the Championship itself would continue to survive.

It was at this nadir of the game's fortunes that Rex Williams, a former Boys and Junior champion nearly twenty years previously before he turned professional at the age of seventeen and concentrated almost exclusively on Snooker, decided to challenge McConachy, now seventy-three, for the World Professional Billiards title which the veteran had held unchallenged since 1951. When he was sixteen, Williams had made a 510 break which was still his personal best and had also beaten Beetham for the Midland Amateur title so his basic technique was extremely sound and would probably have earned him the Amateur Championship in due course.

Though he had played very little Billiards as a professional – because there was no public for it – Williams never completely forgot it and a Snooker tour to Australia gave him the opportunity, backed by a useful sponsorship from John Haig, the whisky distillers, to stop off in Auckland to play McConachy.

The New Zealander's great days were, of course, well in the past, but, his cue-arm shaking from Parkinson's disease, he fought with unquenchable spirit to retain his title. In an attempt to control "the shakes" he had adopted an ever heavier cue until finally he played with a monster 36 ounce model which, like all his others, he had made himself. Never a fast player, his physical disability – having virtually to time the delivery of his cue as best he could in relation to the shaking in his arm – and his age made his rate of scoring excruciatingly slow. With gimlet clear eyes shining beneath his characteristic, stiff-peaked, green eyeshield and the fine general physical condition he still maintained with daily running and exercises, McConachy did not wilt until the sixth and final day which he began only 17 behind after tailing by 543 with two days to go. The table was much slower and covered with a coarser cloth than Williams was accustomed to – factors which helped McConachy's nursery cannons – but the scoring was nevertheless disappointing. A break of 293 by Williams in the fourth session was the highest of his 7 centuries, none of which were made in the last two days. McConachy made 11 centuries with 236 and 200 as his highest.

Some eight thousand spectators paid to see this almost unique spectacle of a septuagenarian national hero battling with enormous relish for a world title. The standard of play was modest but the epic struggle did at least bring the Championship back into circulation.

But what problems were to ensue! Williams, having had the enterprise to challenge and get himself financed, not unreasonably stipulated a £250 guarantee to defend. Fred Davis was nominated as challenger but no British promoter, bearing in mind other promotional expenses and the lack of any proven paying public for Billiards, came forward with such a guarantee and his challenge lapsed. This was far from the end of the story, but it was the end for the time being.

A change of chairmanship from Harold Phillips to Jack Karnehm led to better administration and, on September 1, 1968, a revision of the rules to limit consecutive spot strokes to five (after which the red was placed on the middle spot), a move which restored Billiards to something much nearer its traditional character. The adoption of Lancashire's proposal that affiliations should be five shillings per club instead of three guineas per league or association aroused bitter opposition but nevertheless put a healthier complexion on the association's finances. It also paved the way for the present system of proportional representation (one council member for each hundred clubs affiliated) and led to the axis of power swinging from London to the North. Karnehm also arranged for the 1969 World Amateur Billiards to be staged at the Victoria Halls, London, an event which was to expose the association's out of date and inefficient approach by attracting embarrassingly small crowds.

Karnehm, whose suspect temperament had apparently doomed him never to win the English title, earned his place in the Championship by beating Thompson (who had beaten Dagley by 19) by 333 in the Southern final and Wildman by over 1,000 in the national final at Huddersfield. Marshall came out of a six year retirement to win the 1969 Australian title with a top break of 295 and six more over 200, not vintage Marshall but still useful; though, as it turned out, his lay-off and the lightning speed of the table – which ran seven lengths – made him appear even more a shadow of his former self in London. Ferreira, playing in his third World Championship, and Satish Mohan, who made a new Indian record of 584 to beat him for their national title, constituted a strong challenge from India. Francisco, Lafir, the Maltese Paul Mifsud, the Welshman Roy Oriel, and two New Zealanders, Alan Twohill and Frank Holz, made it a record nine nations competing.

The order of play favoured Karnehm, who opened the proceedings with four hours of minimally interrupted practice against Holz prior to tackling Lafir who, as runner-up in Colombo, had some reason to expect a gentler opening match. Karnehm won by 693 and with his next three matches against the players who, with Holz, were to fill the last four places, was able to record five wins while the other fancied contenders were pitched straight into important matches against each other.

Francisco started well by beating Mohan by 184 after being 390 behind at the interval and Marshall by 876 after Marshall had won an exciting match against Ferreira by 75. Marshall then put Mohan virtually out of the running; then Oriel (who had made a 297 and only just lost to Ferreira by 172 after the Indian had needed a 353 break to level the scores with less than an hour to go) upset Francisco's applecart by beating him by 140.

The topsyturvy sequence of results continued: Ferreira lost to Wildman, who then suffered his first loss to Francisco; Lafir beat Mifsud by 69 after being 320 behind with thirty minutes to go – but then suffered a 65 point defeat by Ferreira. This last match finished just before eleven p.m. but in the nine o'clock session against Karnehm the next morning, Ferreira occupied the last fifty-five minutes with a superb 604 unfinished, a world record under the new rules, which he completed to 629 on the resumption. Karnehm thus suffered what was to prove his only defeat though his most difficult matches were yet to come.

Wildman suffered a second loss to Oriel but Francisco had still only one defeat against him when he met Karnehm in what was to be the key match. The tension was heightened by the fact that both displayed characteristic signs of nerves. Francisco, who had failed against Driffield in Colombo when he virtually had the match won and who throughout his career was to fall victim to fatal inhibitions when he had chances to amass unassailable leads, was in front for all but a few seconds of the match. Karnehm was also guilty of many bad lapses and it seemed inconceivable, when he trailed by 152 with seventeen minutes remaining that he would play out time with 161 unfinished, his only century of the match, to win by 9.

However, this storybook conclusion for Karnehm – a traumatic experience for Francisco – undoubtedly strengthened the Englishman's mental fibre for his tests against Marshall and Oriel. He trailed the Australian by 166 with thirty-five minutes to go but came through with a 62 unfinished to win by 120 and Oriel led him narrowly at the interval, but the tide was by now running in Karnehm's favour. He was making fewer mistakes and the cornerstone of his technique – the in-off game – was yielding a consistently high return. He made only four breaks over 200 in the forty hours he played during the tournament but it was sound, functional and ultimately winning match Billiards.

Coming down the final straight, Lafir showed a glimpse of the form which was to give him the world title in Bombay in 1973 when he scored 930 in the first eight visits against Marshall and ended with the best match average of 52.8. Francisco suffered a third defeat to Ferreira, so on the final day the latter had to defeat Mohan and Karnehm had to lose to Wildman to make a play-off necessary. Mohan, though, produced his best display of the Championship so Karnehm was already champion when he began the final session against Wildman.

Karnehm's victory was achieved over a field of a higher overall standard than ever before. Though breaks and averages (when the latter were kept) were much inferior to those world events which featured Marshall, Cleary and Driffield in their prime – and they were playing to more difficult rules – no less than eight of the eleven competitors made at least one break over 200. Nine wins out of ten matches in this company was an achievement of real substance but Karnehm's greatest victory was possibly that which he achieved over himself and his temperament. Over a period of many years, no one could have practised harder and few could have kept going in the face of such a persistently extravagant disproportion between his impressive statistics in practice (and sporadically in matches) and his unimpressive showings in the English Championships.

Winning the title was a supreme effort. He did not play again as an amateur. Shortly afterwards he resigned the chairmanship of the B.A. and C.C. after a stormy period in office. He turned professional and became well regarded as a coach and in the Billiard trade through the company of which he was a director, Karnehm and Hillman. In office his dual role as player and administrator exposed him to criticism and it was certainly unfortunate that he should be Chairman at a time when Driffield, a member of the council, who had turned professional in October 1968, challenged for the title in July 1969.

Williams was ordered to defend the title within six months but this period elapsed before any proposal was placed before him as to terms or venue. In the meantime, he accepted an offer to defend against Albert Johnson in Australia (terms having been agreed) but the B.A. and C.C. quashed this and insisted that he play Driffield, who at this time was not even a member of the Professional Players Association. At the eleventh hour, it was verbally suggested that Williams should defend against Driffield in the B.A. and C.C.'s new headquarters and match hall at Haringey. He declined and was forthwith stripped of the title.

The professionals had had a number of disagreements with the B.A. and C.C. or, more specifically, over Karnehm's handling of affairs. They felt strongly that they were not being fairly treated and even that there was a hidden intention for Driffield to play Karnehm, who was known to be considering turning professional, for the professional title. So, on December 12, 1970, the P.B.P.A. disaffiliated from the B.A. and C.C., reformed themselves as the World Professional Billiards and Snooker Association, and declared their autonomy in organising the professional game, a step which immediately dried up all sources of income (affiliations and professional membership fees plus five per cent of all earnings from the World Professional Snooker Championship) which the professional game had directly contributed to the amateur.

The professionals' worst suspicions were confirmed when Driffield and Karnehm duly did meet for the B.A. and C.C. version of the world title at Middlesbrough Town Hall in June 1971, Karnehm having simultaneously resigned the B.A. and C.C. chairmanship at their February AGM and announced that he had turned professional. Driffield (with a top break of 352) won a farcically easy 9,029–4,342 victory. *The Middlesbrough Evening Gazette* commented: "It is doubtful whether the enthusiasm of the Teesside fans could wear another flop like this – even for nothing."

Williams's first defence under the aegis of the W.P.B.S.A. was also something of a farce. Bernard Bennett, a second class professional with no substantial previous Billiards achievement, fulfilled the conditions set by the W.P.B.S.A. in guaranteeing Williams £250 for a week's title match at Bennett's own club, The Castle in Southampton. Williams displayed his fine top of the table technique in breaks of 480, 372, 325 and 302. Bennett only twice exceeded the hundred.

Eventually, both Driffield and Karnehm, who for some time were the only two professionals to continue to recognise the B.A. and C.C. as the governing body for the professional as well as the amateur game, abandoned this position and became members of the W.P.B.S.A.

Driffield never challenged Williams again but Karnehm did so in September 1973 at the Marconi Athletic Club, Chelmsford, where Williams played some of the finest Billiards seen in Britain since the war and dispelled any lingering feeling that he was in any way an unworthy champion. A session average of 217 (when he averaged 96 for the day), a match average of 50.7, and a break of 528 as the highest of his 31 centuries were all achieved largely through a top of the table technique so fluent that he made nonsense of the permitted five reds from the spot. From hand he missed only two middle pocket in-offs and one top pocket in-off in the entire match and generally looked, if an incentive could have been provided for him to play Billiards for months on end, well capable of making thousand breaks.

It was a similar story in Williams's next two defences, both against Eddie Charlton in Australia. At Geraldton in 1974, Williams led by over 1,000 after a day's play and it was not until the second part of the week, when he won two sessions and made breaks of 488 and 401, utilising the five pots from the spot to the full, that Charlton struck form appropriate to the event. At Geelong in 1976, Williams averaged 121.3 in the ninth session and 65, 67 and 85 in the last three. Charlton succeeded in obtaining high financial guarantees for the matches and without his efforts the Championship would have lain dormant. But it was sad that there were no promotional offers for a Williams/Davis Championship match for Davis was probably the only professional with the class to threaten the title holder.

In the amateur game it was undoubtedly the Dagley era for he was to win the English title six times in succession from 1970–1975 and the World Amateur title at the Malta Hilton in 1971 and at Auckland Town Hall in 1975. He did not compete in the 1973 World Championship at the Cricket Club of India, Bombay, because of eye trouble.

A silky-smooth cueist, Dagley attributed much of his success to "being thrashed night after night" by Reg Wright at the Earl Shilton Institute in the depths of Leicestershire. These sessions certainly ingrained in his mind all the correct moves and sequences of shots, the importance of never missing an in-off from hand and the scoring potentialities of top of the table play. Unlike his mentor, however, who often lacked the confidence to play top of the table in matches, Dagley was also blessed with an ice-calm match temperament and a serene faith in his own ability. These latter qualities had already earned him some spectacular victories in the English Championship and he was to call upon them at crucial moments in countless matches he played during these six remarkable years of success.

He never looked like losing in any of these six English finals. A 467 break spanning the end of the first and beginning of the second session of his 1970 final against Nolan at Prescot was his highest English Championship break for, unlike Driffield, he had little taste for breakmaking as such. He tended to produce his best under pressure but it was not all that often that he found himself in this position.

After a comfortable retention of the English title in 1971, he started favourite in the World Amateur Championship at the Malta Hilton where the ten competitors were divided into two groups of five with two qualifying from each for a final group of four. Dagley started with a very easy win over Ferreira who, despite his good showings in Pukekohe, Colombo and London, was still very much Indian number two to Mohan, who won five of the six Indian titles between 1968 and 1973. As Mohan had also been drawn in this group, Ferreira began his match with Dagley already feeling under pressure. He did not make a century against Dagley and only one in losing very easily to Mohan and, though he did achieve a remarkable win over Clive Everton (Wales) by 6 points after being 101 behind with six minutes to go, he failed to qualify. Dagley got home by only 70 against Wilfred Asciak, Malta's number two, but by the time he lost to Mohan in the last match of the group both were assured of qualifying.

The other group was not of such a high standard. Mannie Francisco disposed conclusively of all his opponents and Lafir, who was below the form he had shown in Colombo and London, filled second place. Ill in bed for thirty days before the Championship, Lafir arrived in Malta late for his first match, carrying only his cue as his luggage had mysteriously gone on to Rome. With his seven stone engulfed in one of the fifteen stone Ferreira's shirts, he was pushed straight to the table to play his first match against David Sneddon (Scotland) when a break of 204, his only contribution over 50, proved just about his winning margin.

In the play-off group, Francisco beat Lafir 1,423–790 before Dagley and Mohan came together for what proved to be the crucial match. Dagley led 927–399 at the interval and by 518 with an hour to go but Mohan, an amazingly quick player with not only good control but a dazzling array of recovery shots, replied with breaks of 192 and 304 with only one scoreless visit between.

Dagley, who had reclined in his seat languidly smoking a cigarette as he witnessed his overwhelming lead being reduced to a paltry 24, then made 26 and left Mohan apparently safe, but a brilliant cushion cannon put the Indian in again before he failed at a thin in-off. Supremely calm, as if nothing particular had been happening, Dagley then compiled a completely unruffled 170, his face never betraying anything but faint amusement, to win the match 1,462–1,202.

A break of 348 helped Dagley to a 2,014–639 win over Lafir and, with Francisco's earlier form negated by tension, he disposed of the South African 1,565–871 to clinch the title. Francisco, more relaxed, made breaks of 353, the highest of the tournament, and 230 within three visits in beating Mohan 1,687–1,045 for second place.

The three weeks at the Malta Hilton were also notable for a stormy meeting at which a World Council, a new one nation, one vote body, was formed, initially as the supreme body for World Amateur Championships but intended also, by some nations, eventually to take over all the international functions of the B. & S.C.C.

Traditionally, the B. & S.C.C. had governed the game internationally but it was, in structure and preoccupation, an English domestic body whose meetings were always held in England and attended only by English representatives. Discontent and dissatisfaction had been simmering abroad for some time but England gave ground very grudgingly and, indeed, fought a desperate rearguard action not only to prevent more of its international functions being taken away but to regain control of the World Amateur Championships themselves. The B. & S.C.C. continued its autocratic line, flourished an alleged but actually doubtful world copyright on the rules in the faces of other national associations, and reneged on various promises to separate its international and domestic functions.

Overseas nations unanimously condemned the aspect of the B. & S.C.C. constitution which gave Lancashire and Yorkshire alone the voting power to overrule all the other main Billiards and Snooker nations – even in the unlikely event of them all sending a delegate to the regular meetings in England. But a perhaps misplaced nervousness about upsetting England and a desire to preserve some kind of unity led to a succession of attempted compromises. The World Council was watered down in title to the International Billiards and Snooker Federation and its annual meetings, held to coincide with World Amateur Championships, were generally acrimonious as the progressives grappled with the reactionaries, with those who were simply nervous of change (or unable to visualise Billiards and Snooker administration in any different form to that which it had always taken) somewhere in between.

Billiards and Snooker had outgrown its administration not only on the amateur but on the professional side and all too many officials, instead of considering new ideas in relation to their potential force for progress, reacted to them almost solely in terms of the threat they constituted to their own personal positions.

Though Dagley successfully defended his English title in 1972 and 1973, he competed neither in an unofficial World Open organised by Frank Holz in Pukekohe that year nor in the World Amateur in Bombay in 1973. Driffield, by now a professional, won the World Open despite losing to both Ferreira and Mohan in round robin play. Mohan finished the round robin undefeated with eleven wins, a 305 break and a 70.8 session average being the best statistics from a series of inspired displays in which his superiority was so pronounced that he had margin for more than a few careless mistakes.

But with six to qualify for the concluding knock-out, all his superiority in the round robin went for naught. Paddy Morgan who, having concentrated on Snooker since leaving his native Belfast (having won Irish Championships at both Billiards and Snooker) to turn professional in Australia, played the game of his life, having only just scraped into the play-offs, to beat Mohan 2,173–1,719 in the semi-finals, breaks of 201, 88 and 215 in his first five visits giving him the start he needed.

Driffield beat Ferreira 1,859–1,678 in the other semi-final and, with Morgan's inspiration fading, won the final comfortably 3,055–2,404.

Though neither Williams, the World Professional champion, nor Fred Davis accepted invitations to compete and Dagley was unable to do so, the field was otherwise representative of the strength of both the amateur and professional sides of the game. Although the professionals played for fixed fees rather than prize money, the event did at least show that a genuine World Open Championship was possible.

With all restrictions on amateurs accepting prize money having been abolished in 1971 (so that professionals were defined as "members of the World Professional Billiards and Snooker Association" or those who "declared themselves professionals"), Billiards even more than Snooker would have benefited from the regular promotion of official World Open Championships but lack of money and to some extent the unwillingness of certain professionals to risk their reputations against non-professionals – particularly for what they judged to be small rewards – prevented significant progress being made.

Despite his loss to Morgan in Pukekohe, Mohan started favourite for the 1973 World Amateur in Bombay but the pressure of home crowd expectation and a certain instability of temperament seemed to weigh crucially not only on him but on Ferreira. They finished second and third while victory went to

115

Lafir, who was twice the player in ninety degrees that he had been in Malta or New Zealand, where in seventy degrees he had worn a pullover under his shirt and waistcoat and still contrived to have hands like blocks of ice. In the 1974 World Amateur Snooker, in a Dublin winter, he was reduced to huddling over a portable gas fire between shots, warming his hands on a cup of coffee, but Bombay removed not only this problem but that of diet, for his eating during visits to the Western world had to be largely confined to the hot tasting and strong smelling dried fish he carried with him in a glass jar.

He also received significant assistance from his great friend, Bert Demarco, the Scotsman who, since meeting him in the 1966 World Amateur Snooker in Karachi, had become his firmest friend and supporter. Some six months before the Championship, this friendship took the form of a vital gift of a set of billiard balls.

The previous year the Composition Billiard Ball Supply Co., whose association with the B. & S.C.C. had, in effect, given them a ball monopoly, announced that they were discontinuing the manufacture of Crystalate, the Championship ball, in favour of a new ball, the Super Crystalate. The B. & S.C.C. tamely accepted this – in fact the Super Crystalate was used for the 1972 English semi-finals and final after the earlier rounds had been played with Crystalate – and the new ball was adopted for all recognised Championships.

There were teething problems: an extra coating of high lustre finish was discontinued when it was found to be contributing to an unpredictably wide "throw" of the cue-ball in certain shots and to an unusual number of "kicks". Snooker players tended to welcome the greater ease with which screw shots could be executed and the new ball tended to make big breaks easier to compile, but Billiards players proved much more reluctant to accept it, chiefly because, even without the high lustre finish, it tended to be less predictable than the old. To countries with foreign exchange difficulties one problem posed by the adoption of the new ball was simply that of availability. Demarco's gift provided Lafir with what was until after the Championship the only set of Super Crystalate balls in the whole of Sri Lanka.

Lafir, who had learnt to play Billiards on his family dining table, using a broomstick for cue, marbles for balls, a sarong for cloth and a cycle tube for cushions, had other worries. The government had recently banned horse racing so his job as a commission agent had, in one of his characteristically picturesque phases, "gone for a walk". Having no money of his own and a family to support, Lafir lived on £50 which Demarco had sent him and miscellaneous help from friends who kept his mind free from immediate worries so that he could practise for the Championship. When he compiled 27 breaks over 500 in the six months before the Championship, including one of 500 unfinished in the Sri Lanka Championship, it was clear he had a great chance to win but it was only by 14 that he scraped home against Everton in a desperate finish in his first match. Lafir then beat Ferreira by 386 and rewarded his friend Demarco (his next opponent) for all his help by amassing a new world amateur record aggregate for four hours of 2,850 with breaks of 428, 404, 318 and 302. (Later Demarco was also to be on the receiving end of four world records by Ferreira – 3,202 [four hour aggregate], 1,688 [two hour aggregate], 10 centuries in a session and 16 centuries in a four hour match.)

With Mohan beating Ferreira by 158, he and Lafir were the only undefeated players when they met on the eleventh day in front of a capacity crowd with hundreds turned away. Lafir led by 420 at the interval but added only 11 in his first five visits after the resumption. Mohan halved the gap but Lafir came to life with 394 and with 3 further centuries and a 350 unfinished, triumphantly averaged 71.5 to win 2,213–1,079.

Playing with supreme confidence, Lafir then smashed the world amateur break record with an 859 against Eric Simons (New Zealand), almost all of it postman's knock, in forty-nine minutes forty-seven seconds, before he missed a middle pocket pot red from the spot end with position lost.

Mohan kept in pursuit by beating (with a 468 break) Philip Tarrant (the best Australian since the legendary Marshall, Cleary and Long) who had hitherto lost only to Ferreira, but once Lafir had also beaten Tarrant by 494 the Championship was virtually his. Ultimately his last match proved irrelevant as Everton surprisingly beat Mohan by 128 to leave him an unassailable position as he made a 584 in his last match against Mifsud.

In Britain Dagley's reign continued. Nolan, 125 behind with thirteen minutes to go, pipped Everton by 19 in the 1974 English semi-final at Grimsby and made a great effort in the last session of the final, reducing his arrears from 503 to 196 with forty-five minutes to go before Dagley again trod on the accelerator. This capacity to pluck out a break when he needed it was again in evidence in the 1975 final when Bob Close, playing in front of his highly partisan supporters in his own club, Western Social, Middlesbrough, followed his semi-final win over an off-colour Nolan by making his highest competitive break to date, 217, in reducing Dagley's lead of 437 to only 2 with forty minutes left. At this stage Close, in attempting a very thin in-off white, sent his cue-ball straight into the pocket – a foul stroke under a rule amendment of 1972 prohibiting misses except when the striker was in hand and no ball out of baulk. Electing to have the balls spotted, Dagley compiled a 117 and went away to win by 224.

Dagley and Close thus travelled as England's representatives in the World Amateur in New Zealand in September 1975. Dagley was never in the slightest danger in his group, in which he recorded breaks of 300, 348, 374 and 477, but the second qualifier was not the Indian number two, Girish Parikh, as had been expected, but Sneddon who, inexperienced but fast and very determined, beat him by 59 in the vital match.

Ferreira who, earlier that year, with Mohan having emigrated to Australia, had set a world record session average of 128.4 and a record match average of 69.7 in the Indian Championship, topped the second group with breaks of 330 and 411 in a second session average of 69.3 against Close as the highlight. Everton took Wales into the semi-finals by beating Close by 363 after the Englishman had gained a bizarre win over Long, who produced the barest shadow of the form of his great days. With five minutes to go, Long led by 20 with perfect top of the table position only to nervously drop his cue on the cue-ball; then, 22 behind but still with time to win, Long dropped the cue-ball under the table and wasted precious seconds ferreting it out. He was still in play, 9 short, when the bell rang.

Dagley (against Everton) and Ferreira (against Sneddon) both won their semi-finals easily, Ferreira perhaps too easily for he made 6 centuries in each session for an average of 50.4.

The key to the final, after the Indian had led by 8 at the first interval, was the second of the four sessions, for Dagley took a small unfinished break to 200 and made it 3 double centuries in as many visits with further contributions of 228 and 202 in a forty-seven minute spell which destroyed Ferreira's touch and fluency. Ferreira made a slight recovery but late in the session Dagley piled on 314 and 185 (averaging 65.6 for the session) to lead by 714 overnight. A gritty 281 helped the Indian reduce his deficit to 469 at the third interval but 116 and 141 early in the final session assured Dagley of his second world title.

There seemed nothing to prevent Dagley from increasing his total of English title successes to a record nine but Everton, in the same year that he took his fourth Welsh title, played the game of his life to beat him by 83 in the semi-final in Middlesbrough, a 61.1 second session average proving the crucial statistic. Reaction set in in the final, however, for after Everton's 287 break in the opening session and a lead of 333 early in the second, Close replied with a lifetime highest break in competition of 259 and, averaging 51.5 for this session, gradually pulled the match round to win by 219.

A similar thing happened in 1977 when Beetham, a veteran of sixty-seven, dipped into his past to produce his best performance for years to beat Dagley by 76 in the quarter-final before beating Everton by 197 in the semi and fading against Close in the final.

At the end of the year, Close reached a new personal peak by eliminating Dagley in the six hour semi-final of the World Amateur Championship at the Palm Lake Motel, Melbourne. Even 5 centuries and a 99 in the second session of one of his group matches against David Pratt (Scotland) did not fully prepare pundits for a first session against Dagley in which he made a 234 and 4 other centuries to finish 519 ahead. He extended his lead to 701 but Dagley made a great effort to narrow the gap to 180 with fifteen minutes to go before he ran out of time.

In the other semi-final, Ferreira comfortably disposed of Everton who, having displaced a joint in his back two days before the Championship, had achieved second place in Dagley's group despite severe pain and a makeshift stance. Ferreira, who had made a break of 519 and six more over 300 in winning each of his five group matches, had nevertheless looked vulnerable under pressure and was perhaps fortunate, in the eight hour final, that Close had expended precious reserves of nervous energy in beating Dagley.

Though Close led by 250 after ninety minutes, 2 quick centuries put Ferreira just in front at the first interval before Close, with a 231 which proved the highest break of the match, led by 124 overnight. Close widened the gap to 249 but as he faded Ferreira gradually gained confidence with his best session of the match – averaging 37.1 – to start the final period with a 323 advantage. However, the Englishman's determination combined with the Indian's insecurity within sight of victory to produce a thrilling finish, Close getting to within 26 before the Indian, whose highest break in the final session was a paltry 70, virtually fell over the line to win by 119.

Ironically, Ferreira's form in winning the title – he averaged only 20.8 in the final – had been much inferior to that he had often shown in Championships in which ultimate success had eluded him. There was, at the best, however, a fluency, certainty and speed which bore witness to the intensive practice and preparation which he would have found impossible to sustain without his deep love of, and dedication to, the game.

He immediately went to Christchurch, New Zealand, for an unofficial World Open organised by Frank Holz and won this also, surviving a close finish by a mere 82 in the semi-final against his compatriot Parikh, before setting a new world amateur session average record of 189.8 – the 1,709 session total included breaks of 333, 239, 347, 515 and 190 unfinished – in beating Wildman, who, after what he described as "seven years in the wilderness", had played his best competitive Billiards for years, 3,461 (51.6) – 1,309 (19.3) in the final.

John Barrie, outstanding in his youth and nominated to play McConachy for the World Professional title in 1951, competed in a major tournament for the first time since beginning his recovery from a recurrent depressive condition which had put him into virtual retirement for over twenty years. He made a break of 687 and two more over 600 in finishing second in the round robin section before losing to Wildman, formerly his pupil, in the semi-final. During the event, Wildman made a break of 449, Parikh of 330, Brian Kirkness (New Zealand) of 304 and George Ganim jnr. (Australia) of 400.

It was a tournament which emphasised again, through its high general standard, the need to work towards official World Open Championships as a way of sustaining competitive interest for, with no new challenger on the horizon, Williams continued to hold the world professional title unopposed. It also underlined the fact that leading players were making such liberal use of the "five pots from the spot" rule that breaks were escalating, perhaps to an unacceptable level. Big breaks made by repetitive stroke sequences had always damaged Billiards as a public spectacle, notoriously through the nursery cannon specialists of the 1930's, and fears that the game's modest revival might be hindered if breaks again grew too large began to be expressed. Almost all leading players were part of a groundswell of opinion that consecutive pots from the spot should be limited to two (thus returning to the "pure" Billiards of before the disastrous "15 pots" amendment of 1964) or at most three.

Further support for this argument was provided by the manner of Dagley's record ninth English amateur title when, in much better playing conditions than the event had enjoyed for the previous couple of years at Western Social, Middlesbrough, he set a new world amateur break record of 862 in the semi-final against G.M. "Nip" Wright and set five other new English Championship records: a two hour average of 116.6 (v Wright); the highest two and a half hour average, 98.9; the highest ten hour aggregate, 4,611; the highest five hour aggregate, 2,381; and the highest final average, 67.8. The latter were all achieved in his 4,611–2,309 final victory over Close in which he made breaks of 563, 305 and three more over 200. In losing by 2,302, Close averaged a far from negligible 34.5.

# CHAPTER XIII

# The Snooker Boom
*(Snooker 1971–1976)*

The early 70's were to see the presentation of Snooker transformed from a low key, low budget affair in obscure venues to a professionally staged sporting spectacle.

Television discovered a popular formula for televised professional Snooker – one frame sudden death – at the same time as television programmes began to be shown in colour. Since Snooker is the only game in which colour is an intrinsic part of the rules, this change had a spectacular effect. The first programme of the first series of "Pot Black", the progenitor of many television Snooker series, was seen on BBC2 on July 23, 1969. It was a series which was to introduce Snooker to sections of the community who had previously scarcely known of its existence. It was to make reputations, for those players who appeared on it, which reached far beyond the traditional bounds of the Snooker world. A player invited to appear on "Pot Black" almost automatically found himself in much greater demand for the club exhibitions which still yielded the bulk of his income.

As sponsorship became an accepted part of the game, sponsors and their advisers tried to ensure that they received value for their investment. Sponsored tournaments, particularly those for which a sponsor engaged a public relations consultancy, therefore tended to be more efficiently run and better publicised.

The legalisation of gaming machines – one armed bandits – in clubs sparked a revolution: as Jack Rea, who had slogged round the club exhibition circuit in the dark days of the 50's and early 60's put it: "A lot of clubs were tin shacks when I first played there. When I went back in the 70's, I looked for a tin shack and found a palace standing in its place."

The clubs, then, had more money to play with but ultimately all depended on the new cast of players which was offered to the public. Three of these, Spencer, Reardon and Higgins, all of whom were to win the Championship, were to be the outstanding figures of these years.

Spencer's golden years were from 1969–1971. His long potting, dazzling screw shots and general lack of inhibition in his play made him unquestionably number one at this time despite the occasional reverse.

Indeed, even when Reardon began his four year tenure of the world title in 1973, Spencer had the better record in non-Championship tournaments only to suffer a series of failures in the Championship itself.

On his return from Australia with a then record first prize cheque for the

1970 Championship for £2,333 in his pocket, Spencer launched, in January 1971, into the first Park Drive £2,000 tournament, a round robin event in which he, Owen, Pulman and Williams each played each other three times in seven frame matches before the top two played off for the first two prizes of £750 and £550.

The Park Drive £2,000 was not only Snooker's first whiff of tournament sponsorship – outside the World Championship – since *The News of the World* tournament but the initial involvement in the sport of West and Nally, a fresh, young, London public relations firm specialising in the rapidly developing world of sports sponsorship. The concept of this tournament was original: eighteen one night stands in clubs with the final, also in a club, on television, the first professional tournament match which had been televised for over fifteen years. The involvement of West and Nally was also to lead to the first lengthy and level headed appraisal – from the outside – of what Snooker had to offer as a public entertainment and where its lamentably out of date methods of presentation had to be improved.

Peter West, a television commentator and compere of wide experience, and Patrick Nally, a boundlessly energetic motivator and ideas man, improved Snooker's relationship with television sports departments – "Pot Black" was and still is produced by BBC's light entertainment division – and established it as a sport in which a sponsor might extract a reasonable commercial return, particularly in the fields of tobacco and drink. It was the first time Snooker had had a high-powered, media-orientated outfit behind it and its role in the Snooker boom of the 70's has never been sufficiently acknowledged.

Higgins, meanwhile, was about to burst through to the top with all the irresistible crest of a wave force his nickname "Hurricane" implies. The draw for the World Championship, made in February 1971 – the final was played in February 1972 – placed Higgins in one of the qualifying sections. He was to have to play six matches to win the title.

Spencer won the first Park Drive £2,000; Reardon rounded off his win in the Park Drive £600, an event specially devised for Yorkshire Television, with a break of 127, the highest thus far seen on the screen; John Dunning, eleven times Yorkshire Amateur champion, brought off the shock of the season by beating Spencer 13–10 in the Willie Smith Trophy in Leeds before Higgins beat him easily in the final; Higgins and Spencer played to packed houses in a series of £200 challenge matches; Reardon beat Spencer 4–3 on the final black after needing a snooker on the pink in the final of the second Park Drive £2,000 (after Spencer had won seven matches in the round robin to Reardon's four); and Spencer, with the help of the livelier Candian ball, Vitalite, and the more generous Canadian pockets, made 29 centuries (21 of them of 124 or over including his first 147) and 60 breaks over 80 in ninety-eight frames against Cliff Thorburn in Calgary and Edmonton.

It was a visit which opened Thorburn's eyes to a world beyond the pool rooms of Canada and the United States which had been his habitat for almost ten years but it was also one which left Spencer exhausted, for on his return he struggled past Charlton with great difficulty in the world semi-final – a match which carried a personal side stake of £750 – before winning the third Park Drive £2,000 with a 4–3 win over Higgins the very evening before they started their world final in the unpretentious concert hall of Selly Park British Legion, Birmingham.

The Story of Billiards and Snooker

Higgins had survived his semi-final against Williams only by winning the last of the sixty-one frames, casting away frames when he was in a winning position and winning them from losing positions with equal abandon. He ended Rea's twenty-one year tenure of the Irish Professional title by beating him 28–12 with the aid of a fabulous 9–0 third session and beat Reardon handsomely in a big match at the City Hall, Sheffield.

Spencer was nevertheless a clear favourite to retain his title but Higgins played with sublime confidence to become, a few days after his twenty-third birthday, the youngest ever champion. A miners' strike and the consequent power failures contributed not only to the capacity afternoon attendances but to a bizarre incident on the second evening when, with conventional lighting out of action and no heating in the room on this February night, the players agreed to continue under the dull and inadequate lighting produced by a mobile generator. Amazingly, the first three frames were concluded in thirty-five minutes.

The hall bulged with a jam packed crowd accommodated on seats placed on stacked beer crates, which were used as a rough form of tiered seating, or hanging precariously from any point of vantage. Snooker was simply not used to the idea of paying customers being so desperate to see a match. Even Fleet Street Sports Editors conceded that there was a degree of interest in the contest.

Not all the referees were up to such an important occasion. After two ghastly howlers, the unprecedented – and never repeated – step of appointing "linesmen", one sitting on either side of the table, to assist adjudication when the referee was in doubt or to settle appeals, was taken.

Amidst it all, Higgins missed no more than two pots in the entire week that he might reasonably have been expected to get and an unforgettable 6–0 win in the Thursday evening session put him very much in the driver's seat. Spencer fought hard and made the only two centuries of the match but Higgins was not to be denied. He clinched the title early in the final session, 37–32, and Snooker was never the same again.

Higgins's capture of the World Professional title in February 1972 convinced West and Nally of Snooker's wider potentialities. Under their direction, the fourth Park Drive £2,000 was staged in October when Spencer, in front of a crowd of two thousand at Belle Vue, Manchester, beat Higgins 5–3 for the £750 first prize, his fourth first prize (plus two seconds) out of the four £2,000 and two £600 tournaments which Park Drive had sponsored. (Reardon made a break of 146 in one of them which is the highest tournament break of all time.)

This crystallised Patrick Nally's burgeoning scheme to convert the World Professional Championship from an unwieldy event, lasting several months in different venues with no continuity of interest and scant media interest into a lavishly staged, Wimbledon-style spectacle with play taking place on eight tables in different arenas in the same large venue. With the sponsorship of Park Drive, West and Nally promoted at City Exhibition Halls, Manchester – to their immediate financial loss but the game's ultimate gain – a Championship condensed into a fortnight, with £8,000 prize money, television coverage (the first time the world final had ever received it), public bars and (for the first time) public restaurants, a Ladbroke betting tent and carefully nurtured press coverage from every national newspaper.

The publicity bandwagon, already rolling, gathered momentum when a documentary, "Hurricane Higgins", reached twenty-fifth place in the joint ITV/BBC ratings for the week. It was a film which showed that a lonely wait for a train and some rather desperate tinselly gaiety was as much a part of this young genius' life as an incredible exhibition at a Northern workingmen's club or a serious match with Spencer at Wallasey Town Hall. It was no public relations exercise but it helped confirm Higgins in the minds of a great section of the uncommitted public as the only Snooker player it had ever heard of. His partiality to wine, women and gambling, heavily publicised in an opportunist spread in *The Sunday People* and elsewhere, and his propensity for getting involved in disturbances, coupled with his dash, skill and bravado, made him a popular hero. At the table he behaved immaculately (except in a few club exhibitions when he was the worse for drink). Away from it he made it quite clear – self-destructively so at times – that he did not give a damn for anyone or anything. West and Nally attempted to manage him but retired badly bruised.

The publicity build-up for the 1973 Championship was centred round Higgins, not least because it was easy to write colourfully about him. He was seeded to meet Spencer in the final but those who expected a repeat of the 1972 final or the epic £1,000 a side struggle at Radcliffe Town Hall, which Spencer won 38–37, were disappointed as neither reached the final.

There was trouble in Higgins's first match when he arrived twenty-two minutes late for his evening session with Houlihan. In the absence of precise tournament regulations, the tournament director, Bruce Donkin, ticked off Higgins (who was later fined £100 by the W.P.B.S.A.) in no uncertain manner but Higgins, after a placatory speech had been unenthusiastically received, won the crowd over within five minutes with a dazzling break of 78.

His quarter-final against Fred Davis uniquely included a stoppage for rain. Even in Manchester this was a bit thick – but the position was duly marked, the covers were put on and play ceased until the offending leak in the roof had been plugged. The clash of styles between the impetuous, brilliant Higgins and the calm, reflective, steady Davis, not to mention the element of what many saw as Young Upstart versus a member of Snooker's royal family, erupted to a nerve wrenching climax. Davis led 14–12, missed a pink which would have put him one up with 2 to go, and went down 16–14 as Higgins played with all his death or glory bravery to snatch a semi-final place.

This, though, was the end of the road as Charlton won the first six frames of their semi-final and in the same inexorable manner ground out a 23–9 win. The Higgins bubble had burst.

While this was happening, the other semi-final seemed to be proceeding quietly towards a routine win for Spencer, who led Reardon 19–12 and then, at 19–14, missed an easy black which would have put him 20–14. Instead, Reardon recovered to only 4 behind and added the remaining three frames of the penultimate session to trail only 18–19 at the interval. Reardon's revival had coincided with the end of the Higgins/Charlton match, the spectators from which now flooded into the hitherto half-empty arena where he and Spencer were playing. More sensitive to atmosphere, perhaps, than any of the other leading players, Reardon's adrenalin was now well and truly flowing and after innumerable thrills and vicissitudes, he clinched victory in the deciding frame, 23–22.

This traumatic psychological blow seemed to affect Spencer deeply: he won many matches and many tournaments and regained the Championship in 1977 but all without recapturing more than fleetingly the easy confidence and sublime form of his greatest years.

Reardon also suffered his reaction – merely a temporary one – when, next day, he lost the first seven frames of the final, another absorbing match in which Reardon's flair and wider range of shots were pitted against Charlton's dogged consistency. Reardon led 17–13 after the fourth session and kept in front to 27–25 until the eighth session broke the pattern into which the match had settled. After only a few minutes under the blinding, newly installed television lights it was obvious that Charlton could see but Reardon could not. Two frames went to the Australian with ludicrous ease and a third after Reardon's protests had led to two of the largest floodlights, which in any event were needed only to illuminate the crowd, had been switched off. Further discussion took place at the mid-session interval during which Reardon was also able to compose himself. He emerged to win four of the five remaining frames of the day to lead 31–29 and, as if conscious the crisis of the match had passed, forged steadily ahead to win 38–32.

Higgins, apparently temperamentally unfitted to cope either with success or failure, went to Australia where he was thrown out of one club after calling Norman Squire "an old no hoper" – he was allowed in again after writing an abject apology on a piece of toilet paper – and out of an hotel for wrecking his room. A projected tour of India lasted only one day for, after starting his first exhibition at Bombay Gymkhana with a break of 109, he so offended the members of this gentlemanly club by his drinking, the stripping off of his shirt and his insulting behaviour that the B.A. and C.C. of India, his hosts, put him on the next plane home. A childish threat not to complete his commitments in the "Pot Black" series recorded at the end of 1972 was not carried out but was punished by his omission from the 1973 and subsequent series. Wild, uncontrollable, wilful, Higgins seemed bent on self-destruction.

Reardon, the new champion, predictably flourished. He toured India at short notice to repair the damage done by Higgins to professional Snooker's reputation; made 65 public centuries in a four month tour of South Africa; and compiled a second 147 maximum (the first had been at Pontins, Broadreeds, in July 1972) shortly after his return. He was to take this total to seven by mid-1978. Snooker Promotions, the subsidiary West and Nally had set up to tackle their increasing Snooker commitment, organised, with Ladbroke sponsorship, two gala dinner/Snooker evenings at the Cafe Royal in 1973 and 1974, prompted Ladbroke's, a little prematurely, to sponsor a ranking list and, most important, obtained a valuable new sponsor, Norwich Union, whose tournament at the Piccadilly Hotel brought big time Snooker back to London.

Though it did not justify its billing as a World Open Championship, the field was internationally representative both of the professional and amateur sides of the game except that Reardon chose not to compete and Williams and Davis were engaged on the Watney exhibition series which occupied a good part of their British winters from 1968–1976.

Higgins, whose brilliance had grown more and more fitful, fell 8–2 to Spencer in one semi-final while, more surprisingly, Pulman, who had done nothing of note since 1970, overcame Charlton 8–3 in the other. The final provided exciting television, for Spencer led 6–2 and, repeating his semi-final blunder against Reardon in the World Championship, missed a chance to make it 7–2. This was all the encouragement Pulman needed for, revelling in the mounting tension, he recovered to 7–7 and looked like winning the decider before he missed a not too difficult green.

Spencer, who won £1,500 to Pulman's £750, also took part in another Snooker Promotions exercise, the televised Norwich Union Transatlantic Challenge, the first serious attempt in Britain to establish any meaningful contact between the hitherto utterly self-contained worlds of Snooker and American Pool, though Williams and Charlton had both played Pool in the United States. Steve Mizerak, the United States Open Pool champion, predictably beat Spencer 3–0 at Pool and, rather less predictably, beat him 2–1 at Snooker which, even though Spencer was not buckling down with maximum determination, indicated that the top American Pool players possessed the basic cuemanship, even allowing for vast differences in the size of balls, pockets and tables, to become Snooker players of good professional standard.

Mizerak's visit stimulated British interest in Pool. Indeed, Pool was to become one of the great growth areas in the 70's though, ironically, this growth was to occur primarily in pubs, amusement arcades, hotel foyers and in other places not otherwise associated with Snooker tables. The growth occurred almost entirely with coin-operated tables and was to be controlled principally by operators experienced in other coin-operated fields like amusement machines and juke boxes, though Williams's own firm, Rex Williams Leisure, was a notable exception.

Save in the fact that it may have accustomed some people to using a cue who subsequently progressed to Snooker, the growth of Pool in Britain was to have no discernible influence on Snooker even though this new activity widened the market for cues, balls and other accessories. The variety of Pool which was adopted was not the Championship game – 14.1 continuous – but the simpler and quicker Eight Ball, a game which lent itself particularly neatly to a coin-operated set-up.

West and Nally founded another subsidiary, Mister Billiards, to sell Pool tables and equipment and with an enterprising Snooker and Pool stand at the Ideal Home Exhibition on which they staged matches featuring Spencer, then a director of Mister Billiards, and other top professionals, again contributed to the rising tide of interest in the game. Cliff Thorburn, resident professional for the show, recorded a four frame sequence of breaks of 94, 100, 146 and 130 though elsewhere Spencer and Higgins both went one better by completing century breaks in four consecutive frames.

But disappointments were round the corner. Park Drive increased the prize money for the 1974 World Championship but the vast, concrete floored, aircraft hangar-like hall at Belle Vue, Manchester, did not prove a successful choice of venue. This might not have mattered if the main box office attractions had not lost early but, as it was, Reardon retained his title with consummate ease. Only Marcus Owen who had turned professional after winning the English Amateur title in 1973, extended him in a 15–11 quarter-final. Spencer went out in his first match 15–13 to Mans (who was subsequently quashed 15–4 by Williams), Charlton did likewise 15–13 to Dunning, and Higgins lost an epic quarter-final 15–14 to the sixty-one year old Davis, just recuperating from his second heart attack. Higgins led 13–9 before, at 13–11, he was controversially called for a push stroke, a decision which was instrumental in Davis pulling up to 12–13. Higgins led 14–12 but Davis, showing remarkable stamina, won the last three frames to win 15–14.

The modern world championship format, cramming into a fortnight a number of frames which in the old days would have taken several weeks, threw additional physical and mental stress on the participants so it was not too surprising that Davis was submerged 15–3 in one semi-final by Reardon while Graham Miles, who had sprung from obscurity by coming into "Pot Black" as a late replacement for Davis and winning it not only that year but the year following, beat Dunning and Williams to qualify from the other half. Miles, a very unorthodox sighter of the ball in that his cue runs not under his chin but under his left ear, had displayed, notably in a 131 semi-final break, much touch and positional skill but his inspiration had burnt out by the time he contested the final and Reardon won very easily 22–12.

Immediately after the tournament, Snooker Promotions presented to the W.P.B.S.A. meeting a schedule of their ambitious plans for an international tournament circuit, only for these to be rejected so vehemently that West and Nally's interest in Snooker was henceforth to be confined to servicing tournaments in a public relations capacity for sponsors they had obtained. What the company had achieved for Snooker became a matter not for gratitude but envy, jealousy and distrust. The 1975 World Championship was awarded to Eddie Charlton Promotions; Park Drive disappeared from Snooker; and the niggling and internecine strife which had so disfigured the game in the past, disfigured it again. Charlton, who dominated the Australian scene in every way, and Williams, chairman of the W.P.B.S.A. and proprietor of Powerglide Cues, recognised as the leaders of that market, emerged as the dominant personalities of the professional scene and, because there were personal differences with Bruce Donkin, who had by now become the day to day director of business at Snooker Promotions and Mister Billiards, a parting of the ways was almost inevitable.

Though this contretemps retarded the prospect of a full tournament circuit, a new tournament immediately after the 1974 Championship was to become, through its initial success, a permanent feature of the calendar. Pontins, the holiday camp empire where Spencer, Reardon and David Taylor had long-standing contracts to play summer exhibitions, organised at their Prestatyn camp a Festival of Snooker which consisted not only of an eight-man professional event but an Open where twenty-five amateur qualifiers (each receiving 25 points per frame) joined the professionals in the last 32.

Reardon, 9–4 up, beat Spencer 10–9 to win the £1,000 first prize in the professional event but an Open, where twenty-five amateur qualifiers (each professional but then only an unpredictable if talented amateur, win the £1,000 first prize by beating Reardon and Spencer in the last two rounds.

It was an event which emphasised the Snooker world's intimate, democratic qualities. The holiday makers mixed for the week with the stars of their sport, some of them earning a chance for glory and cash against the big names, all of them having the opportunity to watch top class matches and talk Snooker as much as they liked. To a degree unparalleled in the Snooker world, it brought the Snooker family closer together.

Jim Williamson's Northern Snooker Centre in Leeds, a purpose-built Snooker club with a match arena, staged its first big event, the £3,000 Watneys Open, in the latter part of the year when Higgins, who had learnt a great deal about safety play and the less spectacular arts of the game to replace the loss of the fine edge of his potting ability, beat Reardon 13–11 and Davis (who had beaten Spencer 13–12) 17–11 to take the £1,000 first prize.

As four-man and eight-man tournaments proliferated, Spencer retained the Norwich Union Open title with a 10–9 win over Reardon which again revealed his difficulty in clinching winning positions. Spencer led 8–4 (despite a 130 break from his opponent) but was caught at 8–8 and was eventually indebted to a fluke to give him a crucial advantage in the deciding frame.

Reardon, just returned from an exhausting four week tour of Australia and New Zealand, suffered the effects of jet lag during the tournament and in so doing made it clear that Snooker players had now joined other sportsmen in travelling hectically about the globe in pursuit of their profession. He beat Higgins 9–8 in a spellbinding semi-final while Thorburn, who had beaten Davis and Pulman, demonstrated his improvement by extending Spencer to 9–7 in the other.

Despite packed houses and abundant television coverage, Norwich Union afterwards withdrew their sponsorship but the Snooker calendar gained a valuable new event – again through West and Nally – when, after Park Drive's withdrawal from the sport, another Gallaher brand, this time at the top of the market, Benson and Hedges, backed a Masters tournament. Though later housed at the New London Theatre, the initial Benson and Hedges Masters, was first held at the West Centre Hotel in an atmosphere of plush and glitter which established the event, as intended, as the Ascot of the Snooker world. Spencer and Reardon again reached the final though Reardon got home only 5–4 on the final pink against Williams, who had beaten Higgins.

The final followed a familiar pattern of Spencer leading and Reardon equalising until, leading 8–6, Reardon looked a certain winner. The standard was poor, perhaps because, night after night, the leading players were now experiencing more pressure, more general wear and tear on the nervous system, than in any previous era. Eventually Spencer levelled at 8–8 and held a commanding lead in the decider only to throw it away. Reardon then had a golden chance to win but was distracted on the crucial pink by a bevy of Benson and Hedges promotion girls rising in their seats, presumably to be on hand for the prize giving ceremony. The frame ended in a tie before Spencer somehow summoned one of his best pots of the session to despatch the extra black for the £2,000 first prize.

Since Spencer (who made 4 centuries in consecutive frames in an exhibition at Peterborough Conservative Club) and Reardon were clearly two of the top or probably the top two players, there was uproar when the seedings for the 1975 World Professional Championship, playing in various venues all over Australia, placed Reardon, at 1, and Spencer, at 8, to meet in the quarter-finals. The fact that the draw was made contrary to W.P.B.S.A. conditions was allowed to pass and it did not escape the attention of the cognoscenti that not only Reardon and Spencer but Higgins were all in the opposite half of the draw to the promoter, Charlton.

In quality, the quarter-final was the best match these two players ever played, countless frames turning on a single half chance or being won from 50 or 60 behind. Trailing 16–17, Reardon won the next three frames to win 19–17 and, from 10–10, beat Higgins 19–14 in the semi.

In the opposite half, Dennis Taylor, a young Blackburn-based Irishman, made his first significant impact on the Championship by beating Mans 15–12, Davis 15–14 and Gary Owen 19–9 but had to endure a choppy plane trip from Sydney to Brisbane on the morning of his semi-final against Charlton and never recovered from a poor start.

It was an extraordinary final. Reardon led 16–8 but Charlton strung together the next nine frames to lead 17–16. It was 22–20 to Reardon but, when Charlton led 28–23, the title seemed certain to go to Australia for the first time. However, the match began to turn when Reardon potted a daring pink to win the last frame of the penultimate session to keep in the match at 25–29. When Charlton missed a frame ball brown of the type he rarely misses before losing the first frame of the evening session by going in-off the black, his recovery gathered momentum. Reardon extended his winning streak to 7 to lead 30–29 before the crowd in the Nunawading Basketball Stadium saw Charlton equalise at 30–30. After a tense opening to the decider, when the Australian held the initiative, Reardon fashioned a break of 62 to give him the £4,000 first prize and his third consecutive title.

A week later, Reardon was back on the other side of the world winning both the professional and Open sections at Pontins – and another £2,000 – but it was in 1975 that the professional game itself suffered a chaotic disruption through the involvement of 'Q' Promotions, a management and promotions company run by Maurice Hayes, at that time also the Vice-Chairman of the B. & S.C.C.

Hayes began promisingly by organising several small professional tournaments and handling bookings for a number of players. When he obtained the sponsorship of W.D. and H.O. Wills, under their Embassy banner, for the 1976 World Championship, some went as far as to hail him as the game's new Messiah, but as his involvement escalated so did he find it at first more difficult and then impossible to control. There were confusions over bookings, confusions in the pre-organisation of the Championship and ever more desperate efforts to hold things together.

The three Embassy sponsored subsidiary events to the Championship, a Women's Open (which recognised that more women were playing Snooker than ever before), an invitation amateur tournament and an open to all amateur tournament, all good ideas in themselves, proved to the sponsors more trouble than they were worth. The decision to run the top half of the draw at Middlesbrough Town Hall and the bottom half and the final at Wythenshawe Forum proved administratively unwieldy and dissipated the unity of place which had been such a virtue of the West and Nally organised Championships.

Having taken the £2,000 first prize in the Benson and Hedges Masters by beating Charlton, excitingly, 5–4 and Miles, easily, 7–3, Reardon was in a class of his own at Middlesbrough where the hasty and incomplete blackout, the clatter of spectators moving from one arena to another or to the bar or toilet and other small but irritating imperfections claimed most of the press attention.

At Wythenshawe, too, the Championship began controversially when Charlton claimed, correctly, that the pockets of the table on which he was playing Pulman were larger than standard. This was put right – Charlton made a 137 break in this match while Spencer made a 138 on the other table – but criticism of the table conditions was to be redoubled when one table was taken out and the other re-set for the semi-final and final.

Higgins, still wayward and unpredictable in a personal sense, had meanwhile started to regain some of the ground he had lost since his title win in 1972. Still willing to chance his arm, but more balanced and technically more complete, he had beaten Spencer in the final of a big £2,000 Open at the Castle Club, Southampton, and had, amazingly, added to his four 147 maximums a 146 at Leicester in which, profiting initially from taking a free ball as the "extra" red, he had taken, in addition, the usual 15 reds and all the colours, the first such clearance ever recorded. Still searching for consistency, however, Higgins was on the brink of defeat when Thorburn confirmed his emergence as a world class player to lead 14–12 before a surge of inspiration, backed by some luck, carried Higgins to a 15–14 victory. After leading 14–12, Higgins also needed the last frame to beat Spencer 15–14 and, to the delight of some of Snooker's most vociferous supporters, won a third close finish, 20–18 against Charlton, to reach the final.

The final began farcically, the glare and dazzle from the newly installed television lighting being altogether unacceptable. Reardon, who had the additional disadvantage of having played all his previous matches in Middlesbrough, fumed visibly as he slipped to a 2–4 deficit at the first interval. The champion won six of the seven evening frames to lead 8–5 but there was more trouble on the second afternoon when Reardon, with every justification, complained bitterly about the running of the table. Attempts were made to put things right in the interval (by which time Higgins was again ahead 10–9) and Reardon, shrewdly playing a cautious and limited game despite his far from happy state of mind, again won the evening session 6–1 to lead 15–11. Higgins won the first two frames the following day but a failure at a shot he attempted left-handed cost him the next frame. This miss and the loss of the next two frames from winning positions virtually signalled the end of the contest.

Reardon's 27–16 win earned him a new record first prize of £6,000, which he supplemented by another £1,000 from the Pontins professional the following week, before Higgins beat him 6–4 for the £1,000 first prize in the Canadian Club tournament at the Northern Snooker Centre, Leeds, on Yorkshire Television.

Within weeks, though, 'Q' Promotions had folded up. Some of the good they did lingered on – pre-eminently bringing Embassy into Snooker – but in general they can be said to have added to rather than diminished the anarchy within the game.

In contrast to the brisk movement between the amateur and professional ranks of the preceding two years, the 1969–1975 period was to be dominated in the amateur world by three players, two of whom never – and the third not until much later – seriously considered such a change, partly because in 1972 the B. & S.C.C. removed all restrictions on amateurs accepting fees or prize money. A professional thus came to be defined as a member of the W.P.B.S.A. or one who "declares himself a professional". In practice this meant that an amateur could earn as much as any but the top eight or ten professionals, so it was pointless to turn professional unless this kind of status could be achieved with some certainty. A young man, particularly if he was single, tended to view the prospect of endless one-night exhibition stands away from home in a different light to a player of more mature years, married and with a responsible job. Those in the latter category had to give up something tangible in return for rewards that were uncertain.

Ray Edmonds, Sid Hood and Jonathan Barron between them filled ten of the fourteen places in the English finals of this period. Edmonds, manager of a painting and decorating merchants in Grimsby, Barron, an antique dealer and souvenir shop proprietor in Mevagissey, and Hood, a Grimsby docker with a particular relish for the social life of amateur Snooker, contested some gripping matches.

Edmonds, after four unsuccessful appearances in the Northern final, recovered from 3–7 to beat Barron 11–9 in the 1969 final at Grimsby, the year in which a popular London competitor, Bill Smith, died during his match against Houlihan in the Southern section at Great Windmill Street. It was also the year of the first official amateur Snooker international, instigated by Wales, who received England in a special match at the Afan Lido, Port Talbot, on June 7, 1969 to mark the investiture of Prince Charles as Prince of Wales. The success of the venture led to triangular series with Scotland the following year, with the Republic of Ireland making it a four cornered contest a year later.

In 1970, Barron recorded the first of his hat-trick of titles when he beat Hood 11–10. Both men went to Edinburgh for the 1970 World Amateur Championship and both, after some early alarms, won their groups to contest the final. Barron lost his first match 4–1 to Jack Rogers (Rep. of Ireland) whose two breaks of 65 were the highest of the tournament. Rogers could finish only fifth in his group but his last 4–3 win over Des May, when May potted the black only to go in-off, deprived the Welsh champion of a play-off with Barron for first place. Hood was swamped 4–0 by Paul Mifsud but the Maltese then lost a close match to Mohammed Lafir (Sri Lanka) when he could have forced a play-off if he had won. Barron won a somewhat scrappy final 11–7 and, having made two successful defences of his English title, 11–9 against Doug French at Harringay and 11–9 against Edmonds at Truro, he defended his world title in Wales in what was officially the 1972 Championship but which actually finished in the early days of 1973.

The Championship was originally scheduled for Colombo, but a rule which the new World Council, the one-nation, one vote body which had taken from the B. & S.C.C. the control of the World Amateur Championships at a meeting at the Malta Hilton in 1971 (see page 114) had adopted an application which was not originally envisaged. Some national representatives, when discussing in Malta the granting of the 1976 World Amateur Snooker Championship to South Africa, were nervous that invitations would not be issued to "black" nations like India and Sri Lanka. Accordingly, a rule was agreed whereby "the host national association must invite entries from every affiliated national association."

Ironically, the policy of the South African government became to invite competitors of all colours while the governments of India and Sri Lanka not only forbade their nationals to compete in South Africa but refused to allow their national associations to invite South Africans to compete in events in their own countries. The net result was that Sri Lanka, after a postal vote, were deprived of their right to stage the Championship and Wales, at short notice, stepped into the breach.

The popular Jimmy Van Rensburg, the acceptance of whose entry the Scottish Association had had to withdraw at the eleventh hour for the 1970 Championship in Edinburgh because of pressure from anti-apartheid interests, came to Wales, as did another South African, Mannie Francisco. The Edinburgh entry, with ten nations represented among the fourteen competitors, had been the strongest to date but the eighteen competitors from ten nations who competed in Wales were of even higher overall standard.

Four round robin groups reduced the field to eight and two more groups of four produced the qualifiers for the knock-out semi-finals. On the opening night in Wrexham, Barron was beaten 4–3 by Alwyn Lloyd, a short, well-rounded Welshman with a rumbustious attacking style, and then only just beat the Maltese number two, Alfred Borg, 4–3, and Francisco, 4–3, to qualify in second place in group two to the South African.

Mifsud beat Edmonds 4–2 to top group three though Edmonds recorded a 101 break against Rogers. Van Rensburg was undefeated in group one where the New Zealander Kel Tristram also qualified on a frames countback after losing two of his three matches. The dashing sixteen stone Indian, Arvind Savur – Tornado Fats in some newspapers – and Max Williams, a tough, consistent Australian with an energetic cue action, both came through with two wins out of three in group four while David Sneddon (Scotland), who also had two wins, was eliminated on countback.

If these groups were painfully close, the groups at Abercwmboi which produced the semi-finalists were closer still. Group two opened with Francisco beating Van Rensburg 4–2 after making breaks of 53 and 70 in taking a 3–0 lead and Williams, with a 51 in the decider, beating Edmonds 4–3. Edmonds, when a second defeat would have effectively eliminated him, then beat Francisco 4–3 while Van Rensburg beat Williams 4–2. Thus the winner of the last two matches in this group went through. Edmonds beat Van Rensburg 4–2 and, in one of the great amateur contests of all time, Francisco beat Williams 4–3, winning the first frame 115–0, losing the third 101–0 en route to trailing 1–3 (Williams making breaks of 54 and 78) before winning the last two frames 90–10 and 83–11.

In the other group Barron was undefeated, though he trailed Savur 0–2 and Mifsud 1–2. Savur, with the final flourish of a 68 break to complete his 4–2 win over Mifsud, was the other qualifier.

Savur looked well set for the final when, with breaks of 51 and 72 in the first two frames, he led Francisco 4–0 in their fifteen frame semi-final at the Sophia Garden Pavilion, Cardiff, where the Indian felt the low temperature so intensely that his bridge hand cramped up with cold, a condition for which he attempted several remedies, among them massaging his hands with whiskey. Francisco adopted the correct tactics in slowing the Indian down with liberal doses of safety play and gradually fought his way into the match. At 7–7, Savur potted green, brown, blue but, playing with the rest, he wobbled the pink, which would have put him in the final, in the jaws. Francisco took the pink and, after a safety exchange on the black, potted it in a deathly silence to win 8–7.

In the other semi-final, Barron lost his title when Edmonds won a scrappy match 8–6. Barron, a fine competitor with the knack of potting the really important balls, had often, even in his three year spell of unbroken success in major events between 1969 and 1972, looked as if the strain of the occasion was about to prove too much for him. Burying his brow in his hands between shots, like a man with a blinding headache, Barron doubtless looked – much like the great Olympic champion Emil Zatopek – much worse than he felt, but not all the strain was apparent rather than real for, after the 1973 English Championship, when he lost in the Southern semi-final to Marcus Owen, he retired from Championship Snooker, a mysterious internal complaint (which had started in 1972) and the strain of travelling and competing leading him to switch his attentions to Golf, a game he could play well without having to endure the pressure of top level competition.

The final provided for Francisco a reversal of his great recovery against Savur for he won the first six frames and led 6–1 overnight. On the resumption, Francisco led 7–2 but Edmonds recovered to 6–8 at the interval by sinking a long bold black for game after Francisco had needed only an easy pink, almost straight across the table, for a 9–5 lead, a blunder which both players subsequently agreed proved to be the crucial point of the match. The South African nevertheless led 9–6 but Edmonds invariably looked cooler in moments of crisis and won the next four frames to lead 10–9. Francisco levelled at 10–10 but Edmonds always had his nose in front in the decider and half an hour after midnight, after the players had occupied the table for seven and a half hours that evening, he clinched the match 11–10.

The result, a tribute to Edmonds's heart and determination, was a sadder commentary on Francisco's inability to clinch a winning position which his excellent technique, cue-ball control and tactical acumen had earned. Nevertheless, to have finished second in World Amateur Championships at both Billiards and Snooker effectively underlines his claim to be regarded as the outstanding amateur all rounder of his time.

Edmonds went on to retain the Northern section of the English Championship by beating John Virgo 6–4 but the organisation of the national final fell into such disarray that it did not take place in Birmingham until mid May, by which time Edmonds's inspiration and concentration had faded, and Owen regained the title after not entering for six years. Owen then turned professional but failed to make the impact in the Professional Championship that he assuredly would have made if he had done so at his peak between 1958 and 1963.

The following year, however, Edmonds did win the English title with a comfortable 11–7 over Patsy Fagan, a Putney-based Irishman who typified a new breed of young players which was thriving amidst the general air of high activity in the Snooker world by playing money matches against both amateurs and professionals. Under the management and backing then of Peter Careswell and later of George Jackson, Fagan established himself as a fine player in a situation not unlike that which used to commonly exist in Boxing when a local businessman/sportsman would take up a local hopeful and, in return for the thrill of involvement and a percentage of earnings, nurture his career.

Another young player, Willie Thorne (Leicester), who had shown great promise in winning the British Boys Championship in 1970 and Junior Championship in 1973 and becoming England's youngest international in 1973, came through by capturing the Southern title in a blaze of glory in 1975 with breaks of 91, 71 and 80 in his 8–5 win over Chris Ross (Woking) in the final. Having beaten him five times out of five, Thorne was expected to beat Hood (who, with Edmonds withdrawing in favour of a South African tour, had won the Northern title) in the national final at Hull but after winning the first frame with an 86 break he fell victim to the most determined and sustained effort Hood made in his long career. Hood won 11–6 and the twenty-one year old Thorne turned professional the following November when, in view of his obvious talent and a defeat of Spencer in an international tournament in Toronto, he was invited to compete in "Pot Black".

Edmonds had retained the World Amateur Championship at the Crofton Airport Hotel, Dublin, in November 1974 in a field inferior to that of 1972. England sent no second representative; Malta nominated Borg but not Mifsud; and South Africa, whose nomination of Silvino Francisco or Mike Hines had originally been accepted, was forced to withdraw after the Irish Transport and General Workers Union made it clear that their support for the Anti-Apartheid Movement would otherwise lead to the event being crippled by industrial action, demonstrations and disruptions.

The field of eighteen was divided into two groups. Edmonds, despite losing his opening match 4–3 to Lafir, won group A while Alwyn Lloyd, who had won the 1973 and 1974 Welsh Championships as Welsh standards of play rose and the organisation of their association began to be geared more to the international game, won group B undefeated. Lloyd, who made breaks of 97 against Sneddon and 104 against N.J. Rahim (Sri Lanka), played some of the best Snooker of the Championship but all this went for naught when he was beaten 4–2 by his compatriot Geoff Thomas, the 1972 Welsh champion, in the quarter-finals.

The system of allowing the top four from each group through to the knock-out quarter-finals actually appeared to give a psychological advantage to those who qualified in fourth place. Thomas, for instance, with four defeats, only qualified on frames after a late run and thus played against Lloyd like a man unexpectedly reprieved and with everything to gain and nothing to lose. The same nearly happened to Edmonds for Lou Condo, the Australian who had finished fourth in the other group, played his best Snooker of the tournament to lead 3–1 before the holder won 4–3.

In the semi-finals, Edmonds beat Eddie Sinclair, the Scottish champion, 8–4 and Thomas beat the Republic of Ireland champion, Pascal Burke, 8–2 after Burke had ended Lafir's hopes of the second leg of a unique World Billiards/World Snooker double by beating him 4–3 in the quarters.

When Edmonds led Thomas 5–2 in the final it looked odds-on an early finish but the Welshman recovered to 7–7 at the second interval and again showed his tenacity by converting 7–9 into 9–9. But Thomas, it seemed, could not quite picture himself as world champion and, after missing a green with the rest which would have given him a 10–9 lead, he lost this and the following frame for Edmonds, like Gary Owen in 1963 and 1966, to win his second World Amateur title.

Edmonds and Lloyd subsequently constituted a British team which won one and drew two of three Tests in South Africa, where Edmonds and another leading English amateur, Chris Ross, had previously made tours at the invitation of the South African Association.

South Africa's unprecedented offer to pay air fares for one competitor and one delegate from each affiliated country to the World Amateur Championship in Johannesburg in 1976 was made and confirmed, thus enabling some of the more impoverished national associations to be represented and others who would have been refused a grant by their governments to be represented at no cost to themselves. Twenty-four players were divided into three groups with three qualifying from each and two of the third place finishers being drawn by lot to contest a match to reduce the field to eight. India and Sri Lanka were forbidden by their governments to compete but the entry was nevertheless of very high overall quality.

England was represented in the lavish Championship setting of the President Hotel, Johannesburg, by Edmonds, the defending champion; Ross, who after years of near misses had finally won the English title by beating Fagan in the Southern final – despite his opponent equalling with 115, Thompson's English Championship break record; and Roy Andrewartha in the grand final. Andrewartha also made the trip as it had been decided, for this Championship only, to allow three competitors from the country of the defending champion and three from the host country instead of the usual two. South Africa eventually had a fourth representative through the late withdrawal of Malta's number two.

The tournament was, however, to see the end of England's domination, an out of touch Ross finishing fourth in his group, Andrewartha falling 0–4 to the 1975 Welsh champion, Terry Griffiths, in the round before the quarter-finals, and Edmonds going out 5–1 in the quarters to Mifsud, who was to give Malta a World Amateur finalist for the first time.

Wales, home international champions in 1975 and 1976, emphasised their rising status on the international scene by supplying a quarter-finalist, Griffiths, and the new champion, Doug Mountjoy, who epitomised a new breed of player which had flourished since the abolition of all restrictions on amateurs accepting prize money or exhibition fees.

Though he had won the Welsh Amateur title in 1968, Mountjoy had remained for several years a player whose outstanding natural ability was frequently obscured by inconsistency. Having become the first amateur to win a £1,000 first prize in the first Pontin's Open at Prestatyn in 1974 (see page 126), Mountjoy had played full time without risk of losing his amateur status.

Playing full time gradually matured Mountjoy's game though he needed all his new found steadiness and composure to beat Dai Thomas 7–6 in the Welsh semi-final, after Thomas had twice been within a ball of victory, and Lloyd 8–6 in the final. Even his 4–2 quarter-final win over Geoff Thomas, in which he set a new Welsh record break of 103, was far from plain sailing.

Mountjoy won all seven of his Group one matches though he had to recover from 1–3 to beat Peter Reynolds (Isle of Man) 4–3 and overcome two outrageous refereeing decisions against him before beating Jimmy van Rensburg (South Africa) 4–2. Later he made a break of 107 in his 4–1 over the Maori, Norman Stockman, which, but for a disappointing failure at the last red, looked certain to develop into a new World Amateur record. As it was, Ratan Bader's 122 stood until December 1977 when Brian Kirkness (New Zealand) recorded a 128, missing the pink, in the Snooker tournament supplementary to the unofficial World Open Billiards Championship in Christchurch.

Van Rensburg (two defeats) and Edmonds (three) – but with a lower frames against total than either Stockman or Eddie Sinclair (Scotland), who were also beaten three times – were the other qualifiers from this group.

In Group two, Mifsud and Silvino Francisco, the younger of the South African brothers, both finished with one defeat and Griffiths with two. The Welshman ultimately qualified only through fluking the final pink to beat the

Canadian, Bob Paquette, who would otherwise have gone through.

From Group three, slightly weaker than the other two, the qualifiers were Mannie Francisco (one defeat), Ron Atkins (Australia) (one) and Andrewartha, who made a break of 100 in beating Atkins 4–1, (two).

Atkins impressed with a solid, efficient, consistent style reminiscent of his professional compatriot, Charlton, and even more so through his courage in overcoming the loss of a leg in a teenage shooting accident, but was unlucky enough to find Mountjoy at his most dominating in their quarter-final as he clinched a 5–1 win with an 80 break in the last frame.

Van Rensburg, a clever tactician, ended visions of an all Welsh final by beating Griffiths 5–3 and Mifsud squashed Edmond's hopes of a hat trick of titles by beating him 5–1, not a surprising result in view of the Englishman's patchy form throughout the tournament.

More surprising in terms of past results was Silvino's 5–1 win over Mannie, twelve years his senior, in the clash between the Francisco brothers, but whereas Silvino had impressed as an outstanding potter (if with a puzzling streak of exaggerated caution in his make-up) Mannie's always suspect temperament had deteriorated since reaching the 1972 final in Cardiff.

Mifsud, going boldly for every chance, then beat Van Rensburg 8–4 but the final saw Mountjoy outclass him 11–1 just as he had overwhelmed Francisco 8–2 in the semi. There was no mistaking that Mountjoy was top professional class. Next day, having submitted a post dated application, he became a professional, and Ross and Andrewartha, less successfully, turned a few weeks later.

In his first professional tournament, Mountjoy illustrated how narrow was the gap between top amateur and professional standards when he beat Pulman 4–2, Davis 4–2, Higgins 5–3 and Reardon, in a wonderfully exciting finish, 7–6 on the final pink to win the Benson and Hedges Masters in February 1977.

# CHAPTER XIV

# The Television Age
*(Snooker 1977–1978)*

The Snooker boom continued: the equipment firms transacted an unprecedented volume of business; professionals were not only more numerous but busier than ever before; amateur activity, to an even greater extent than professional, completely outgrew its administration. There were developments of all kinds but each seemed to occur independently.

Where there should have been an overall coherence, there was all too often, on the professional side, an unseemly, every man for himself scramble for the rich final rewards the game could now offer. The W.P.B.S.A., thanks to some devoted work by Williams, until his disillusioned resignation in May 1977, exerted a measure of control over the World Championship but, largely because it comprised professional players, each of whom had his own interests to consider, it failed (or lacked the muscle) to guide development in all but the most immediate matters. Alliances, formal or otherwise, were formed within the professional ranks and decisions on all too many issues appeared to hinge on short term profit rather than any long term vision.

One of the W.P.B.S.A.'s mistakes was to approve a so-called World Professional Matchplay Championship in Melbourne in November 1976. Charlton beat Reardon to win it and financially the players did well out of it but the indiscriminate application of the word "world" to a tournament which was no more than a pale carbon copy of the genuine Championship was no more than an exploitation of the Australian public and, in the dilution of the authentic article and confusion which was sown among the unknowledgable as to who was the real world champion, a disservice to the game. Charlton, who also promoted the 1976 event, was refused the W.P.B.S.A.'s permission to promote a repeat in 1977 but in 1978 his offer of $35,000 prize money conditional (to guarantee, it was said, the support of television and sponsorship) on the word "world" appearing in the title, was unanimously accepted by the W.P.B.S.A. committee.

On the amateur front Snooker had progressed, in little more than a decade, from having no international contact at amateur level to an established World Amateur Championship which many national associations eagerly sought to hold. There was in the British Isles an established Home International Series which, though dominated by England and Wales, gave Scottish and Irish players a measure of top class matchplay which had previously been unavailable to them. International contacts of all sorts had been fostered and though British standards in depth were by the end of this period much higher than ever before, other nations were also producing some of the best players in their history.

The central problem of administration was not seriously tackled. The Home International Series was run by a committee on which the four national associations had equal representation and the one nation, one vote International Billiards and Snooker Federation (which to soothe the B. & S.C.C.'s feelings had changed its title from 'World Council' in 1973) controlled World Amateur Championships but the B. & S.C.C. fought tooth and nail any suggestion that they should either separate their (English) domestic and international functions or recognise the I.B.S.F. rather than itself as the world amateur governing body.

The B. & S.C.C., which held all its meetings in England, gave each county, through its archaic constitution, one council member (and one vote) for every hundred clubs affiliated while an overseas nation was entitled to only one representative. It was manifestly absurd that Australia, New Zealand, India and other distant nations would send representatives all the way to England only to be outvoted by Lancashire and Yorkshire alone but the B. & S.C.C., through its forceful chairman, Bill Cottier, an ex-policeman from Bootle, resisted change so bitterly that, rather than force the issue, the overseas nations settled for the most part for a policy of allowing time to do its evolutionary work.

At home, the B. & S.C.C., with support from the Billiard Traders Association, made some progress with coaching and a significant advance with the appointment, in 1977, of a development officer, David Ford, certainly the first B. & S.C.C. administrator to move with confidence through the labyrinthine channels of local government, a vital skill in seeking to ensure that Snooker facilities would be provided in the new sports centres which had become a feature of the 1970's and were being planned for the 1980's. He also demonstrated an encouraging appreciation of the need to encourage Snooker's development in sport's mainstream rather than leave it, as had been overwhelmingly the case in the 1950's and 1960's, within the province of the licensed clubs, a tradition which nevertheless is likely always to have an important role.

But with sponsorship having become an accepted part not only of the professional but the amateur scene the B. & S.C.C.'s difficulty in retaining amateur sponsors underlined its inability and that of amateur officials in general to appreciate that sponsorship was not a handout to the needy but a commercial investment on which they had a responsibility to help provide a return.

Some sponsors were so ill used that they departed as quickly as they came. Watneys had sponsored a British Pairs Championship in 1969 but, disenchanted with such official blunders as the arranging of one of the quarter-finals in a temperance hall, did not renew their interest. Joe Coral, the bookmakers, adopted the event from 1974. Players No 6 sponsored a British Championship for teams of three in 1968 and 1969 and Langs, the whisky distillers, did so in 1974. Double Diamond sponsored a Championship for teams of two in 1975 and 1976 but, like their predecessors, then withdrew. Canadian Club, who sponsored a national Snooker handicap from 1976–1978, were also lost.

At first supported by Accles and Pollock, manufacturers of metal cues, and then by the Composition Ball Co., the B. & S.C.C. had taken over the running of the Boys and Junior Championship from the author (who had revived them in 1968 after the Snooker events had lapsed for a year and the Billiards for longer), instituted Inter-County Championships in 1975 and an unsponsored national three-a-side Championship in 1977.

Regional and local sponsorships and tournaments, not to mention leagues, flourished in large numbers and, despite the setbacks and general lack of co-ordination, the game was in a very healthy state. Problems there remained, but many of these were at least now posed by success rather than failure, by the need to live up to what was now expected from the game rather than that of living down the impecunious and cloth-capped image of its past.

\*　　\*　　\*

After the chaos of the 1976 World Professional Championship it seemed long odds against Embassy wanting to be involved again. Fortunately, their long debated decision to continue the sponsorship with a new promoter, Mike Watterson, at a new theatre-in-the-round venue, the Crucible Theatre, Sheffield, was triumphantly vindicated. Streamlined organisation, excellent playing conditions, a total attendance of over twenty thousand, record prize money of £17,000 (including a new record first prize of £6,000) and increased television coverage all contributed to an aura of success so heady and unmistakable that Snooker itself had clearly made a significant step forward. These gains were to be spectacularly consolidated in 1978.

Meanwhile, the 1977 Championship, was to interrupt, albeit briefly, Reardon's reign as champion. His supply of adrenalin drying up and his concentration wayward, he went out tamely 13–6 to Spencer in the quarter-finals.

Even then, Spencer did not stand out as the likely champion for, after his 1969 and 1970 titles, he had slid slowly down the W.P.B.S.A. rankings until, at number eight, he only just rated a seeding. This was in part due to the W.P.B.S.A. system of assessing rankings entirely on the basis of the three previous World Championships, a method which rendered wins in other major tournaments irrelevant and which aroused heated protests from relative newcomers to the professional ranks on the grounds that it was unfair to players who had been professionals for less than three years. (Indeed, before the malcontents called an Extraordinary General Meeting, which voted to end the system whereby two qualifiers joined the top fourteen in the rankings in the competition proper in favour of eight qualifiers joining the top eight, the system favoured the established professionals even more.)

Of the qualifiers, Virgo led Spencer 7–4 before going down 13–9 in the first round; Mountjoy, with the most daring of pots down the side cushion, beat Higgins 13–12 on the final black; Dennis Taylor reached the semi-final for the second time in three years with 13–11 wins over both Perrie Mans and Mountjoy; Pulman, with his best competitive Snooker for some years, beat Davis 13–12 and Miles 13–10 and led Spencer 7–3 in the semi-final before losing 18–16; and Thorburn became the first Canadian ever to reach the final with wins of 13–6 over Williams, 13–12 over Charlton (after a sixty-two minute deciding frame) and 18–16 (including a 111 break in the penultimate frame) over Taylor.

When, in the final, Thorburn led 15–11, it seemed as if the first non-British world professional champion was about to be crowned but Spencer, as had happened so often during the tournament, played with great determination and nerve to level. Throughout the Championship, he had demonstrated a priceless ability to hang on when not playing well. It was a sharp contrast to the easy natural fluency with which he had played in the early 70's but it proved that courage, tenacity and tactical acumen can still be made to count for a great deal.

Starting the last day level at 18–18, Spencer, not normally an early riser, rose at seven-thirty for an hour's stroll in the park to clear his mind for the eleven o'clock start, a course which had occurred to him through surveying his comparatively poor showing in morning sessions. He won the first three frames and finally clinched victory at 25–21.

It was a success in which not the least remarkable element was that he achieved it with a cue which he used for less than two months prior to the Championship. This exploded two myths: first that it takes months or even years to become accustomed to a new cue, a view supported by most professionals using the same cue for their entire careers; second, that top class Snooker could not be played with a two-piece cue, hitherto considered suitable only for the smaller American Pool tables.

Both finalists, in fact, used two-piece cues. As Canadians, long under American influence, had always done so, it would have been surprising if Thorburn had used anything else, but for Spencer to discard, so near the Championship, the "old faithful" cue with which he had recorded all his successes in favour of what was regarded in the British game as little better than a new-fangled gimmick, was looked upon almost as a symptom of insanity. What only Spencer himself knew was that his old cue, broken into four pieces in a car accident shortly before the 1974 Norwich Union Open, had never, despite the masterly cue surgery of Cliff Curtis, played quite the same after it had been pinned together. He gradually lost confidence in it but laboured on indecisively until, on a visit to Canada, he picked a two-piece cue out of stock. Still he hovered until he decided to use it through a week's tour of Cornwall. Five century breaks within the week convinced him that he could use it in the Championship. Ironically, some months after becoming champion, he discarded this cue in favour of another two-piece model made in Japan.

Spencer added another £1,500 to his bank balance by beating Pulman 7–5 to win the Pontins Professional title a few days later but the highlight of that week was Higgins's capture of the £1,500 first prize from the Pontins Open in which he took advantage of a new dispensation by which non-invited professionals could compete on condition that, conceding 21 start, they played through the qualifying competition, most of which was conducted not on glossy match tables but in the 14 table billiard room ordinarily used by holidaymakers with no specialist interest in Snooker.

The professionals invited to play at Pontins were automatically those invited to play in "Pot Black", still clocking up its regular three or four million viewers per week on BBC 2. This link arose through Ted Lowe, back in the 1940's and 50's manager of Leicester Square Hall and now "Pot Black" commentator, not only having the most influential voice in the selection of players for the programme but in acting as consultant to Pontins.

Higgins, who, after the BBC had taken a poor view of his threat to walk out halfway through recording the 1973 series, had been dropped from the "Pot Black" line-up in subsequent years, was thus, until 1977, effectively debarred from Pontins as well, a situation which displeased a large section of the Snooker public on the grounds that, as one of the top players, he should figure in the game's major events.

But it was a situation which, just as riding in to the 1972 world title on the crest of a wave starting way out in an amorphous sea of the qualifying competition had done, saw his challenge gradually gather an irresistible momentum. Drawn in group fourteen of an eight hundred and sixty-four entry qualifying competition, in which matches were decided on the aggregate score of two frames, Higgins, in only his second match, trailed Bill Kelly, a top class amateur from Manchester, by 104 with only 4 reds remaining in the first frame before recovering to win 133–121.

Two amateur internationals, Murdo McLeod (Scotland) in the last 32, and Doug French (England) in the last 16, took him to the deciding frame of seven only to waver in the uniquely charged emotional atmosphere which Higgins's matches created. His 4–0 defeat of Reardon in the quarters was an execution. Another 4–0 win over Davis in the semi, followed by a 7–5 win, conceding 21 of course, over Terry Griffiths, who a month previously had demolished Hood 13–3 to win the English Amateur Championship, were also achieved on a tidal wave of support reminiscent of the 1972 world final but even more an expression of identification with a star who had remained, like his most intensive supporters, an outsider still more at ease with the kind of people he had grown up with and with no desire to change his social position or pursue security.

Each successive victory brought a pop idol's reception from the supporters who, in overpowering volume, found in him a hero who did not represent the conventional values they had rejected. This Snooker equivalent of the Stretford End had no sympathy with a professional Establishment yearning at heart for the days of Leicester Square Hall when everybody wore tuxedos, when there were just one hundred and fifty polite, well heeled spectators, when everybody knew who was boss and who was supposed to beat whom. Right or wrong – and he was often in the wrong – they supported Higgins.

Snooker – indeed most sports – had moved on: a great mass of enthusiasts had grown resentful and frustrated that their game, as they saw it, was being taken away from them. In the dark days, when a great deal of Snooker was played but with no glamour or publicity attaching to it, the Snooker world had been a kind of sub-culture whose values were more often those of private rather than conventional codes. Higgins grew up in such a climate and, for all the media's subsequent attention, always returned to it.

As Snooker, through television, newspapers and sponsorship, began to develop as a business, the traditional and often unconsidered supporters were disturbed and even angered by decisions made for reasons they could not understand. When, for instance, a player of Higgins's ability was constantly omitted from tournaments, the bitterness and resentment of those not "in the know" was focused on the "right people" who appeared to hold the strings and the other "right people" who benefited. Thus, when Higgins, from the outsider's humble initial status of "just another qualifier" came through to win,

Leslie Driffield

Alex Higgins

Jonathan Barron

Bob Marshall

John Spencer

Gary Owen

Ray Reardon (left) talks to Doug Mountjoy between frames of the 1977
Benson and Hedges Masters final

Michael Ferreira

celebration was uproarious. "What about 'Pot Black' then?" called a small section of the crowd, none too good humouredly, as he received his prize.

Higgins registered another notable success four months later, winning the Canadian National Exhibition Centre tournament in Toronto which, from 1974, had become an annual feature in late August/early September on the permanent Canadian National Exhibition site. As Thorburn won in 1974, Higgins in 1975 and Spencer in 1976, the event not only acquired higher status as an accepted fixture on the international scene but became a focus for the rise of Canadian Snooker itself; though the game had been popular in Canada since the 1920's, it had been almost entirely in the context of gambling with little or even no formal competitive structure. It was largely through Thorburn, a player, and two Billiard traders, Terry Haddock and Doug McDonald, between whom a keen rivalry existed, that Canada entered Snooker's mainstream. Haddock organised the C.N.E. tournament while McDonald involved himself chiefly with the amateur side, organising Canadian participation in the 1976 World Amateur Championship in Johannesburg and, as Canadian delegate at the International Federation meeting there, securing Canada's right to stage the 1982 Championship.

Due to an administrative difficulty, the 1977 C.N.E. tournament was accommodated not in one of the exhibition's permanent buildings but, as the only alternative to cancellation, in a large tent. A steel band, a non-stop dance band and a circus in the nearest tents, not to mention a plague of flies in a hundred degree temperatures and sunlight in the afternoon sessions, tested the concentration of competitors but for $15,000 prize money, a fifty per cent increase on the previous year, the show went on.

The development, amidst Canada's Snooker boom, of a crop of young players of high quality was confirmed. In 1976, Bernie Mikkelsen, a twenty-six year old, six foot five inch beanpole, had made a 141 break in the deciding frame to beat Pulman 9–8 in the quarter-finals; in 1977, Kevin Robitaille, nineteen, beat Mountjoy 9–8; Mario Morra, twenty, led Spencer 7–5 before losing 9–7; Jim Wych, twenty, lost only 9–8 on the final black to Dennis Taylor and Kirk Stevens, eighteen, led Reardon 5–3 before losing 9–6. Eventually Higgins beat Reardon 9–7 and Spencer 17–14 to win the tournament.

Meanwhile, Britain too was producing young players of exceptional quality. Steve Davis, when only nineteen, made a 147 maximum, as did Tony Meo, only eighteen, a few weeks after he won the 1977 Warners Open, an event on similar lines to, if a smaller scale than, the Pontins Open. Opportunities for young players – with the opening of more and more new Snooker centres, almost all with standards of comfort and amenity which were a great improvement on the old billiards halls, and with the promotion of a wide variety of tournaments offering prize money which a few years previously would not have been sniffed at even by professionals – grew out of all recognition. Davis was given a five year contract and managed by Barry Hearn, the young go-ahead chairman of Lucania, a long established Snooker club chain; Meo and the exceptionally talented Jimmy White, the 1977 National Under Sixteen champion, operated from the Ron Gross Snooker Centre in Neasden and the Pot Black Snooker Centre in Clapham, the latter a venture of Noel Miller Cheevers, a Dublin-born but London based property millionaire who, in a non-commercial capacity, also started the International Snooker League in which teams of wealthy enthusiasts from England, Ireland, the United States,

Canada, Bermuda and South Africa met annually in keen but sociable competition.

Tirfor, a lifting and pulling equipment company, put £1,000 into an open junior tournament offering a £400 first prize (won by Meo). White, only sixteen, made a break of 119 at his first visit to the table in his first match, followed by one of 97 in the next frame.

Not merely junior but amateur standards in general inched up all the time through competition, partly through established Amateur Championships run by the B. & S.C.C. and regional and local events by their respective amateur associations, but principally through the clubs and promoters who organised open or invitation events. First prizes of £300, £400 or even £500 began to become common.

Amidst the boom, fringe operators, middlemen, managers or simply people attracted to the Snooker world who wanted to carve out some distinctive niche within it, hustled endlessly; informal gambling and money matches, a feature of Snooker throughout its history, proliferated; one-man or two-man maintenance and equipment firms mushroomed, some of them lasting long enough to dent the complacency which still distinguished many of the established firms. One way and another, it seemed, everybody wanted to get in on the act.

Some newcomers, of course, brought experience which had been proven in other fields, notably Mike Barrett, the boxing promoter, who began his association with the sport in December 1977 by staging the Dry Blackthorn Cup at the massive Wembley Conference Centre with prize money of no less than £4,000 for a four-man, one-day event.

Fagan, accepted as a professional in 1976 only at his second application to the W.P.B.S.A. – the initial rejection illustrating the inherent problem of a system of election depending solely on players who were already members – scooped half of this with 4–2 wins over Spencer and Higgins to add to £2,000 he had earned a couple of weeks earlier by winning the United Kingdom Professional Championship, an event initiated by promoter Mike Watterson with sponsorship by Super Crystalate at Blackpool Tower Circus.

Blackpool in the depths of winter did not provide the crowds which had supported the spring world finals of the 1950's but there were some lively matches. Reardon went out 5–4 in the first round to Jim Meadowcroft, one of a group of competent players still struggling to establish themselves, who in turn lost 5–4 to Fagan. Spencer went out 5–3 to Mountjoy in the first round and Higgins, after trailing 2–4, survived perilously, 5–4 over David Taylor, who, after winning the world amateur title in 1968, had gradually lost faith in his ability to beat top players.

Overshadowing not only the first round but the whole week, however, was the match – or rather its aftermath – in which Willie Thorne beat Williams, who, in disillusion at the lack of co-operation of other members, had resigned the chairmanship of the W.P.B.S.A. some six months previously.

The match was important to both players: Thorne a young professional making his way, Williams an established figure trying to hold his place in the pecking order. Thorne led 3–1 and 4–2 but at 4–4 it was anybody's match. Then, in the final frame, Williams snookered Thorne on a group of reds in such a way that his opponent was quite likely, in escaping from the snooker, to leave the opening for a frame winning break. When Thorne failed to hit a red but in such a way that the cue-ball returned to a safe position, Williams angrily claimed a foul for a "deliberate miss" – an infringement of rule 5, . . . the player shall, to the best of his ability, endeavour to strike a ball that is on" – and alleged, furthermore, that Thorne had been guilty of other such fouls during the match.

The referee, however, adjudged that Thorne had made a genuine attempt to hit the ball on and play continued until Thorne won 5–4. Williams declined to sign the result sheet and delivered himself of some bitter comments to the press but then drove home, the matter apparently closed. Later that night, in the lounge of the players' hotel, Thorne was allegedly overheard to admit a deliberate miss and an informal and unconstitutional committee of the promoter, the W.P.B.S.A. Secretary, Mike Green, and the senior referee, John Williams, disqualified him without giving him the opportunity to state his case. The promoter rang Williams to inform him that he was reinstated and that he was expected back in Blackpool to play his next match.

But at Blackpool, when Thorne learned of his disqualification, there was uproar. A meeting of the W.P.B.S.A. committee was hastily convened – or at any rate a four man quorum – and, after lengthy debate, Thorne's disqualification was rescinded just in time for Williams to be informed of it on his arrival! It was an incident which illustrated the need for the W.P.B.S.A. to control major tournaments more effectively, through a considered procedural system, rather than deal with crises on a spur of the moment basis. It also emphasised that the "deliberate miss" was, in itself, a growing problem, perhaps exaggerated by a context of high prize money and intense competition, which could only be dealt with by firm, knowledgeable refereeing.

A deliberate miss was actually called in the first session of the final on Mountjoy (and hotly disputed by him), after he had beaten Higgins 9–2 in the semi. It was an early turning point as the decision was instrumental in Fagan's recovery from 2–3 to lead 4–3 at the first interval, though ultimately Mountjoy's failure at the final pink at 9–9 gave Fagan the springboard to win 12–9. In retrospect, though, Fagan's success turned not so much on the final, perhaps, as the semi-final in which he trailed Virgo 5–8 and 60 behind in the next frame before winning 9–8.

That Fagan could win a major tournament (as Mountjoy had won the 1977 Benson and Hedges Masters) proved once again that outstanding amateurs could quickly mature into formidable professionals. There were no wholesale applications for W.P.B.S.A. membership because most could still perceive that unless they reached the top eight or at least top dozen in the professional ranks, the sort of status required for them to receive invitations to the big money tournaments, they were better off as amateurs with a job of work supplemented by tournament earnings.

The World Amateur Championship, which had gained steadily not only in prestige but as a potential commercial asset, also tended to affect the thinking of players contemplating a change of status. Griffiths, English Amateur Champion in 1977, retained this title with some ease but a surprise quarter-final loss in the Welsh Championship to Steve Newbury ruled him out of the November 1978 World Amateur in Malta, Wales nominating Cliff Wilson, their 1977 champion and one of the game's most popular attractions, amateur or professional, and Lloyd, who won in 1978. Rather than wait two more years for the 1980 World Amateur in Australia, Griffiths turned professional.

More surprisingly, Edmonds, who had found problems of motivation, concentration and consistency since winning the world amateur title in 1972 and 1974, also decided, after losing in the 1978 Northern section semi-finals of the English Championship, to try his luck as a professional. More controversially, Steve Davis, winner of the £1,500 first prize at the 1978 Pontin's Open by beating Meo, who took £500, 7–6 in a splendid final, followed a couple of months later. He had had a string of successes but an unexpected defeat in the Southern Section of the English Amateur Championship, which consequently ruled him out of the World Amateur, had raised a question mark not over his outstanding ability but over the more general issue of whether, at the age of twenty, he could still have benefited from another couple of years in the amateur ranks.

In the opposite direction, on January 1, 1977, Ron Gross was reinstated as an amateur. "Look at it this way", he said. "It's £150 to be a member of the W.P.B.S.A., another £50 to enter the World Championship and another £100 or so to go up for the qualifying competiton. Then you've got to beat at least two really good players to get in the money at all."

Proprietor of a flourishing Snooker Centre in Neasden, Gross's urge to play competitively was, ironically, frustrated by his professional status. He was not good enough to get in the tournaments where the real money was and, as a professional, he was debarred from the increasingly remunerative amateur circuit.

With South Africa excluded from participation in Malta, both Francisco brothers, Van Rensburg, Roy Amdol and Derek Mienie turned professional in the belief that, with South Africans likely to be excluded from most international amateur events in the foreseeable future, this offered them a better competitive future.

Throughout 1977 and 1978 each national association held annual Championships to determine its representatives for Malta, a build-up which led to twelve countries taking up their entitlement of two entries, with Sudan participating for the first time, bringing the total competitors to twenty-five. England, as Griffiths and Wilson had contested an all Welsh final to the Southern Area, nominated two Yorkshiremen, Joe Johnson, who had set a record for the Home International Series with a 108 break against Scotland in 1977, and Ian Williamson, whom he had defeated 8–4 in the Northern final at the Northern Snooker Centre, Leeds, one of the best of the new Snooker centres, whose proprietor, Jim Williamson, indefatigably promoted tournaments of all sorts in its match arena.

On the professional scene, with the Benson and Hedges Masters in February forming the centrepiece to the run up to the Embassy World Professional Snooker Championship in April, Higgins maintained his recent ascendancy over Reardon, against whom, indeed, his record over the years had been better than anyone's - with a 5–1 semi-final victory before beating Thorburn 7–5 for the £3,000 first prize. The week prior to the tournament, Higgins swamped Dennis Taylor 21–7 in defending his Irish title in Belfast and the week before the Championship disposed of Fagan in similar style 21–13.

But a rude shock awaited him in the Championship when he lost in the first round to Fagan on the final pink, 13–12, just as he had lost on the final black to Mountjoy a year earlier. Playing either with a hint of the death wish or with an unconscious lust for the spotlight, which made him incapable of concluding the match when he was in a commanding position, Higgins played with all his characteristic bravery and recklessness, determination and prodigality. With a superlative pink and black finish, Higgins led 11–10 and when he went two up with three to play he looked a certainty. In the next frame a superb break of 66 took him within one ball of victory only for a failure at the green to allow Fagan to tie the frame and sink the re-spotted black to keep in the match at 11–12. Fagan won another desperately exciting black ball frame to level at 12–12 and, after Higgins had again looked odds-on in the decider, won this too with a last ditch colours clearance.

There was pandemonium. A young Higgins fan from Barrow-in-Furness, Tony Metcalf, a long time sufferer from a bone marrow disease, was emotionally overcome by the shock. (Next day, the tournament director, Bruce Donkin, organised a collection among the players.) The crowd could hardly believe it. Viewers to BBC 2's nightly fifty minute programme talked about it for days – or at least until another dramatic match superseded it.

In the first round alone there was almost an embarrassment of riches. Mountjoy led Reardon 7–2 before the latter repeated his 12–8 William Hill Welsh Professional Championship victory (another new event held earlier in the season), 13–9; Thorne, leading Charlton 12–9, missed a black which would have given him a famous victory and eventually went down 13–12 to the Australian's break of 98 in the deciding frame; Spencer, the holder, despite breaks of 118 and 138, was for the most part out of touch and went down 13–9 to Mans, a player who had always given him trouble.

The quarter-finals brought another amazing recovery from Charlton who, having trailed Thorburn 3–9 and 8–12, incredibly won the last five frames for a second 13–12 victory. Thorburn's compatriot, the seventeen stone Bill Werbeniuk, who had given Canada, for the first time, a second quarter-finalist by beating Pulman 13–4, fell 13–6 to Reardon who, to overcome his notorious aversion to morning sessions, rose early each morning he was due to play one for an hour's practice at eight a.m. on his friend Gordon Ingham's table on which, incidentally, he had compiled his seventh 147 maximum a few weeks previously.

Davis, who had recovered from 3–7 to beat Virgo 9–8 in the last match of the qualifying section, staged at Romiley Forum, Stockport, with a quality which many previous Championships proper had fallen short of, followed his 13–9 first round win over Dennis Taylor by defeating Fagan 13–10 with a display which recalled his golden years, Mans beat Miles, whose game had lost its edge in the preceding three years, 13–7.

In the semi-finals, Charlton briefly threatened Reardon by leading 12–9 before a 7–0 whitewash prefaced his defeat at 18–14 while Mans, whose spectacular single ball potting was one of the most memorable features of the event, finally ended Davis's bid to regain the title after twenty-two years at 18–16.

As in all the sixty-four year old veteran's matches, the crowd responded with waves of affection to his warm personality, puckish sense of humour and cultured skill, almost overwhelmingly so, as, from 12–16, he recovered to within one ball of 15–16 only to miss a simple straight pink for the frame. At one behind with two to go he was still in the match but Mans, who had borne with patience and dignity the crowd's support for his opponent, made a confident and fluent 60 break to become the first South African ever to reach the final.

For Mans it was an important personal breakthrough. Though a World Championship competitor since 1970, he had spent, as South Africa's only active professional and thus with no domestic opposition, a great deal more time as an insurance agent than as a Snooker player. Indeed, he had bothered to practise only immediately before an overseas trip. With infrequent opportunities for competition, his game did not acquire the positional polish of the other top players but he gradually fashioned a style which was awkward to combat.

"If I left him anything at all in the open", said Davis, "no matter how far away, he invariably potted it and some of his safety shots surprised me. When I had to play safe myself, it always seemed to be difficult to get behind something."

Building up a lead with small contributions without letting his opponent get to close quarters or counterpunching near the end by clearing the last couple of reds and all the colours, the Mans style, allied to the inspiration and elation of being in the final, kept the score to 8–8 at the end of the first day of the final.

Twice on the second afternoon Mans was a frame in front but Reardon finished the session with a 12–11 lead and pushed on to 18–14 at the close. On the resumption, Mans gave it all he had to win the first three frames before Reardon, visibly steadying himself, halted the trend with a 100 break and secured a record first prize of £7,500 at 25–18 by winning seven of the last eight frames.

It was, of course, the television coverage which was to elevate the Championship to a place beside Britain's other great sporting occasions. As early as 1976, Nick Hunter, the executive producer entrusted with the Championship, had wanted to develop BBC's coverage from a glimpse of the final to a portrait of an event. "Pot Black" and other special tournaments for television, notably from Thames and Yorkshire, had proved that the casual, floating viewer was prepared to watch Snooker and it was Hunter's theory that the potential viewing audience for the sport was far in excess of the already respectable three to four million for "Pot Black". Though even more ambitious plans had to be shelved owing to a change of Championship dates, television coverage increased in 1977 quite considerably preparatory to, in 1978, daily coverage by means of a fifty minute compilation, sometimes with live inserts, on each of the thirteen days of the Championship, in addition to Saturday afternoon exposure on BBC 1's "Grandstand" and, a final triumph for Hunter and his men, live coverage of the final on BBC 2 on the second Thursday and Friday and early on Saturday evening.

The very first fifty minute compilation – edited from simultaneous recording of two matches, a total of twenty-six playing hours through the day – attracted a near midnight audience of four million which built to seven million by the end of the tournament. The nation stayed up late and went to work red-eyed as some one hundred and fifty BBC personnel were involved in recording some three hundred miles of video tape during the Championship fortnight. "Backstage at the Crucible", wrote Peter Fiddick, *The Guardian*'s television correspondent, "there is a sense that the result scarcely matters, that something new is happening. The top professionals are very conscious of their new audience and its implications. For them, the game is at least being shown properly, at length, with all its tactics, and the fact that it could prove even more popular that way opens a whole new future even to men said to be potting

£30,000 a year. 'What the public are getting here', says Fred Davis, 'is the feel of what it is like playing under pressure hour after hour, for days on end.'"

Sadly, the pressure told most deeply not on a player but a spectator: Joe Davis, now seventy-seven, swinging in his seat this way and that as he mentally played every shot for his brother, was taken ill at the mid-session interval of the final session of Fred's semi-final against Mans and taken back to his hotel. Two days later, outside his Kensington flat, he collapsed a few seconds after getting out of the car which had brought him back from Sheffield. He survived a six and a half hour operation, related to a serious operation from a haemorrhaged aorta three years previously, but died a few weeks later from a chest infection when he was convalescing in the country. He died with the satisfaction of having seen, at Sheffield and on television, the game which he had pioneered at a peak of popularity and the Championship he had founded established, with events like Wimbledon and the Open Golf Championship, as one of Britain's great annual sporting spectacles.

# Tables

## I Billiards: World Professional Championships

| Date | Winner | Runner-up | Final Scores |
|------|--------|-----------|--------------|
| 1870 Feb. | W. Cook | J. Roberts jun. | 1200–1083 |
| 1870 Apr. | J. Roberts jun. | W. Cook | 1000– 522 |
| 1870 June | J. Roberts jun | A. Bowles | 1000– 759 |
| 1870 Nov. | J. Bennett | J. Roberts jun. | 1000– 905 |
| 1871 Jan. | J. Roberts jun. | J. Bennett | 1000– 637 |
| 1871 Nov. | W. Cook | J. Bennett | 1000– 942 |
| 1872 Mar. | W. Cook | J. Roberts jun. | 1000– 799 |
| 1874 Feb. | W. Cook | J. Roberts jun. | 1000– 784 |
| 1875 May | J. Roberts jun. | W. Cook | 1000– 837 |
| 1875 Dec. | J. Roberts jun. | W. Cook | 1000– 865 |
| 1877 May | J. Roberts jun. | W. Cook | 1000– 779 |
| 1880 Nov. | J. Bennett | W. Cook | 1000– 949 |
| 1881 Jan. | J. Bennett | T. Taylor | 1000– 910 |
| 1885 Apr. | J. Roberts jun. | W. Cook | 3000–2908 |
| 1885 Jun. | J. Roberts jun. | J. Bennett | 3000–1360 |
| 1889 | C. Dawson | J. North | 9000–4715 |
| 1900 | C. Dawson | H.W. Stevenson | 9000–6775 |
| 1901 | H.W. Stevenson | C. Dawson | 9000–6406 |
| 1901 | C. Dawson | H.W. Stevenson | 9000–5796 |
| 1901 | H.W. Stevenson | declared Champion | No contest |
| 1903 | C. Dawson | H.W. Stevenson | 9000–8700 |
| 1908 | M. Inman | declared Champion | No contest |
| 1909 | M. Inman | A. Williams | 9000–7662 |

### Billiards Control Club Rules

| | | | |
|------|--------|-----------|--------------|
| 1909 | H.W. Stevenson | declared Champion | No contest |
| 1910 | H.W. Stevenson | M. Inman | 13370–13212 |
| | | Match abandoned | |
| 1910 | H.W. Stevenson | M. Inman | 18000–16907 |
| 1911 | H.W. Stevenson | M. Inman | 18000–16914 |
| 1912 | M. Inman | T. Reece | 18000– 9675 |
| 1913 | M. Inman | T. Reece | 18000–16627 |
| 1914 | M. Inman | T. Reece | 18000–12826 |
| 1919 | M. Inman | H.W. Stevenson | 16000– 9468 |
| 1920 | W. Smith | C. Falkiner | 16000–14500 |

**1921**

| | | | |
|---|---|---|---|
| C. Falkiner 560 | 7,334 (35.3) | H.W. Stevenson | 5,084 (24.3) |
| T. Newman 467 | 8,000 (54.0) | T. Tothill | 3,267 (22.0) |
| T. Newman 627, 531 | 8,000 (56.7) | C. Falkiner 587 | 6,627 (47.3) |
| T. Reece | (n.r.) | F. Lawrence | (n.r.) |
| T. Newman | 16,000 (n.r.) | T. Reece | 10,744 (n.r.) |

**1922**

| | | | |
|---|---|---|---|
| T. Reece | 8,000 (35.2) | C. McConachy | 6,767 (29.9) |
| T. Newman 561, 512 | 8,000 (52.6) | J. Davis | 5,181 (34.1) |
| C. Falkiner 391 | 8,000 (41.9) | T. Reece 455 | 7,289 (38.2) |
| T. Newman | 16,000 (56.4) | C. Falkiner | 15,167 (52.7) |

**1923**

| | | | |
|---|---|---|---|
| M. Inman | 16,000 (n.r.) | A. Peall | 11,758 (n.r.) |
| C. Falkiner | 16,000 (n.r.) | T. Reece | 14,952 (n.r.) |
| T. Newman 850, 705, 500 × 4 | 16,000 (56.3) | M. Inman 701 | 14,506 (51.1) |
| W. Smith 688 | 16,000 (71.7) | C. Falkiner 782, 620 | 8,695 (29.2) |
| W. Smith 451, 446 | 16,000 (46.4) | T. Newman 638, 629, 575 | 15,180 (44.0) |

**1924**

| | | | |
|---|---|---|---|
| T. Newman 875 | 16,000 (71.4) | C. McConachy 349 | 8,703 (38.9) |
| T. Newman 1021 | 16,000 (43.5) | T. Reece | 14,845 (40.3) |

**1925**

| | | | |
|---|---|---|---|
| T. Newman 957, 672 | 16,000 (68.4) | T. Reece 512 | 10,092 (43.1) |

**1926**

| | | | |
|---|---|---|---|
| T. Newman 637, 574, 558 | 16,000 (82.0) | J. Davis 414 | 9,505 (49.0) |

**1927**

| | | | |
|---|---|---|---|
| M. Inman 459 | 8,000 (n.r.) | T. Reece 1,151 | 6,895 (n.r.) |
| J. Davis 504, 588 | 8,000 (n.r.) | M. Inman | 6,895 (n.r.) |
| T. Newman 787, 1,073, 1,012, 891 | 16,000 (73.0) | J. Davis 2,501, 727 | 14,763 (68.0) |

**1928**

| | | | |
|---|---|---|---|
| T. Carpenter | 8,000 (22.4) | T. Reece | 7,283 (20.5) |
| J. Davis | 8,000 (66.4) | T. Carpenter | 5,602 (41.8) |

| Player | Score | Opponent | Score |
|---|---|---|---|
| J. Davis<br>529, 525, 501, 425,<br>408, 404, 403, 400 | 16,000 (74.4) | T. Newman<br>564, 489, 467, 455,<br>451, 427 | 14,874 (69.5) |

**1929**

| Player | Score | Opponent | Score |
|---|---|---|---|
| T. Newman<br>553 | 8,000 (74.1) | T. Carpenter<br>453 | 5,984 (55.4) |
| J. Davis<br>838, 609, 599 | 18,000 (100.0) | T. Newman<br>723, 691, 672, 647,<br>576 | 17,219 (96.2) |

**1930**

| Player | Score | Opponent | Score |
|---|---|---|---|
| T. Newman<br>1,567, 1,047 | 24,001 (85.1) | M. Inman | 10,104 (35.8) |
| J. Davis | 21,975 (82.0) | C. Falkiner<br>900 | 19,815 (74.0) |
| J. Davis<br>2052, 500 × 9 | 20,918 (113.1) | T. Newman<br>500 × 12 | 20,117 (109.9) |

**1932**

| Player | Score | Opponent | Score |
|---|---|---|---|
| J. Davis<br>1,058, 844, 774 | 25,161 (112.0) | C. McConachy<br>1,432, 916, 889 | 19,259 (98) |

**1933**

| Player | Score | Opponent | Score |
|---|---|---|---|
| W. Lindrum<br>1,578, 984 | 21,470 (n.r.) | T. Newman<br>877, 805 | 20,252 (n.r.) |
| J. Davis<br>995 | 20,136 (n.r.) | C. McConachy<br>675 | 16,110 (n.r.) |
| W. Lindrum<br>1,492, 1,272, 1,013 | 21,815 (92.0) | J. Davis<br>792 | 21,121 (89.0) |

**1934**

| Player | Score | Opponent | Score |
|---|---|---|---|
| W. Lindrum<br>1,065, 807 | 21,903 (n.r.) | C. McConachy<br>892, 829 | 20,795 (n.r.) |
| W. Lindrum<br>1,474, 1,353 | 23,533 (n.r.) | J. Davis<br>824, 728 | 22,678 (n.r.) |

**1951**

| Player | Score | Opponent | Score |
|---|---|---|---|
| C. McConachy<br>481, 438, 425, 397,<br>376 | 6,681 (60) | J. Barrie<br>367, 336 | 5,057 (44.8) |

**1968**

| Player | Score | Opponent | Score |
|---|---|---|---|
| R. Williams<br>293 | 5,499 (n.r.) | C. McConachy<br>236, 200 | 5,234 (n.r.) |

**1971**

| Player | Score | Opponent | Score |
|---|---|---|---|
| R. Williams<br>480, 372, 353, 325,<br>302 | 9,250 (n.r.) | B. Bennett<br>132 | 4,058 (n.r.) |

**1973**

| Player | Score | Opponent | Score |
|---|---|---|---|
| R. Williams<br>528, 363, 309 | 8,360 (50.7) | J. Karnehm<br>215 | 4,336 (26.1) |

**1974**

| R. Williams | 7,017 (43.6) | E. Charlton | 4,916 (30.4) |
|---|---|---|---|
| 506, 365, 308, 307 | | 488, 401 | |

**1976**

| R. Williams | 9,105 (42.1) | E. Charlton | 5,149 (23.9) |
|---|---|---|---|
| 532, 349, 382, 306 | | 333 | |

## II Snooker: World Professional Championships

**1927**

I  M. Inman beat T. Newman 8–5; T. Carpenter beat N. Butler 8–3

II  T.A. Dennis beat F. Lawrence 8–7; A. Cope beat A. Mann 8–6; J. Davis beat J. Brady 10–5; Carpenter beat Inman 8–3

Semis  Davis beat Cope 16–7; Dennis beat Carpenter 12–10

Final  Davis beat Dennis 20–11

**1928**

I  T. Newman beat F. Smith 12–6; A. Mann beat A. Cope 14–9

II  Newman beat T.A. Dennis 12–5; F. Lawrence beat Mann 12–11

III  Lawrence beat Newman 12–7

Final  J. Davis beat Lawrence 16–13

**1929**

I  F. Lawrence beat A. Mann 13–12

Semis  J. Davis beat Lawrence (n.r.s.); T.A. Dennis beat K. Prince 14–6

Final  Davis beat Dennis 19–14

**1930**

I  F. Lawrence beat A. Mann 13–11; N. Butler beat T. Newman 13–11

Semis  J. Davis beat Lawrence 13–2; T.A. Dennis beat Butler 13–11

Final  Davis beat Dennis 25–12

**1931**

Final  J. Davis beat T.A. Dennis 25–21

**1932**

Final  J. Davis beat C. McConachy 30–19

**1933**

I  W. Donaldson beat W. Leigh 13–11

Semis  J. Davis beat Donaldson 13–1; W. Smith beat T.A. Dennis 16–9

Final  Davis beat Smith 25–18

**1934**

Final  J. Davis beat T. Newman 25–23

**1935**

I  W. Smith beat C. Stanbury 13–12

Semis  Smith beat A. Mann 13–4; J. Davis beat T. Newman 15–10

Final  Davis beat Smith 25–20

**1936**

I C. O'Donnell beat S. Lee 16–15; H. Lindrum beat H. Terry 20–11; J. Davis beat T. Newman 29–2; W. Smith beat S. Smith 16–15; C. Stanbury beat A. Mann 22–9

II Alec Brown beat Stanbury 16–15; Lindrum beat O'Donnell 19–6 (retired); J. Davis beat W. Smith 22–9; S. Newman w.o.

Semis Davis beat Brown 21–10; Lindrum beat S. Newman 29–2

Final Davis beat Lindrum 34–27

**1937**

I W.A. Withers beat F. Davis 17–14

II J. Davis beat Withers 30–1; H. Lindrum beat S. Lee 20–11; W. Smith beat T. Newman 16–15; S. Smith beat Alex Brown 18–13

Semis Lindrum beat W. Smith 20–11; Davis beat S. Smith 18–13

Final Davis beat Lindrum 32–29

**1938**

Q1 H. Holt beat C.W. Read 21–10

Q2 F. Davis beat Holt 23–8

I F. Davis beat Alec Brown 14–6 (retired ill); S. Smith beat C. Stanbury 27–4;

remaining scores lost

Final J. Davis beat S. Smith 37–24

**1939**

Q1 W. Donaldson beat H. Holt 18–13; H.W. Laws beat S. Newman 19–12

Q2 Donaldson beat Laws 18–13

I S. Smith beat S. Lee 21–10; W. Donaldson beat C. Falkiner 21–10; T. Newman beat A. Mann 19–12; F. Davis beat C. Stanbury 19–12

II J. Davis beat W. Smith 19–12; F. Davis beat T. Newman 20–11; Alex Brown beat H. Lindrum 17–14; S. Smith beat Donaldson 16–15

Semis J. Davis beat F. Davis 17–14; S. Smith beat Alec Brown 20–11

Final J. Davis beat S. Smith 43–30

**1940**

Q H. Holt beat C. Stanbury 18–13

I W. Donaldson beat Holt 24–7; J. Davis beat Alec Brown 20–11; F. Davis beat S. Lee 20–11; S. Smith beat T. Newman 22–9

Semis J. Davis beat Donaldson 22–9; F. Davis beat S. Smith 17–14

Final J. Davis beat F. Davis 37–36

**1946**

Q1 K. Kennerley beat F. Lawrence 22–9; C. Stanbury beat J. Barrie 18–13; S. Newman beat W. Leight 16–15

Q2 Kennerley beat T. Reece 8–2 (retired); S. Newman beat Stanbury 17–14

Q3 S. Newman beat Kennerley 21–10

I J. Davis beat W. Donaldson 21–10; S. Newman beat S. Lee 19–12; F. Davis beat Alec Brown 24–7; H. Lindrum beat H. Holt 17–14

Semis J. Davis beat S. Newman 21–10; Lindrum beat F. Davis 16–12

Final J. Davis beat Lindrum 78–67

**1947**
- Q1 Albert Brown beat J. Pulman (n.r.s.); W. Leigh beat H.F. Francis 19–16; S. Lee beat J. Lees 19–16; K. Kennerley beat C. Stanbury 23–12
- Q2 J. Barrie beat F. Lawrence 25–10; Albert Brown beat E. Newman 28–7; Kennerley beat A. Mann 23–12; W. Leigh beat S. Lee (n.r.s.)
- Q3 Albert Brown beat Barrie 24–11; Kennerley beat Leigh 21–14
- Q4 Albert Brown beat Kennerley 21–14
- I H. Lindrum beat Albert Brown 39–34; S. Smith beat Alec Brown 43–28; W. Donaldson beat S. Newman 46–25; F. Davis beat C. McConachy 53–20
- Semis Donaldson beat Lindrum (n.r.s.); F. Davis beat S. Smith 39–32
- Final Donaldson beat F. Davis 82–63

**1948**
- Q1 C. Stanbury beat E. Newman 26–9; W. Leigh beat H. Holt 18–17; J. Barrie beat H.F. Francis 19–16
- Q2 Leigh beat Barrie 21–14; J. Pulman beat Stanbury 19–16
- Q3 Pulman beat Leigh 18–17
- I F. Davis beat Alec Brown 43–28; C. McConachy beat J. Pulman 42–29; Albert Brown beat S. Smith 36–35; W. Donaldson beat K. Kennerley 46–25
- Semis F. Davis beat McConachy 43–28; Donaldson beat Albert Brown 40–31
- Final F. Davis beat Donaldson 84–61

**1949**
- Q1 C. Stanbury beat H.F. Francis 18–17
- Q2 C. Stanbury beat J. Rea 18–17
- Q3 C. Stanbury beat J. Holt 18–17
- I W. Donaldson beat Stanbury 58–13; J. Pulman beat Albert Brown 42–29; S. Smith beat Alec Brown 41–30; F. Davis beat Kennerley 50–21
- Semis Donaldson beat Pulman 49–22; F. Davis beat S. Smith 42–29
- Final F. Davis beat Donaldson 80–65

**1950**
- Q1 W. Smith beat W.A. Withers 28–7; H. Holt beat H.W. Laws 26–9; S. Lee beat C. Stanbury 20–15; K. Kennerley beat J. Barrie 21–14
- Q2 Kennerley beat W. Smith 22–13; Lee beat Holt 16–8 (retired ill)
- Q3 Kennerley beat Lee 21–14
- I Albert Brown beat J. Pulman 37–34; W. Donaldson beat Kennerley 42–29; G. Chenier beat P. Mans 37–34; F. Davis beat Alec Brown 44–27
- Semis Donaldson beat Albert Brown 37–34; F. Davis beat Chenier 43–28
- Final Donaldson beat F. Davis 51–46

**1951**
- Q1 J. Barrie beat S. Lee 23–12
- Q2 Barrie beat H.W. Laws 28–7
- I F. Davis beat Barrie 42–29; H. Lindrum beat Albert Brown 43–28; W. Donaldson beat K. Kennerley 41–30; J. Pulman beat S. Smith 38–33

Semis  Donaldson beat Lindrum 41–30; F. Davis beat Pulman 22–14 (retired ill)

Final    F. Davis beat Donaldson 58–39

**1952**
> I  Alec Brown beat R. Williams 39–22; J. Rea beat J. Lees 38–32; Albert Brown beat J. Pulman 32–27; records incomplete

Semis  W. Donaldson beat Albert Brown 31–30

Final    F. Davis beat Donaldson 38–35

**1953**
> Q1  W. Smith beat J. Lees 21–14; K. Kennerley beat R. Williams 25–12
>
> Q2  Kennerley beat W. Smith 42–29
>
> I  Albert Brown beat Alec Brown 35–26; J. Pulman beat J. Rea 36–25; W. Donaldson beat Kennerley 42–19; F. Davis beat J. Barrie 32–29

Final    F. Davis beat Donaldson 37–34

**1954**
> I  J. Pulman beat J. Rea 31–30

Semis  W. Donaldson beat Alec Brown 36–25; F. Davis beat J. Pulman 32–29

Final    F. Davis beat Donaldson 39–21

**1955**
> I  J. Pulman beat R. Williams 22–15; J. Rea beat H. Stokes (n.r.s.)

Semis  F. Davis beat J. Rea 36–25; Pulman beat Alec Brown (n.r.s.)

Final    F. Davis beat Pulman 37–34

**1956**

Semis  J. Pulman beat J. Rea 36–25; F. Davis beat R. Williams 35–26

Final    F. Davis beat Pulman 38–35

**1957**

Semis  J. Pulman beat R. Williams 21–16; J. Rea beat K. Kennerley 25–12

Final    Pulman beat Rea 39–34

No Championships were organised from 1957–1964 when, after a truce with the B.A. and C.C., a new system came into being in which the champion defended his title against a series of single challengers. These matches resulted:

**1964**    J. Pulman beat F. Davis 19–16

**1964**    J. Pulman beat R. Williams 40–33

**1965**    J. Pulman beat F. Davis 37–36

**1965**    J. Pulman beat R. Williams 25–22 (matches)

**1965**    J. Pulman beat F. van Rensburg 39–12

**1966**    J. Pulman beat F. Davis 5–2 (matches)

**1968**    J. Pulman beat E. Charlton 39–34

**1969**
> I  J. Spencer beat J. Pulman 30–19; R. Williams beat B. Bennett 38–11; G. Owen beat J. Rea 25–17; F. Davis beat R. Reardon 25–24

Semis  Spencer beat Williams 55–18; Owen beat Davis 45–28

Final    Spencer beat Owen 46–27

**1970 (APRIL)**
> I  David Taylor beat B. Bennett 11–18

II   J. Pulman beat David Taylor 39–22; G. Owen beat R. Williams (n.r.); R. Reardon beat F. Davis (n.r.); J. Spencer beat J. Rea (n.r.)

Semis   Pulman beat Owen (n.r.), Reardon beat Spencer (n.r.)

Final   Reardon beat Pulman 39–34

## 1970 (NOVEMBER)

Q   J. Spencer beat P. Mans 20–17; beat N. Squire 27–10; beat J. Pulman 23–14

R. Reardon beat P. Mans 22–15; beat E. Charlton 21–16; beat J. Spencer 21–16

W. Simpson lost to P. Morgan 16–21; beat G. Owen 19–18; beat J. Pulman 21–16; beat P. Mans 19–18

E. Charlton beat N. Squire 27–10; beat P. Mans 26–11; beat G. Owen 23–14

G. Owen beat P. Morgan 26–11; beat N. Squire 19–18

J. Pulman beat P. Morgan 25–12; beat N. Squire 26–11

Semis   Spencer beat Reardon 34–15; Simpson beat Charlton 27–22

Final   Spencer beat Simpson 42–31

## 1972

Q1   A. Higgins beat R. Gross 15–6; M. Parkin beat G. Thompson 11–10; J. Dunning beat P. Houlihan 11–10; G. Miles beat B. Bennett 15–6

Q2   Higgins beat Parkin 11–3; Dunning beat Miles 11–5

I   J. Pulman beat Dunning 19–7; Higgins beat J. Rea 19–11

II   J. Spencer beat F. Davis 31–21; E. Charlton beat David Taylor 31–25; Higgins beat Pulman 31–23; R. Williams beat R. Reardon 25–23

Semis   Higgins beat Williams 31–30; Spencer beat Charlton 37–32

Final   Higgins beat Spencer 37–32

## 1973

I   P. Houlihan beat J. Rea 9–2; D. Greaves beat B. Bennett 9–8; G. Miles beat G. Thompson 9–5; P. Mans beat R. Gross 9–2; W. Simpson beat M. Parkin 9–3; C. Thorburn beat Dennis Taylor 9–8; David Taylor beat J. Dunning 9–4

II   F. Davis beat Greaves 16–1; Miles beat J. Pulman 16–10; E. Charlton beat Mans 16–8; G. Owen beat Simpson 16–14; R. Reardon beat J. Meadowcroft 16–10; R. Williams beat Thorburn 16–15; J. Spencer beat David Taylor 16–5; A. Higgins beat Houlihan 16–3

III   Higgins beat Davis 16–14; Spencer beat Williams 16–7; Charlton beat Miles 16–6; Reardon beat G. Owen 16–6

Semis   Charlton beat Higgins 23–9; Reardon beat Spencer 23–22

Final   Reardon beat Charlton 38–32

## 1974

I   B. Bennett beat W. Simpson 8–2; B. Werbeniuk beat G. Thompson 8–3; J. Meadowcroft beat K. Kennerley 8–5; M. Owen beat M. Parkin 8–5; P. Mans beat I. Anderson 8–1; J. Pulman beat S. Lee 8–0; Dunning beat David Taylor 8–6; P. Morgan beat C. Thorburn 8–4

II   Mans beat J. Spencer 15–13; Dunning beat E. Charlton 15–13; M. Owen beat G. Owen 15–8; A. Higgins beat Bennett 15–4; G. Miles beat Morgan 15–7; R. Williams beat Pulman 15–12; F. Davis beat

Werbeniuk 15–5; R. Reardon beat Meadowcroft 15–3
- III Davis beat Higgins 15–14; Reardon beat M. Owen 15–11; Miles beat Dunning 15–13; Williams beat Mans 15–4
- Semis Miles beat Williams 15–7; Reardon beat Davis 15–3
- Final Reardon beat Miles 22–12
- QL J. Dunning beat D. Greaves 8–2; W. Simpson beat J. Rea 8–3; J. Meadowcroft beat P. Houlihan 8–5; C. Thorburn beat A. McDonald 8–3; J. Pulman beat J. Karnehm 8–0; David Taylor beat R. Gross 8–7; M. Owen beat Dennis Taylor 8–1

**1975**

- Q P. Tarrant beat B. Bennett 15–8; L. Condo beat M. Parkin 15–8; D. Greaves beat J. Charlton 15–14.
- I W. Simpson beat R. Mares 15–5; J. Pulman beat P. Tarrant 15–5; David Taylor beat R. King 15–8; I. Anderson beat Condo 15–8; Dennis Taylor beat P. Mans 15–12; G. Owen beat Greaves 15–3; B. Werbeniuk beat J. Meadowcroft 15–9; C. Thorburn beat P. Morgan 15–6
- II R. Reardon beat Simpson 15–11; J. Spencer beat Pulman 15–10; A. Higgins beat David Taylor 15–2; R. Williams beat Anderson 15–4; Dennis Taylor beat F. Davis 15–14; G. Owen beat J. Dunning 15–8; E. Charlton beat Werbeniuk 15–11; C. Thorburn beat G. Miles 15–2
- III Reardon beat Spencer 19–17; Higgins beat Williams 19–12; Dennis Taylor beat G. Owen 19–9; Charlton beat Thorburn 19–12
- Semis Charlton beat Dennis Taylor 19–12; Reardon beat Higgins 19–14
- Final Reardon beat Charlton 31–30

**1976**

- Q1 J. Rea beat I. Anderson 8–5; D. Greaves beat J. Charlton 8–5; J. Meadowcroft beat D. Wheelwright 8–1; R. Gross beat M. Parkin 8–5; L. Condo beat M. Owen 8–6.
- Q2 Rea beat B. Bennett 8–5; David Taylor beat Greaves 8–1; Meadowcroft beat Gross 8–4; W. Thorne beat Condo 8–3
- Q3 David Taylor beat Rea 8–7; Meadowcroft beat Thorne 8–5
- I R. Reardon beat J. Dunning 15–7; Dennis Taylor beat G. Owen 15–9; P. Mans beat G. Miles 15–10; Meadowcroft beat R. Williams 15–7; E. Charlton beat J. Pulman 15–9; F. David beat B. Werbeniuk 15–12; A. Higgins beat C. Thorburn 15–14; J. Spencer beat David Taylor 15–5
- II Reardon beat Dennis Taylor 15–2; Mans beat Meadowcroft 15–8; Charlton beat Davis 15–13; Higgins beat Spencer 15–14
- Semis Reardon beat Mans 20–10; Higgins beat Charlton 20–18
- Final Reardon beat Higgins 27–16

**1977**

- P J. Virgo beat R. Andrewartha 11–1
- Q P. Fagan beat J. Meadowcroft 11–9; Virgo beat J. Dunning 11–6; W. Thorne beat B. Bennett 11–4; J. Pulman w.o. M. Parkin; David Taylor beat D. Greaves 11–0; C. Thorburn beat C. Ross 11–0; Dennis Taylor beat J. Karnehm 11–0; D. Mountjoy beat J. Rea 11–9
- I R. Reardon beat Fagan 13–7; J. Spencer beat Virgo 13–9; G. Miles beat W. Thorne 13–4; Pulman beat F. Davis 13–12; E. Charlton beat

David Taylor 13–5; Thorburn beat R. Williams 13–6; Dennis Taylor beat P. Mans 13–11; Mountjoy beat A. Higgins 13–12

II   Spencer beat Reardon 13–6; Pulman beat Miles 13–10; Thorburn beat Charlton 13–12; Dennis Taylor beat Mountjoy 13–11

Semis   Spencer beat Pulman 18–16; Thorburn beat Dennis Taylor 18–16

Final   Spencer beat Thorburn 25–21

**1978**

P   M. Parkin beat B. Bennett 9–4; R. Andrewartha beat J. Karnehm 9–0; J. Barrie beat D. Greaves 9–3; P. Houlihan beat C. Ross 9–1

Q   D. Mountjoy beat Andrewartha 9–3; P. Fagan beat J. Dunning 9–5; W. Thorne beat R. Williams 9–3; B. Werbeniuk beat Parkin 9–2; P. Mans beat Barrie 9–6; David Taylor beat P. Morgan 9–7; Houlihan beat J. Meadowcroft 9–6; F. Davis beat J. Virgo 9–8

I   Mans beat J. Spencer 13–8; G. Miles beat David Taylor 13–10; Fagan beat A. Higgins 13–12; Davis beat Dennis Taylor 13–9; E. Charlton beat Thorne 13–12; C. Thorburn beat Houlihan 13–8; Werbeniuk beat J. Pulman 13–4; R. Reardon beat Mountjoy 13–9

II   Mans beat Miles 13–7; Davis beat Fagan 13–10; Charlton beat Thorburn 13–12; Reardon beat Werbeniuk 13–6

Semis   Mans beat Davis 18–16; Reardon beat Charlton 18–14

Final   Reardon beat Mans 25–18

# III Billiards: World Amateur Championships

### 1926: LONDON

| | | | | |
|---|---|---|---|---|
| J. Earlham (Eng.) | 4 | 8,000 | 25.6 | 282 | 18 |
| G. Shailer (Aust.) | 3 | 7,394 | 16.8 | 203 | 13 |
| M. Smith (Scot.) | 2 | 6,569 | 12.7 | 130 | 4 |
| P. Rutledge (S.A.) | 1 | 5,902 | 12.5 | 142 | 2 |
| T.M. Cluney (N.I.) | 0 | 5,617 | 11.9 | 144 | 4 |

No red limit

### 1927: LONDON

| | | | | |
|---|---|---|---|---|
| A. Prior (S.A.) | 3 | 6,000 | 16.6 | 184 | 9 |
| H.F. Coles (Wales) | 2 | 5,533 | 12.2 | 164 | 2 |
| L. Steeples (Eng.) | 1 | 5,506 | 14.8 | 236* | 9 |
| M. Smith (Scot.) | 0 | 4,499 | 12.6 | 158 | 1 |

25 red limit

### 1929: JOHANNESBURG

| | | | | |
|---|---|---|---|---|
| L. Hayes (Aust.) | 3 | 6,000 | 15.5 | 136 | 6 |
| A. Prior (S.A.) | 2 | 5,512 | 16.0 | 226 | 7 |
| H.F. Coles (Eng.) | 1 | 5,592 | 14.7 | 170 | 7 |
| P. Rutledge (S.A.) | 0 | 2,882 | 10.9 | 164 | 1 |

*record

## 1931: SYDNEY

| | | | | | |
|---|---|---|---|---|---|
| L. Steeples (Eng.) | 4 | 8,000 | 37.3 | 461* | 24 |
| S. Lee (Eng.) | 3 | 7,126 | 22.1 | 433 | 18 |
| L. Hayes (Aust.) | 2 | 6,113 | 15.3 | 167 | 6 |
| H. Goldsmith (Aust.) | 1 | 4,995 | 13.0 | 179 | 4 |
| W. Hackett (N.Z.) | 0 | 3,549 | 7.7 | 97 | 0 |

## 1933: LONDON

| | | | | | |
|---|---|---|---|---|---|
| S. Lee (Eng.) | 4 | 12,402 | 28.0 | 394 | 31 |
| T. Jones (Wales) | 3 | 9,883 | 18.7 | 144 | 8 |
| A. Prior (S.A.) | 2 | 9,113 | 18.3 | 235 | 13 |
| M. Smith (Scot.) | 1 | 8,292 | 17.5 | 166 | 5 |
| J. Blackburn (N.I.) | 0 | 6,362 | 12.5 | 94 | 0 |

15 red limit

## 1935: LONDON

| | | | | | |
|---|---|---|---|---|---|
| H.F. Coles (Eng.) | 4 | 13,665 | 28.4 | 267 | 33 |
| J. McGhie (Scot.) | 3 | 9,359 | 19.4 | 207 | 11 |
| I. Edwards (Wales) | 2 | 9,814 | 18.1 | 196 | 11 |
| S. Fenning (I.F.S.) | 1 | 9,068 | 17.4 | 161 | 6 |
| P. Deb (India) | 0 | 7,461 | 13.1 | 123 | 5 |

## 1936: JOHANNESBURG

| | | | | | |
|---|---|---|---|---|---|
| R. Marshall (Aust.) | 3 | 8,526 | 22.0 | 248 | 24 |
| A. Prior (S.A.) | 2 | 7,014 | 17.7 | 197 | 11 |
| J. Thompson (Eng.) | 1 | 7,705 | 21.2 | 245 | 15 |
| A. Bowlly (S.A.) | 0 | 4,548 | 9.0 | 93 | 0 |

Three 2¼ hour sessions

## 1938: MELBOURNE

| | | | | | |
|---|---|---|---|---|---|
| R. Marshall (Aust.) | 6 | 17,626 | 39.0 | 427 | 59* |
| K. Kennerley (Eng.) | 5 | 14,528 | 30.1 | 472* | 45 |
| T. Cleary (Aust.) | 4 | 8,535 | 19.7 | 322 | 17 |
| S. Moses (N.Z.) | 2 | 6,727 | 13.1 | 129 | 4 |
| M.M. Begg (India) | 2 | 6,685 | 13.4 | 111 | 2 |
| A. Burke (S.A.) | 1 | 5,993 | 12.0 | 119 | 1 |
| A. Albertson (N.Z.) | 1 | 5,805 | 12.4 | 107 | 1 |

## 1951: LONDON

| | | | | | |
|---|---|---|---|---|---|
| R. Marshall (Aust.) | 6 | 14,735 | 38.1 | 423 | 42 |
| F. Edwards (Eng.) | 5 | 13,459 | 26.7 | 345 | 36 |
| T. Cleary (Aust.) | 4 | 12,373 | 25.5 | 330 | 31 |
| W. Ramage (Scot.) | 3 | 7,638 | 19.1 | 151 | 8 |
| W. Pierce (Wales) | 2 | 6,029 | 13.6 | 225 | 3 |
| W. Jones (India) | 1 | 7,202 | 16.6 | 138 | 10 |
| E. Haslem (N.I.) | 0 | 5,896 | 14.1 | 125 | 3 |

## 1952: CALCUTTA

| | | | | | |
|---|---|---|---|---|---|
| L. Driffield (Eng.) | 5 | 8,529 | 34.5 | 278 | 31 |
| R. Marshall (Aust.) | 3 | 9,237 | 37.3 | 351 | 27 |
| C. Hirjee (India) | 3 | 7,701 | 22.7 | 230 | 14 |

*record

| | | | | |
|---|---|---|---|---|
| W. Ramage (Scot.) | 3 | 6,525 | 20.8 | 211 | 10 |
| W. Jones (India) | 1 | 6,731 | 23.3 | 253 | 6 |
| A. Yunoos (Burma) | 0 | 3,768 | 11.0 | 79 | 0 |

**1954: SYDNEY**

| | | | | |
|---|---|---|---|---|
| T. Cleary (Aust.) | 4 | 11,496 | 33.5 | 682 | 35 |
| R. Marshall (Aust.) | 3 | 11,488 | 36.0 | 407 | 35 |
| F. Edwards (Eng.) | 2 | 9,053 | 24.7 | 328 | 26 |
| W. Jones (India) | 1 | 8,523 | 20.5 | 209 | 17 |
| T.G. Rees (S.A.) | 0 | 6,271 | 16.9 | 207 | 6 |

**1956** Championship not held

**1958: CALCUTTA**

| | | | | |
|---|---|---|---|---|
| W. Jones (India) | 5 | 16,493 | | 501 | 56 |
| L. Driffield (Eng.) | 4 | 14,370 | | 499 | 48 |
| T. Cleary (Aust.) | 3 | 13,626 | | 431 | 52 |
| C. Hirjee (India) | 2 | 12,853 | | 226 | 38 |
| W. Asciak (Malta) | 1 | 6,329 | | 154 | 7 |
| M. Hman (Burma) | 0 | 5,633 | | 215 | 8 |

**1960: EDINBURGH**

| | | | | |
|---|---|---|---|---|
| H. Beetham (Eng.) | 7 | 9,351 | | 277 | 29 |
| J. Long (Aust.) | 6 | 10,634 | | 353 | 26 |
| W. Jones (India) | 5 | 12,397 | | 589 | 30 |
| M. Fransisco | 4 | 7,773 | | 148 | 11 |
| W. Ramage (Scot.) | 3 | 7,938 | | 283 | 12 |
| W. Asciak (Malta) | 2 | 8,408 | | 194 | 11 |
| W. Dennison (N.I.) | 1 | 6,231 | | 155 | 4 |
| A. Ramage (Scot.) | 0 | 5,706 | | 101 | 2 |

**1962: PERTH**

| | | | | |
|---|---|---|---|---|
| R. Marshall (Aust.) | 5 | 12,367 | 35.6 | 348 | 57 |
| W. Jones (India) | 5 | 10,805 | 26.9 | 489 | 34 |
| T. Cleary (Aust.) | 4 | 9,808 | 27.0 | 315 | 27 |
| J.H. Beetham (Eng.) | 3 | 7,626 | 22.9 | 283 | 18 |
| S. Banerjee (India) | 3 | 8,332 | 17.2 | 219 | 9 |
| R.A. Karim (Pakistan) | 1 | 5,657 | 11.9 | 130 | 3 |
| W. Harcourt (N.Z.) | 0 | 5,623 | 14.3 | 123 | 5 |

*Play-off*

Marshall beat Jones 3,623–2,891

**1964: PUKEKOHE**

| | | | | |
|---|---|---|---|---|
| W. Jones (India) | 9 | 16,628 | 24.5 | 294 | 49 |
| J. Karnehm (Eng.) | 8 | 12,953 | 21.8 | 390 | 28 |
| M. Ferreira (India) | 7 | 13,345 | 19.0 | 182 | 29 |
| M. Francisco (S.A.) | 6 | 12,957 | 22.0 | 518 | 38 |
| A. Nolan (Eng.) | 5 | 12,126 | 19.9 | 259 | 26 |
| T. Cleary (Aust.) | 4 | 10,781 | 13.9 | 241 | 19 |
| H. Robinson (N.Z.) | 3 | 7,643 | 10.5 | 85 | 0 |
| T. Yesberg (N.Z.) | 2 | 7,528 | 10.4 | 80 | 0 |
| M. Mavalwala (Pakistan) | 1 | 8,404 | 11.3 | 174 | 1 |
| A.E. Redmond (N.Z.) | 0 | 6,914 | 9.0 | 107 | 1 |

## 1967: COLOMBO

| | | | | | |
|---|---|---|---|---|---|
| L. Driffield (Eng.) | 8 | 13,556 | 30.5 | 421 | 53 |
| M.J.M. Lafir (Ceylon) | 7 | 12,562 | 18.4 | 218 | 31 |
| M. Francisco (S.A.) | 6 | 12,477 | 20.4 | 301 | 32 |
| M. Ferreira (India) | 5 | 11,140 | 19.5 | 507 | 22 |
| J. Long (Aust.) | 4 | 11,068 | 17.5 | 261 | 27 |
| T. Cleary (Aust.) | 3 | 9,252 | 11.6 | 322 | 15 |
| N.J. Rahim (Ceylon) | 2 | 6,895 | 8.8 | 116 | 3 |
| M.S.M. Marzuq (Ceylon) | 1 | 7,153 | 7.9 | 88 | 0 |
| F. Holz (N.Z.) | 0 | 5,350 | 7.1 | 68 | 0 |

## 1969: LONDON

| | | | | | |
|---|---|---|---|---|---|
| J. Karnehm (Eng.) | 9 | 12,902 | nr | 232 | 27 |
| M. Ferreira (India) | 7 | 14,115 | nr | 629 | 34 |
| M. Francisco (S.A.) | 7 | 13,760 | nr | 335 | 35 |
| M.J.M. Lafir (Ceylon) | 7 | 12,934 | nr | 296 | 28 |
| R. Marshall (Aust.) | 6 | 13,033 | nr | 216 | 33 |
| M. Wildman (Eng.) | 6 | 11,739 | nr | 274 | 22 |
| R. Oriel (Wales) | 5 | 13,306 | nr | 297 | 30 |
| S. Mohan (India) | 5 | 13,407 | nr | 219 | 24 |
| P. Mifsud (Malta) | 2 | 10,410 | nr | 173 | 8 |
| A. Twohill (N.Z.) | 1 | 10,016 | nr | 146 | 12 |
| F. Holz (N.Z.) | 0 | 6,061 | nr | 65 | 0 |

## 1971: MALTA
*Group A*

| | | | | |
|---|---|---|---|---|
| M. Francisco (S.A.) | 4 | 6,450 | 321 | 15 |
| M.J.M. Lafir (Sri Lanka) | 3 | 4,757 | 233 | 4 |
| P. Mifsud (Malta) | 2 | 4,142 | 134 | 2 |
| D. Sneddon (Scot.) | 1 | 3,160 | 121 | 2 |
| L. Napper (N.Z.) | 0 | 3,798 | 87 | 0 |

*Group B*

| | | | | |
|---|---|---|---|---|
| S. Mohan (India) | 4 | 5,839 | 188 | 11 |
| N. Dagley (Eng.) | 3 | 5,454 | 330 | 11 |
| M. Ferreira (India) | 2 | 4,423 | 227 | 4 |
| C. Everton (Wales) | 1 | 3,893 | 205 | 5 |
| W. Asciak (Malta) | 0 | 4,511 | 188 | 7 |

*Play-off*

| | | | | |
|---|---|---|---|---|
| Dagley | 3 | 6,041 | 348 | 17 |
| Francisco | 2 | 3,981 | 353 | 11 |
| Mohan | 1 | 3,822 | 327 | 11 |
| Lafir | 0 | 2,514 | 211 | 5 |

## 1973: BOMBAY

| | | | | | |
|---|---|---|---|---|---|
| M.J.M. Lafir (Sri Lanka) | 9 | 16,956 | 34.1 | 859 | 43 |
| S. Mohan (India) | 7 | 17,016 | 30.8 | 468 | 53 |

| | | | | |
|---|---|---|---|---|
| M. Ferreira (India) | 7 | 15,639 | 25.4 | 421 | 41 |
| P. Tarrant (Aust.) | 6 | 13,200 | 24.4 | 372 | 36 |
| C. Everton (Wales) | 5 | 9,921 | 18.2 | 240 | 17 |
| A. Nolan (Eng.) | 4 | 12,709 | 20.8 | 265 | 31 |
| P. Mifsud (Malta) | 4 | 12,253 | 18.8 | 203 | 23 |
| E. Simons (N.Z.) | 2 | 8,521 | 12.4 | 94 | 0 |
| B. Kirkness (N.Z.) | 1 | 8,464 | 13.5 | 195 | 7 |
| L.U. Demarco | 0 | 7,488 | 10.4 | 87 | 0 |

## 1975: AUCKLAND
### Group A

| | | | | |
|---|---|---|---|---|
| N. Dagley (Eng.) | 5 | 9,257 | | 477 | 24 |
| D. Sneddon (Scot.) | 4 | 6,272 | | 124 | 4 |
| G. Parikh (India) | 3 | 6,471 | | 197 | 16 |
| J. Reece (Aust.) | 2 | 4,058 | | 125 | 4 |
| H. Robinson (N.Z.) | 1 | 4,529 | | 123 | 2 |
| M. Shaharwardi (Sri Lanka) | 0 | 4,032 | | 121 | 1 |

### Group B

| | | | | |
|---|---|---|---|---|
| M. Ferreira (India) | 5 | 9,022 | | 411 | 26 |
| C. Everton (Wales) | 4 | 6,043 | | 272 | 13 |
| R. Close (Eng.) | 3 | 5,449 | | 164 | 10 |
| T. Yesberg (N.Z.) | 2 | 4,373 | | 131 | 3 |
| J. Long (Aust.) | 1 | 4,598 | | 157 | 5 |
| B. Bennett (N.Z.) | 0 | 3,684 | | 95 | 0 |

*Play-offs*
Semi-finals: Dagley beat Everton 1,293–755; Ferreira beat Sneddon 2,470–681
Final: Dagley beat Ferreira 3,385–2,268

## 1977: MELBOURNE
### Group A

| | | | | |
|---|---|---|---|---|
| N. Dagley (Eng.) | 5 | 7,546 | | 272 | 16 |
| C. Everton (Wales) | 4 | 4,962 | | 170 | 7 |
| S. Aleem (India) | 3 | 7,028 | | 263 | 11 |
| G. Ganim snr (Aust.) | 2 | 6,322 | | 231 | 6 |
| H. Robinson (N.Z.) | 1 | 4,133 | | 93 | 0 |
| J. Nugent (Scot.) | 0 | 4,131 | | 68 | 0 |

### Group B

| | | | | |
|---|---|---|---|---|
| M. Ferreira (India) | 5 | 12,554 | | 519 | 33 |
| R. Close (Eng.) | 4 | 7,252 | | 207 | 15 |
| G. Ganim jnr (Aust.) | 3 | 6,424 | | 192 | 9 |
| T. Yesberg (N.Z.) | 2 | 4,349 | | 109 | 1 |
| W. Weerasinghe (Sri Lanka) | 1 | 4,364 | | 97 | 0 |
| D. Pratt (Scot.) | 0 | 4,316 | | 108 | 1 |

*Play-offs*
Semi-finals: Ferreira beat Everton 2,155–1,310; Close beat Dagley 1,912–1,781
Final: Ferreira beat Close 2,683–2,564

# IV Snooker: World Amateur Championships

| | Wins | Frames For | Frames Against | Highest Breaks |
|---|---|---|---|---|
| **1963: CALCUTTA** | | | | |
| G. Owen (Eng.) | 4 | 23 | 7 | 71 |
| F. Harris (Aust.) | 3 | 21 | 17 | 52 |
| M.J.M. Lafir (Ceylon) | 2 | 19 | 18 | 67 |
| T. Monteiro (India) | 1 | 14 | 19 | 56 |
| W. Jones (India) | 0 | 7 | 24 | 36 |
| **1966: KARACHI** | | | | |
| G. Owen (Eng.) | 5 | 30 | 7 | 118 |
| J. Spencer (Eng.) | 4 | 26 | 14 | 101 |
| W. Barrie (Aust.) | 3 | 23 | 22 | 73 |
| M. Lafir (Ceylon) | 2 | 22 | 20 | 45 |
| L.U. Demarco (Scot.) | 1 | 14 | 28 | 36 |
| H. Karim (Pakistan) | 0 | 6 | 30 | 60 |
| **1968: SYDNEY** | | | | |
| *Group A* | | | | |
| D. Taylor (Eng.) | 4 | 24 | 13 | 96 |
| J. van Rensburg (S.A.) | 3 | 22 | 14 | n.r. |
| H. Andrews (Aust.) | 2 | 17 | 16 | n.r. |
| T. Monteiro (India) | 1 | 17 | 22 | n.r. |
| L. Napper (N.Z.) | 0 | 9 | 24 | n.r. |
| *Group B* | | | | |
| M. Williams (Aust.) | 3 | 22 | n.r. | n.r. |
| P. Morgan (Rep. of Ireland) | 3 | 19 | n.r. | 88 |
| M. Lafir (Ceylon) | 2 | 19 | 16 | n.r. |
| S. Shroff (India) | 2 | 18 | 19 | n.r. |
| R. Flutey (N.Z.) | 0 | n.r. | 24 | n.r. |

*Semi-finals:* Williams beat van Rensburg 8–7; Taylor beat Morgan 8–3
*Final:* Taylor beat Williams 8–7

| | Wins | Frames For | Frames Against | Highest Breaks |
|---|---|---|---|---|
| **1970: EDINBURGH** | | | | |
| *Group A* | | | | |
| S. Hood (Eng.) | 5 | 20 | 9 | 50 |
| P. Mifsud (Malta) | 4 | 22 | 11 | 61 |
| M.J.M. Lafir (Sri Lanka) | 4 | 20 | 16 | 50 |
| J. Phillips (Scot.) | 4 | 19 | 18 | 62 |
| D. Sneddon (Scot.) | 2 | 17 | 17 | 38 |
| L. Glozier (N.Z.) | 2 | 10 | 21 | 34 |
| J. Clint (N.I.) | 0 | 8 | 24 | 46 |
| *Group B* | | | | |
| J. Barron (Eng.) | 5 | 21 | 13 | 51 |
| D. May (Wales) | 4 | 22 | 18 | 64 |
| S. Shroff (India) | 3 | 18 | 14 | 47 |
| E. Sinclair (Scot.) | 3 | 16 | 16 | 49 |

| | Wins | Frames For | Frames Against | Highest Breaks |
|---|---|---|---|---|
| J. Rogers (Rep. of Ireland) | 3 | 16 | 19 | 65 |
| L.U. Demarco (Scot.) | 2 | 15 | 19 | 32 |
| H. Andrews (Aust.) | 1 | 13 | 22 | 35 |

*Final*
Barron beat Hood 11–7

## 1972: CARDIFF
*Group A*

| | Wins | Frames For | Frames Against | Highest Breaks |
|---|---|---|---|---|
| J. van Rensburg (S.A.) | 3 | 12 | 6 | 45 |
| K. Tristram (N.Z.) | 1 | 8 | 8 | 50 |
| G. Thomas (Wales) | 1 | 6 | 8 | 32 |
| L.U. Demarco (Wales) | 1 | 6 | 10 | 41 |

*Group B*

| | | | | |
|---|---|---|---|---|
| M. Francisco (S.A.) | 3 | 15 | 5 | 47 |
| J. Barron (Eng.) | 3 | 15 | 10 | 50 |
| A. Borg (Malta) | 2 | 12 | 11 | 59 |
| A. Lloyd (Wales) | 2 | 11 | 14 | 41 |
| T. Monteiro (India) | 0 | 3 | 16 | 46 |

*Group C*

| | | | | |
|---|---|---|---|---|
| P. Mifsud (Malta) | 4 | 16 | 5 | 61 |
| R. Edmonds (Eng.) | 3 | 14 | 7 | 101 |
| J. Rogers (Rep. of Ireland) | 2 | 8 | 8 | 36 |
| M. Berni (Wales) | 1 | 7 | 12 | 47 |
| B. Bennett (N.Z.) | 0 | 3 | 16 | 30 |

*Group D*

| | | | | |
|---|---|---|---|---|
| A. Savur (India) | 2 | 10 | 6 | 38 |
| M. Williams (Aust.) | 2 | 9 | 7 | 48 |
| D. Sneddon (Scot.) | 2 | 9 | 9 | 34 |
| D. May (Wales) | 0 | 6 | 12 | 42 |

*SEMI-FINAL GROUPS*

*Group A*

| | | | | |
|---|---|---|---|---|
| Barron | 3 | 12 | 4 | 35 |
| Savur | 2 | 10 | 8 | 68 |
| Tristram | 1 | 6 | 8 | 29 |
| Mifsud | 0 | 6 | 12 | 50 |

*Group B*

| | | | | |
|---|---|---|---|---|
| Francisco | 2 | 11 | 9 | 70 |
| Edmonds | 2 | 11 | 9 | 39 |
| Van Rensburg | 1 | 8 | 10 | 51 |
| Williams | 1 | 9 | 11 | 78 |

*Semi-finals*
Edmonds beat Barron 8–6; Francisco beat Savur 8–7 (51, 72)

*Final*
Edmonds beat Francisco 11(40) – 10

## 1974: DUBLIN

### Group A

| | Wins | Frames For | Frames Against | Highest Breaks |
|---|---|---|---|---|
| R. Edmonds (Eng.) | 7 | 31 | 11 | 66 |
| M.J.M. Lafir (Sri Lanka) | 6 | 30 | 19 | 77 |
| E. Sinclair (Scot.) | 6 | 28 | 21 | 67 |
| G. Thomas (Wales) | 4 | 24 | 22 | 43 |
| D. Sheehan (Rep. of Ireland) | 4 | 25 | 24 | 43 |
| P. Donnelly (N.I.) | 3 | 21 | 28 | 42 |
| S. Shroff (India) | 3 | 16 | 26 | 44 |
| N. Stockman (N.Z.) | 2 | 18 | 29 | 51 |
| J. Sklazeski (Canada) | 1 | 18 | 31 | 79 |

### Group B

| | Wins | Frames For | Frames Against | Highest Breaks |
|---|---|---|---|---|
| A. Lloyd (Wales) | 8 | 32 | 14 | 104 |
| W. Hill (N.Z.) | 5 | 26 | 21 | 58 |
| P. Burke (Rep. of Ireland) | 4 | 26 | 20 | 71 |
| L. Condo (Aust.) | 4 | 26 | 21 | 53 |
| A. Borg (Malta) | 4 | 27 | 23 | 37 |
| D. Sneddon (Scot.) | 4 | 23 | 21 | 54 |
| A. Savur (India) | 4 | 24 | 23 | 50 |
| R. Cowley (Isle of Man) | 3 | 16 | 27 | 50 |
| N.J. Rahim (Sri Lanka) | 0 | 2 | 32 | 25 |

*Quarter-finals*
Edmonds beat Condo 4 (60) – 3; Sinclair beat Hill 4–2; Burke beat Lafir 4–3; Thomas beat Lloyd 4–2

*Semi-finals*
Edmonds beat Sinclair 8 (54) – 4 (79); Thomas beat Burke 8–2
Final: Edmonds beat Thomas 11–9

## 1976: JOHANNESBURG

### Group A

| | Wins | Frames For | Frames Against | Highest Breaks |
|---|---|---|---|---|
| D. Mountjoy (Wales) | 7 | 28 | 9 | 107 |
| J. van Rensburg (S.A.) | 5 | 24 | 16 | 72 |
| R. Edmonds (Eng.) | 4 | 20 | 18 | 77 |
| N. Stockman (N.Z.) | 4 | 21 | 19 | 45 |
| E. Sinclair (Scot.) | 4 | 21 | 21 | 51 |
| P. Burke (Rep. of Ireland) | 2 | 17 | 25 | 48 |
| J. van Niekerk (S.A.) | 1 | 17 | 27 | 35 |
| P. Reynolds (Isle of Man) | 1 | 14 | 27 | 46 |

### Group B

| | Wins | Frames For | Frames Against | Highest Breaks |
|---|---|---|---|---|
| P. Mifsud (Malta) | 6 | 25 | 9 | 47 |
| S. Francisco (S.A.) | 6 | 27 | 12 | 68 |
| T. Griffiths (Wales) | 5 | 23 | 14 | 69 |
| C. Ross (Eng.) | 4 | 19 | 17 | 58 |
| R. Paquette (Canada) | 4 | 22 | 22 | 72 |
| E. Swaffield (N.I.) | 1 | 16 | 26 | 59 |
| L. Heywood (Aust.) | 1 | 13 | 27 | 46 |
| L. Watson (Rep. of Ireland) | 1 | 9 | 27 | 45 |

*Group C*

| | | | | |
|---|---|---|---|---|
| M. Francisco (S.A.) | 6 | 27 | 12 | 62 |
| R. Atkins (Aust.) | 6 | 25 | 12 | 45 |
| R. Andrewartha (Eng.) | 5 | 25 | 14 | 100 |
| J. Clint (N.I.) | 4 | 17 | 18 | 33 |
| L.U. Demarco (Scot.) | 3 | 21 | 21 | 75 |
| B. Mikkelsen (Canada) | 3 | 19 | 22 | 60 |
| K. Tristram (N.Z.) | 1 | 9 | 27 | 46 |
| R. Cowley (Isle of Man) | 0 | 11 | 28 | 41 |

*Elimination Match:*
Griffiths beat Andrewartha 4 (51) – 0

*Quarter-finals*
Mountjoy beat Atkins 5 (80) – 1; van Rensburg beat Griffiths 5–3 (52); S. Francisco beat M. Francisco 5–1; Mifsud beat Edmonds 5–1

*Semi-finals*
Mountjoy beat S. Francisco 8 (51) – 2; Mifsud beat van Rensburg 8 (50) – 4

*Final*
Mountjoy beat Mifsud 11 (62, 79) – 1

# V Billiards: National Amateur Championships

## England

| | | | |
|---|---|---|---|
| 1888 | H.A.O. Lonsdale | J. Tither | 500– 356 |
| 1888 | A.P. Gaskell | H.A.O. Lonsdale | 1500–1349 |
| 1889 | A.P. Gaskell | declared Champion | |
| 1889 | A.P. Gaskell | E.W. Alabone | 1500–1278 |
| 1890 | A.P. Gaskell | S.H. Fry | 1500–1395 |
| 1890 | A.P. Gaskell | N. Defries | 1500–1395 |
| 1890 | W.D. Courtney | A.P. Gaskell | 1500–1141 |
| 1891 | W.D. Courtney | A.P. Gaskell | 1500– 971 |
| 1891 | A.P. Gaskell | W.D. Courtney | 1500–1188 |
| 1892 | A.R. Wisdom | "Osbourne" | 1500–1094 |
| 1892 | S.S. Christey | S.H. Fry | 1500– 928 |
| 1893 | A.R. Wisdom | Mr. Buxton | 1500– 852 |
| 1893 | S.H. Fry | A.R. Wisdom | 1500–1239 |
| 1893 | A.H. Vahid | S.S. Christey | 1500–1395 |
| 1894 | H. Mitchell | A. Vinson | 1500–1464 |
| 1894 | W.T. Maughan | H. Mitchell | 1500–1202 |
| 1896 | S.H. Fry | W.T. Maughan | 1500–1439 |
| 1899 | A.R. Wisdom | S.H. Fry | 1500–1297 |
| 1900 | S.H. Fry | A.R. Wisdom | 1500–1428 |
| 1901 | S.S. Christey | W.S. Jones | 1500–1305 |
| 1902 | A.W.T. Good | S.S. Christey | 2000–1669 |
| 1902 | A.W.T. Good | A.J. Browne | 2000–1689 |
| 1903 | A.R. Wisdom | A.W.T. Good | 2000–1783 |
| 1903 | S.S. Christey | G.A.V. Diehl | 2000–1314 |
| 1904 | W.A. Lovejoy | A.W.T. Good | 2000–1733 |
| 1905 | A.W.T. Good | G.A. Heginbottom | 2000–1739 |

| | | | |
|---|---|---|---|
| 1906 | E.C. Breed | A.W.T. Good | 2000–1620 |
| 1907 | H.C. Virr | J. Nugent | 2000–1896 |
| 1908 | H.C. Virr | G.A. Heginbottom | 2000–1841 |
| 1909 | Major Fleming | H.C. Virr | 2000–1501 |
| 1910 | H.A.O. Lonsdale | Major Fleming | 2000–1882 |
| 1911 | H.C. Virr | Major Fleming | 3000–2716 |
| 1912 | H.C. Virr | Major Fleming | 3000–2993 |
| 1913 | H.C. Virr | J. Nugent | 3000–1956 |
| 1914 | H.C. Virr | J. Nugent | 3000–1962 |
| 1915 | A.W.T. Good | G.A. Heginbottom | 2000–1444 |
| 1916 | S.H. Fry | G.A. Heginbottom | 2000–1417 |
| 1917 | J. Graham-Symes | S.H. Fry | 2000–1540 |
| 1918 | J. Graham-Symes | "Osbourne" | 2000–1121 |
| 1919 | S.H. Fry | J. Graham-Symes | 2000–1729 |
| 1920 | S.H. Fry | W.B. Marshall | 3000–2488 |
| 1921 | S.H. Fry | J. Graham-Symes | 3000–2591 |
| 1922 | J. Graham-Symes | W.P. McLeod | 3000–2661 |
| 1923 | W.P. McLeod | J. Graham-Symes | 3000–2867 |
| 1924 | W.P. McLeod | J. Graham-Symes | 3000–2862 |
| 1925 | S.H. Fry | W.B. Marshall | 3000–2778 |
| 1926 | J. Earlam | C.M. Helyer | 3000–1751 |
| 1927 | L. Steeples | H.F.E. Coles | 3000–2449 |
| 1928 | A. Wardle | A.W.T. Good | 3000–2189 |
| 1929 | H.F.E. Coles | S. Lee | 3000–2215 |
| 1930 | L. Steeples | H.F.E. Coles | 3000–2462 |
| 1931 | S. Lee | M.A. Boggin | 3793–3134 |
| 1932 | S. Lee | F. Edwards | 4674–3508 |
| 1933 | S. Lee | H.F.E. Coles | 4458–3237 |
| 1934 | S. Lee | F. Edwards | 3929–3509 |
| 1935 | H.F.E. Coles | M.A. Boggin | 3707–3272 |
| 1936 | J. Thompson | J.H. Beetham | 3179–3149 |
| 1937 | K. Kennerley | J. Thompson | 4703–3633 |
| 1938 | K. Kennerley | J. Thompson | 4714–3925 |
| 1939 | K. Kennerley | A. Spencer | 4423–3264 |
| 1940 | K. Kennerley | A. Spencer | 3931–3749 |
| 1941–45 | No contests | | |
| 1946 | M. Showman | J.H. Beetham | 3077–2539 |
| 1947 | J. Thompson | A. Hibbert | 4104–3185 |
| 1948 | J. Thompson | H.G. Terry | 5202–2816 |
| 1949 | F. Edwards | J. Tregoning | 4813–3297 |
| 1950 | F. Edwards | J. Tregoning | 4968–3385 |
| 1951 | F. Edwards | J. Tregoning | 5015–3791 |
| 1952 | L. Driffield | J.H. Beetham | 2894–2793 |
| 1953 | L. Driffield | F. Edwards | 4136–3016 |
| 1954 | L. Driffield | F. Edwards | 4165–3030 |
| 1955 | F. Edwards | A. Nolan | 4194–3206 |
| 1956 | F. Edwards | L. Driffield | 3395–3327 |
| 1957 | L. Driffield | F. Edwards | 4464–2894 |
| 1958 | L. Driffield | J.T. Wright | 4483–2587 |
| 1959 | L. Driffield | J.H. Beetham | 4968–3385 |

| | | | |
|---|---|---|---|
| 1960 | J.H. Beetham | R.C. Wright | 3426–2289 |
| 1961 | J.H. Beetham | R.C. Wright | 4060–2043 |
| 1962 | L. Driffield | J.H. Beetham | 3412–2993 |
| 1963 | J.H. Beetham | N. Dagley | 4052–2759 |
| 1964 | A. Nolan | L. Driffield | 3455–2188 |
| 1965 | N. Dagley | A. Nolan | 2983–2757 |
| 1966 | N. Dagley | A. Nolan | 3018–2555 |
| 1967 | L. Driffield | C. Everton | 3395–2328 |
| 1968 | M. Wildman | C. Everton | 2652–2540 |
| 1969 | J. Karnehm | M. Wildman | 3722–2881 |
| 1970 | N. Dagley | A. Nolan | 4467–2372 |
| 1971 | N. Dagley | W.J. Dennison | 3672–2019 |
| 1972 | N. Dagley | A. Nolan | 3115–2469 |
| 1973 | N. Dagley | C. Everton | 2804–1976 |
| 1974 | N. Dagley | A. Nolan | 2961–2677 |
| 1975 | N. Dagley | R. Close | 2917–2693 |
| 1976 | R. Close | C. Everton | 2413–2194 |
| 1977 | R. Close | H. Beetham | 2951–2031 |
| 1978 | N. Dagley | R. Close | 4611–2309 |

N.B. 1931–1970: twelve hour finals. 1971 onwards: ten hour finals.

## EIRE

| | | | | |
|---|---|---|---|---|
| 1933 J. Ayres | S. Fenning | | 1963 J. Bates | P. Fenelon |
| 1934 S. Fenning | | | 1964 J. Bates | L. Codd |
| 1935 S. Fenning | | | 1965 L. Codd | J. Shortt |
| 1936 S. Fenning | | | 1966 L. Codd | G. Connell |
| 1937 T. O'Brien | | | 1967 P. Morgan | L. Codd |
| 1948 W. Brown | | | 1968 P. Morgan | T. Doyle |
| 1949 S. Fenning | | | 1969 J. Rogers | L. Codd |
| 1952 M. Nolan | T. McCusker | | 1970 L. Drennan | T. Doyle |
| 1953 D. Turley | M. Nolan | | 1971 L. Codd | P. Fenelon |
| 1954 M. Nolan | D. Barry | | 1972 L. Codd | |
| 1955 M. Nolan | D. Barry | | 1973 T. Martin | |
| 1956 M. Nolan | S. Fenning | | 1974 T. Doyle | A. Roche |
| 1957 M. Nolan | E. Morrissey | | 1975 P. Fenelon | T. Martin |
| 1958 W. Dennison | K. Smith | | 1976 J. Rogers | P. Fenelon |
| 1959–60 No official contests | | | 1977 E. Hughes | T. Martin |
| 1961 K. Smyth | J. Hanlon | | 1978 E. Hughes | R. Brennan |
| 1962 K. Smyth | F. Murphy | | | |

## NORTHERN IRELAND

| | | | | |
|---|---|---|---|---|
| 1925 T. McCluney | B. Craig | | 1930 J. Blackburn | |
| 1926 T. McCluney | J. Sloan | | 1931 J. Blackburn | W. Mills |
| 1927 J. Sloan | R. Mulholland | | 1932 W. Lowe | R. Mulholland |
| 1928 A. Davison | S. Stranaghen | | 1933 W. Mills | J. Dubois |
| 1929 J. Blackburn | W. Morrison | | 1934 W. Lowe | J. Presley |

| 1935 W. Morrison | W. Lowe |
|---|---|
| 1936 J. Blackburn | G. Hutton |
| 1937 J. Blackburn | E. Haslem |
| 1938 W. Lowe | W. Mills |
| 1939 W. Lowe | E. Haslem |
| 1940 No Championship | |
| 1941 E. Haslem | R. Scleater |
| 1945 E. Haslem | W. Webb |
| 1946 J. Holness | C. McErlean |
| 1947 J. Bates | J. Sloan |
| 1948 J. Bates | E. Haslem |
| 1949 J. Bates | E. Haslem |
| 1950 J. Bates | E. Haslem |
| 1951 E. Haslem | H.J. Bates |
| 1952 R. Taylor | D. Turley |
| 1953 W. Sanlon | C. McErlean |
| 1954 W. Sanlon | W. Dennison |
| 1955 D. Turley | J. Stevenson |
| 1956 J. Stevenson | R. Lough |
| 1957 W. Sanlon | R. Taylor |

| 1958 W. Hanna | R. Hanna |
|---|---|
| 1959 W. Hanna | W. Dennison |
| 1960 W. Dennison | R. Taylor |
| 1961 R. Hanna | D. Anderson |
| 1962 N. McQuay | D. Turley |
| 1963 W. Hanna | W. Ashe |
| 1964 D. Anderson D. Turley | Joint |
| 1965 W. Ashe | W. Loughran |
| 1966 D. Anderson | P. Morgan |
| 1967 W. Loughran | D. Anderson |
| 1968 D. Anderson | W. Loughran |
| 1969 W. Loughran | D. Anderson |
| 1970 S. Crothers | P. Donnelly |
| 1971 J. Bates | |
| 1972 No Championship | |
| 1973 No Championship | |
| 1974 P. Donnelly | M. Osborne |
| 1975 P. Donnelly | D. Anderson |

## SCOTLAND

| 1933 A. Ramage | |
|---|---|
| 1934 N. Canney | |
| 1935 H. King | |
| 1936 N. Canney | R. Pollock |
| 1937 J. McGhee | J.S. Patterson |
| 1938 J. McGhee | |
| 1946 J. Levey | R. McKendrick |
| 1947 A. Ramage | G. Aitken |
| 1948 W. Ramage | A. Ramage |
| 1949 W. Ramage | A. Ramage |
| 1950 A. Ramage | W. Ramage |
| 1951 W. Ramage | G. Jardine |
| 1952 J. Murray | R. Gillon |
| 1953 J. Bates | W. Ramage |
| 1954 J. Bates | J. Murray |
| 1955 W. Ramage | A. Ramage |
| 1956 W. Ramage | A. Ramage |

| 1957 W. Ramage | M. Morrin |
|---|---|
| 1958 W. Ramage | P. Spence |
| 1959 W. Ramage | W. Taylor |
| 1960 A. Ramage | C. Spence |
| 1961 P. Spence | W. Ramage |
| 1962 W. Ramage | A. Kennedy |
| 1963 W. Ramage | A. Kennedy |
| 1964 W. Ramage | A. Kennedy |
| 1965 W. Ramage | A. Kennedy |
| 1966 W. Ramage | B. Demarco |
| 1967 W. Ramage | A. Kennedy |
| 1968 A. Kennedy | B. Demarco |
| 1969 A. Kennedy | R. Eprile |
| 1970 D. Sneddon | B. Demarco |
| 1971 D. Sneddon | R. Eprile |
| 1972 B. Demarco | D. Sneddon |
| 1977 J. Nugent | B. Demarco |

## WALES

| 1920 H.F.E. Coles | |
|---|---|
| 1921 H.F.E. Coles | |
| 1922 H.F.E. Coles | |
| 1923 H.F.E. Coles | |
| 1924 H.F.E. Coles | |
| 1929 J. Tregoning | |

| 1931 L. Prosser |
|---|
| 1932 T. Jones |
| 1933 T. Jones |
| 1935 I. Edwards |
| 1936 J. Tregoning |
| 1937 B. Gravenor |

| Year | Winner | Runner-up |
|---|---|---|
| 1938 | J. Tregoning | |
| 1946 | T.G. Rees | |
| 1947 | T.C. Morse | R. Smith |
| 1948 | J. Tregoning | I. Edwards |
| 1949 | I. Edwards | T. Jones |
| 1950 | W. Pierce | W.T. Jones |
| 1951 | W. Pierce | – |
| 1952 | J. Tregoning | L. Davis |
| 1953 | B. Sainsbury | W. Pierce |
| 1954 | R. Smith | R. Keats |
| 1955 | J. Tregoning | R.W. Oriel |
| 1956 | A.J. Ford | A. Davies |
| 1957 | R. Smith | A.J. Ford |
| 1958 | R.W. Oriel | A.J. Ford |
| 1959 | A.J. Ford | E. Marks |
| 1960 | C. Everton | P.J. Morris |
| 1961 | R.W. Oriel | P.J. Morris |
| 1962 | R.W. Oriel | E. Marks |
| 1963 | R.W. Oriel | P.J. Morris |
| 1964 | R.W. Oriel | D.E. Edwards |
| 1965 | R.W. Oriel | N. Jaynes |
| 1966 | R.W. Oriel | A. Davies |
| 1967 | R.W. Oriel | C. Jenkins |
| 1968 | D. Edwards | R.W. Oriel |
| 1969 | R.W. Oriel | T.J. Entwistle |
| 1970 | R.W. Oriel | D.E.G. Edwards |
| 1971 | R.W. Oriel | C. Everton |
| 1972 | C. Everton | R.W. Oriel |
| 1973 | C. Everton | J. Terry |
| 1974 | R.W. Oriel | C. Everton |
| 1975 | R.W. Oriel | C. Everton |
| 1976 | C. Everton | R.W. Oriel |
| 1977 | C. Everton | R.W. Oriel |

# AUSTRALIA

| Year | Winner | Runner-up |
|---|---|---|
| 1929 | L.L. Beauchamp | |
| 1913 | G.B. Shailer | |
| 1920 | J.R. Hooper | C.T. Von Luft |
| 1921 | G.B. Shailer | D. Sutherland |
| 1922 | G.B. Shailer | D. Sutherland |
| 1923 | G.B. Shailer | A. Tricks |
| 1924 | E. Eccles | – |
| 1925 | G.B. Shailer | C. Coleman |
| 1926 | L.W. Hayes | – |
| 1927 | L.W. Hayes | G.C. Sutherland |
| 1928 | L.W. Hayes | A. Sakzewski |
| 1929 | A.H. Hearndon | G.C. Sutherland |
| 1930 | S. Ryan | G.B. Shailer |
| 1931 | H.L. Goldsmith | A. Sakzewski |
| 1932 | A. Sakzewski | L.W. Hayes |
| 1933 | L.W. Hayes | W.H. Carter |
| 1934 | L.W. Hayes | A. Sakzewski |
| 1935 | L.W. Hayes | T. Cleary |
| 1936 | R. Marshall | A.G. Bull |
| 1937 | R. Marshall | T. Cleary |
| 1938 | R. Marshall | T. Cleary |
| 1939 | R. Marshall | A. Sakzewski |
| 1940–45 | No contests | |
| 1946 | R. Marshall | J. Harris |
| 1947 | T. Cleary | A.G. Bull |
| 1948 | R. Marshall | T. Cleary |
| 1949 | R. Marshall | T. Cleary |
| 1950 | T. Cleary | R. Marshall |
| 1951 | R. Marshall | J. Harris |
| 1952 | R. Marshall | J. Long |
| 1953 | R. Marshall | T. Cleary |
| 1954 | R. Marshall | T. Cleary |
| 1955 | R. Marshall | T. Cleary |
| 1956 | J. Long | O. Pitman |
| 1957 | R. Marshall | T. Cleary |
| 1958 | T. Cleary | O. Pitman |
| 1959 | R. Marshall | T. Cleary |
| 1960 | J. Long | T. MacLaughlin |
| 1961 | R. Marshall | T. Cleary |
| 1962 | R. Marshall | T. Cleary |
| 1963 | R. Marshall | T. Cleary |
| 1964 | J. Long | G. Ammon |
| 1965 | T. Cleary | K. Lord, |
| | | G. Ammon, |
| | | W. Barrie (tied) |
| 1966 | T. Cleary | J. Long |
| 1967 | J. Long | T. Cleary |
| 1968 | J. Long | T. Cleary |
| 1969 | R. Marshall | F. Harris |
| 1970 | R. Marshall | J. Collins |
| 1971 | M. Williams | B. Stevens |
| 1972 | P. Tarrant | J. Collins |
| 1973 | P. Tarrant | J. Reece |
| 1974 | J. Reece | G. Ganim |
| 1975 | J. Long | J. Reece |
| 1976 | G. Ganim jnr. | |
| 1977 | G. Ganim jnr. | |
| 1978 | G. Ganim jnr. | |

## INDIA

| | | | |
|---|---|---|---|
| 1931 M.M. Begg | J. Buchanan | 1956 C. Hirjee | W. Jones |
| 1932 P.K. Deb | H.D. Bhadra | 1957 W. Jones | C. Hirjee |
| 1933 Major Meade | M.M. Begg | 1958 C. Hirjee | W. Jones |
| 1934 Mg. Ba Sin | J. Buchanan | 1959 T. Cleary | W. Jones |
| 1935 P.K. Deb | M.M. Begg | 1960 W. Jones | S.N. Banerjee |
| 1936 P.K. Deb | M.M. Begg | 1961 W. Jones | S.N. Banerjee |
| 1937 M.M. Begg | P.K. Deb | 1962 R. Marshall | W. Jones |
| 1938 P.K. Deb | S.H. Lyth | 1963 W. Jones | M. Ferreira |
| 1939 P.K. Deb | S.H. Lyth | 1964 W. Jones | M. Ferreira |
| 1940 S.H. Lyth | P.K. Deb | 1965 W. Jones | M.J.M. Lafir |
| 1941 V.R. Freer | P.K. Deb | 1966 W. Jones | M. Ferreira |
| 1942 V.R. Freer | H.H. Nilsen | 1967 A. Savur | S. Mohan |
| 1943–45 No Championship | | 1968 S. Mohan | A. Savur |
| 1946 C. Hirjee | C.C. James | 1969 M. Ferreira | S. Mohan |
| 1947 C. Hirjee | T.A. Selvaraj | 1970 S. Mohan | S. Ferreira |
| 1948 V.R. Freer | P.K. Deb | 1971 S. Mohan | G.C. Parikh |
| 1949 T.A. Selvaraj | W. Jones | 1972 S. Mohan | M. Ferreira |
| 1950 W. Jones | T.A. Selvaraj | 1973 S. Mohan | A. Savur |
| 1951 W. Jones | T.A. Selvaraj | 1974 M. Ferreira | G.C. Parikh |
| 1952 W. Jones | C. Hirjee | 1975 G.C. Parikh | M. Ferreira |
| 1953 L. Driffield | W. Ramage | 1976 M. Ferreira | |
| 1954 W. Jones | C. Hirjee | 1977 M.J.M. Lafir | M. Ferreira |
| 1955 W. Jones | C. Hirjee | | |

## MALTA

| | | | |
|---|---|---|---|
| 1947 V. Micallef | J. Debatista | 1963 J. Bartolo | W. Caruana |
| 1948 No Championship | | 1964 W. Asciak | P. Cosaitis |
| 1949 E. Bartolo | P. Debono | 1965 A. Asciak | J. Bartolo |
| 1950 W. Asciak | V. Micallef | 1966 A. Asciak | F. Farrugia |
| 1951 W. Asciak | R. Aquilina | 1967 A. Asciak | |
| 1952 W. Asciak | E. Bartolo | 1968 | |
| 1953 W. Asciak | R. Lautier | 1969 P. Misfud | J. Debattista |
| 1954 W. Asciak | J. Reginiano | 1970 W. Asciak | P. Misfud |
| 1955 W. Asciak | G. Taliana | 1971 P. Mifsud | W. Asciak |
| 1956 A. Asciak | J. Reginiano | 1972 W. Asciak | P. Mifsud |
| 1957 A. Asciak | J. Debattista | 1973 P. Mifsud | J. Bartolo |
| 1958 A. Asciak | J. Agius | 1974 P. Mifsud | P. Grech |
| 1959 A. Asciak | R. Lautier | 1975 P. Mifsud | P. Grech |
| 1960 A. Asciak | P. Cosaitis | 1976 P. Mifsud | |
| 1961 A. Borg | S. French | 1977 P. Mifsud | |
| 1962 J. Bartolo | P. Cosaitis | 1978 J. Grech | P. Mifsud |

## NEW ZEALAND

| | | |
|---|---|---|
| 1908 J. Ryan | 1911 F. Lovelock | |
| 1909 no contest | 1912 H. Valentine | |
| 1910 F. Lovelock | 1913 H. Valentine | |

1914 N. Lynch
1915 W.E. Warren
1916 H. Siedeberg
1917 H. Siedeberg
1918 W.E. Warren
1919 H. Siedeberg
1920 W.E. Warren
1921 H. Siedeberg
1922 E.V. Roberts
1923 E.V. Roberts
1924 R. Fredatovich
1925 C. Mason
1926 E.V. Roberts
1927 E.V. Roberts
1928 A. Bowie
1929 L. Stout
1930 W.E. Hackett
1931 A. Duncan
1932 C. Mason
1933 A. Albertson
1934 H. McLean
1935 L. Holdsworth
1936 S. Moses
1937 S. Moses
1938 L. Holdsworth
1939 R. Carrick
1940 S. Moses
1941 R. Carrick
1942 R. Carrick
1943 A. Albertson
1944 S. Moses
1945 J. Shepherd
1946 R. Carrick

1947 C. Peek
1948 R. Carrick
1949 R. Carrick
1950 R. Carrick
1951 R. Carrick
1952 L. Stout
1953 A. Twohill
1954 A. Twohill
1955 A. Twohill
1956 A. Twohill
1957 A. Twohill
1958 A. Albertson
1959 A. Twohill
1960 W. Harcourt
1961 A. Albertson
1962 W. Harcourt
1963 H.C. Robinson
1964 T. Yesberg
1965 L. Napper
1966 A. Twohill
1967 A. Twohill
1968 A. Twohill
1969 E. Simons
1970 L. Napper
1971 W. Harcourt
1972 B. Kirkness
1973 H. Robinson
1974 H. Robinson
1975 T. Yesberg
1976 H. Robinson
1977 B. Kirkness
1978 B. Kirkness

**SOUTH AFRICA**
1950 T.G. Rees
1951 I. Drapin
1952 T.G. Rees
1953 T.G. Rees
1954 F. Walker
1955 F. Walker
1956 G. Povall
1957 F. Walker
1958 R. Walker
1959 M. Francisco
1960 R. Walker
1961 M. Francisco
1962 M. Francisco

1963 M. Francisco
1964 M. Francisco
1965 M. Francisco
1966 M. Francisco
1967 J. van Rensburg
1968 M. Francisco
1969 M. Francisco
1970 M. Francisco
1971 M. Francisco
1972 S. Francisco
1973 S. Francisco
1974 M. Francisco
1975 S. Francisco

**SRI LANKA**

| | |
|---|---|
| 1948 A.C. Cambal | 1963 M.H.M. Mujahid |
| 1949 M.J.M. Lafir | 1964 M.J.M. Lafir |
| 1950 M.J.M. Lafir | 1965 – |
| 1951 M.J.M. Lafir | 1966 M.J.M. Lafir |
| 1952 M.J.M. Lafir | 1967 J.K. Bakshani |
| 1953 M.J.M. Lafir | 1968 – |
| 1954 A.C. Cambal | 1969 M.J.M. Lafir |
| 1955 T.A. Selvaraj | 1970 M.J.M. Lafir |
| 1956 T.A. Selvaraj | 1971 – |
| 1959 M.J.M. Lafir | 1972 M.J.M. Lafir |
| 1960 M.J.M. Lafir | 1973 M.J.M. Lafir |
| 1961 M.J.M. Lafir | 1974 M. Shaharawardi |
| 1962 M.J.M. Lafir | |

# VI Billiards: Women's Professional Championships

| | | | |
|---|---|---|---|
| 1930–3 (3 wins) | Joyce Gardner | 1940 | Thelma Carpenter |
| 1034–5 | Ruth Harrison | 1941–47 | No contests |
| 1935–8 (4 wins) | Joyce Gardner | 1948–50 | Thelma Carpenter |
| 1939 | Ruth Harrison | | |

# VII Billiards: Women's Amateur Championships

| | | | |
|---|---|---|---|
| 1931 | Ruth Harrison | 1959 | Muriel Hazeldine |
| 1932 | Thelma Carpenter | 1960 | Maureen Barrett |
| 1933 | Thelma Carpenter | 1962 | Thea Hindmarch |
| 1934 | Thelma Carpenter | 1963 | Sadie Isaacs |
| 1935 | Vera Seals | 1964 | Maureen Baynton |
| 1936 | Vera Seals | | (née Barrett) |
| 1937 | Grace Philips | 1965 | Vera Youle |
| 1938 | Mrs. V. McDougall | 1966 | Maureen Baynton |
| 1939 | Mrs. V. McDougall | 1967 | Thea Hindmarch |
| 1940–46 | No contests | 1968 | Maureen Baynton |
| 1947 | Sadie Isaacs | 1969 | Thea Hindmarch |
| 1948 | Mrs. E. Morland Smith | 1970 | Vera Selby |
| 1949 | Mrs. M. Keeton | 1971 | Vera Selby |
| 1950 | Helen Futo | 1972 | Vera Selby |
| 1951 | No contests | 1973 | Vera Selby |
| 1952 | Mrs. E. Morland Smith | 1974 | Vera Selby |
| 1953 | Mrs. E. Morland Smith | 1975 | no championship |
| 1954 | Helen Futo | 1976 | Vera Selby |
| 1955 | Maureen Barrett | 1977 | Vera Selby |
| 1956 | Maureen Barrett | 1978 | Vera Selby |

# VIII Snooker: National Amateur Championships

**ENGLAND**

| | | | |
|---|---|---|---|
| 1916 | C.N. Jacques | | |
| 1917 | C.N. Jacques | | |
| 1918 | T.N. Palmer | | |
| 1919 | S.H. Fry | | |
| 1920 | A.R. Wisdom | | |
| 1921 | M.J. Vaughan | S.H. Fry | 384–378 |
| 1922 | J. McGlynn | C. Cox, jun. | – |
| 1923 | W. Coupe | E. Forshall | 432–337 |
| 1924 | W. Coupe | H.G. Olden | 413–333 |
| 1925 | J. McGlynn | W.L. Crompton | 392–308 |
| 1926 | W. Nash | A.W. Casey | – |
| 1927 | O.T. Jackson | F. Whittall | – |
| 1928 | P.H. Matthews | F.T.W. Leaphard (Morley) | 383–356 |
| 1929 | L. Steeples | F. Whittall | 5–4 |
| 1930 | L. Steeples | F. Whittall | 5–1 |
| 1931 | P.H. Matthews | H. Kingsley | 5–4 |
| 1932 | W.E. Bach | O.T. Jackson | 5–3 |
| 1933 | E. Bedford | A. Kershaw | 5–1 |
| 1934 | C.H. Beavis | P.H. Matthews | 5–2 |
| 1935 | C.H. Beavis | D. Hindmarch | 5–3 |
| 1936 | P.H. Matthews | C.H. Beavis | 5–3 |
| 1937 | K. Kennerley | W.H. Dennis | 6–3 |
| 1938 | P.H. Matthews | K. Kennerley | 6–5 |
| 1939 | P. Bendon | K. Kennerley | 6–4 |
| 1940 | K. Kennerly | A. Brown | 8–7 |
| 1941–45 | No contests | | |
| 1946 | H.J. Pulman | A. Brown | 5–3 |
| 1947 | H. Morris | C.A. Kent | 5–1 |
| 1948 | S. Battye | T. Postlethwaite | 6–3 |
| 1949 | T.C. Gordon | S. Kilbank | 6–4 |
| 1950 | A. Nolan | G. Owen | 6–5 |
| 1951 | R. Williams | P. Bendon | 6–1 |
| 1952 | C. Downey | J. Allen | 6–1 |
| 1953 | T.C. Gordon | G. Humphries | 6–5 |
| 1954 | G. Thompson | C. Wilson | 11–9 |
| 1955 | M. Parkin | A. Nolan | 11–7 |
| 1956 | T. Gordon | R. Reardon | 11–9 |
| 1957 | R. Gross | S. Haslam | 11–6 |
| 1958 | M. Owen | J.T. Fitzmaurice | 11–8 |
| 1959 | M. Owen | A. Barnett | 11–5 |
| 1960 | R. Gross | J. Price | 11–4 |
| 1961 | A. Barnett | R. Edmonds | 11–9 |
| 1962 | R. Gross | J. Barron | 11–9 |
| 1963 | G. Owen | R. Gross | 11–3 |
| 1964 | R. Reardon | J. Spencer | 11–8 |
| 1965 | P. Houlihan | J. Spencer | 11–3 |
| 1966 | J. Spencer | M. Owen | 11–5 |

| 1967 | M. Owen | S. Hood | 11–5 |
| 1968 | D. Taylor | C. Ross | 11–6 |
| 1969 | R. Edmonds | J. Barron | 11–9 |
| 1970 | J. Barron | S. Hood | 11–10 |
| 1971 | J. Barron | D. French | 11–9 |
| 1972 | J. Barron | R. Edmonds | 11–9 |
| 1973 | M. Owen | R. Edmonds | 11–6 |
| 1974 | R. Edmonds | P. Fagan | 11–7 |
| 1975 | S. Hood | W. Thorne | 11–6 |
| 1976 | C. Ross | R. Andrewartha | 11–7 |
| 1977 | T. Griffiths | S. Hood | 13–3 |
| 1978 | T. Griffiths | J. Johnson | 13–5 |

## EIRE

| 1933 S. Fenning | J. Ayres | 1963 J. Rogers | G. Hanway |
| 1935 S. Fenning | | 1964 J. Rogers | G. Buffini |
| 1937 P.J. O'Connor | | 1965 W. Fields | J. Grace |
| 1940 P. Merrigan | S. Fenning | 1966 G. Hanway | J. Rogers |
| 1947 C. Downey | P. Merrigan | 1967 P. Morgan | J. Rogers |
| 1948 P. Merrigan | | 1968 G. Hanway | T.G. Hearty |
| 1949 S. Fenning | | 1969 D. Dally | J. Rogers |
| 1952 W. Brown | S. Fenning | 1970 D. Sheehan | P. Thornton |
| 1953 S. Brooks | W. Brown | 1971 D. Sheehan | J. Webber |
| 1954 S. Fenning | J. Redmond | 1972 J. Rogers | D. Sheehan |
| 1955 S. Fenning | W. Brown | 1973 F. Murphy | J. Bannister |
| 1956 W. Brown | S. Fenning | 1974 P. Burke | P. Miley |
| 1957 J. Connolly | G. Gibson | 1975 F. Nathan | J. Weber |
| 1958 G. Gibson | F. Murphy | 1976 P. Burke | L. Watson |
| 1959–60 No official contests | | 1977 J. Clusker | F. Murphy |
| 1961 W. Brown | F. Murphy | 1978 E. Hughes | N. Lowth |
| 1962 J. Webber | G. Buffini | | |

## NORTHERN IRELAND

| 1927 G. Barron | G.R. Duff | 1941 J. McNally | A. Heron |
| 1928 J. Perry | | 1945 J. McNally | C. Downey |
| 1929 W. Lyttle | Capt. J. Ross | 1946 J. McNally | J. Rea |
| 1930 J. Luney | | 1947 J. Rea | J. Bates |
| 1931 J. McNally | W.R. Mills | 1948 J. Bates | E. Haslem |
| 1932 Capt. J. Ross | W.R. Mills | 1949 J. Bates | J. Stevenson |
| 1933 J. French | J. Chambers | 1950 J. Bates | J. Dickson |
| 1934 Capt. J. Ross | W. Price | 1951 J. Stevenson | E. Haslem |
| 1935 W. Agnew | Capt. J. Ross | 1952 J. Stevenson | D. Turley |
| 1936 W. Lowe | S. Brooks | 1953 J. Stevenson | J. Thompson |
| 1937 J. Chambers | J. Blackburn | 1954 W. Seeds | J. Stevenson |
| 1938 J. McNally | W. Sankon | 1955 J. Stevenson | M. Gill |
| 1939 J. McNally | S. Brooks | 1956 S. Brooks | G. Lyttle |

| | | | |
|---|---|---|---|
| 1957 M. Gill | D. Anderson | 1967 D. Anderson | S. Crothers |
| 1958 W. Agnew | W. Hanna | 1968 A. Higgins | M. Gill |
| 1959 W. Hanna | W. Seeds | 1969 D. Anderson | A. Higgins |
| 1960 M. Gill | D. Anderson | 1970 J. Clint | N. McCann |
| 1961 D. Anderson | M. Gill | 1971 S. Crothers | |
| 1962 S. McMahon | D. Anderson | 1974 P. Donnelly | S. Pavis |
| 1963 D. Anderson | J. Clint | 1975 J. Clint | S. McMahon |
| 1964 P. Morgan | M. Gill | 1977 D. McVeigh | |
| 1965 M. Gill | S. Crothers | 1978 D. McVeigh | L. McCann |
| 1966 S. Crothers | W. Caughey | | |

## SCOTLAND

| | | | |
|---|---|---|---|
| 1946 J. Levey | N. McGowan | 1963 E. Sinclair | D. Miller |
| 1947 J. Levey | T. Gray | 1964 J. Phillips | E. Sinclair |
| 1948 I. Wexelstein | R. Walls | 1965 B. Demarco | P. Spence |
| 1949 W. Ramage | P. Spence | 1966 B. Demarco | P. Spence |
| 1950 W. Ramage | R. McKendrick | 1967 E. Sinclair | B. Demarco |
| 1951 A. Wilson | A. Wishart | 1968 E. Sinclair | J. Zonfrillo |
| 1952 D. Emerson | P. Spence | 1969 A. Kennedy | B. Demarco |
| 1953 P. Spence | H. Thompson | 1970 D. Sneddon | M. McLeod |
| 1954 D. Edmond | P. Spence | 1971 J. Phillips | D. Miller |
| 1955 B. Demarco | P. Spence | 1972 D. Sneddon | B. Demarco |
| 1956 W. Barrie | R. McKendrick | 1973 E. Sinclair | J. Zonfrillo |
| 1957 T. Paul | H.D. Thompson | 1974 D. Sneddon | E. Sinclair |
| 1958 J. Phillips | J. Ferguson | 1975 E. Sinclair | J. Phillips |
| 1959 J. Phillips | E. Sinclair | 1976 E. Sinclair | D. Sneddon |
| 1960 E. Sinclair | A. Kennedy | 1977 R. Miller | E. McLaughlin |
| 1961 J. Phillips | B. Demarco | 1978 J. Donnelly | E. McLaughlin |
| 1962 A. Kennedy | B. Demarco | | |

## WALES

| | | | |
|---|---|---|---|
| 1947 T. Jones | R. Smith | 1963 R.D. Meredith | J.R. Price |
| 1948 R. Smith | A.J. Ford | 1964 M.L. Berni | A.J. Ford |
| 1949 A.J. Ford | C. Coles | 1965 T. Parsons | A.J. Ford |
| 1950 R. Reardon | A.J. Ford | 1966 L.L. O'Neill | D. Mountjoy |
| 1951 R. Reardon | – | 1967 L.L. O'Neill | K. Weed |
| 1952 R. Reardon | A.J. Ford | 1968 D. Mountjoy | J. Terry |
| 1953 R. Reardon | A. Kemp | 1969 T. Parsons | T. Prosser |
| 1954 R. Reardon | A.J. Ford | 1970 D.T. May | G. Thomas |
| 1955 R. Reardon | A.J. Ford | 1971 D.T. May | R.W. Oriel |
| 1956 C. Wilson | V. Wilkins | 1972 G. Thomas | T. Griffiths |
| 1957 R.D. Meredith | N. Williams | 1973 A. Lloyd | G. Thomas |
| 1958 A. Kemp | R.D. Meredith | 1974 A. Lloyd | G. Thomas |
| 1959 J.R. Price | M.L. Berni | 1975 T. Griffiths | G. Thomas |
| 1960 L. Luker | A.G. Kemp | 1976 D. Mountjoy | A. Lloyd |
| 1961 T. Parsons | J.R. Price | 1977 C. Wilson | D. Thomas |
| 1962 A.J. Ford | M.L. Berni | 1978 A. Lloyd | S. Newbury |

## AUSTRALIA

| | | | |
|---|---|---|---|
| 1953 W. Simpson | R. Marshall | 1965 W. Barrie | A. Cuffe |
| 1954 W. Simpson | F. Edwards (Open) | 1966 M. Williams | R. Atkins |
| 1955 E. Pickett | J. Harris | 1967 M. Williams | R. King |
| 1956 R. Marshall | W. Simpson | 1968 M. Williams | R. Mares |
| 1957 W. Simpson | N. Squire (Open) | 1969 W. Barrie | M. Williams |
| 1957 W. Simpson | R. Marshall | 1970 M. Williams | H. Andrews |
| 1958 F. Harris | W. Simpson | 1971 M. Williams | G. Miller |
| 1959 K. Burles | F. Harris | 1972 M. Williams | B. McLass |
| 1960 K. Burles | R Marshall | 1973 M. Williams | B. McLass |
| 1960 F. Davis | K. Burles (Open) | 1974 L. Condo | J. Campbell |
| 1961 M. Williams | L. Rahilly | 1975 R. Atkins | F. Thomas |
| 1962 W. Barrie | J. Lyons | 1976 R. Atkins | L. Heywood |
| 1963 F. Harris | W. Barrie | 1977 R. Atkins | J. Bonner |
| 1964 W. Barrie | F. Harris | 1978 K. Burles | R. Atkins |

## INDIA

| | | | |
|---|---|---|---|
| 1939 P.K. Deb | M.M. Begg | 1960 W. Jones | M.J.M. Lafir |
| 1940 P.K. Deb | H.P. Smith | 1961 M.J.M. Lafir | W. Jones |
| 1941 V.R. Freer | P.K. Deb | 1962 R. Marshall | B. Komti |
| 1942 P.K. Deb | V.R. Freer | 1963 M.J.M. Lafir | T. Monteiro |
| 1943–45 No Championship | | 1964 S. Shroff | T. Monteiro |
| 1946 T.A. Selvaraj | S.J. Coelho | 1965 S. Shroff | T. Monteiro |
| 1947 T. Sadler | A. Wali | 1966 T. Monteiro | S. Shroff |
| 1948 W. Jones | T. Sadler | 1967 S. Shroff | T. Monteiro |
| 1949 T.A. Selvaraj | W. Jones | 1968 S. Mohan | T. Monteiro |
| 1950 F. Edwards | T.A. Selvaraj | 1969 S. Shroff | A. Savur |
| 1951 T.A. Selvaraj | W.A. Reed | 1970 S. Shroff | A. Savur |
| 1952 W. Jones | C. Hirjee | 1971 T. Monteiro | A. Savur |
| 1953 L. Driffield | C. Hirjee | 1972 S. Shroff | S. Aleem |
| 1954 W. Jones | C. Hirjee | 1973 S. Shroff | T. Monteiro |
| 1955 T.A. Selvaraj | T. Sadler | 1974 M.J.M. Lafir | A. Savur |
| 1956 M.J.M. Lafir | C. Hirjee | 1975 M.J.M. Lafir | A. Savur |
| 1957 M.J.M. Lafir | C. Hirjee | 1976 A. Savur | |
| 1958 W. Jones | C. Hirjee | 1977 M.J.M. Lafir | A. Savur |
| 1959 M.J.M. Lafir | T. Cleary | | |

## MALTA

| | | | |
|---|---|---|---|
| 1947 L. Galea | G. Taliana | 1954 W. Asciak | J. Reginiano |
| 1948 T.B. Oliver | V. Reginiano | 1955 A. Borg | W. Asciak |
| 1949 L. Galea | V. Naudi | 1956 W. Asciak | A. Borg |
| 1950 W. Asciak | V. Micallef | 1957 W. Asciak | A. Borg |
| 1951 W. Asciak | L. Galea | 1958 W. Asciak | A. Borg |
| 1952 A. Borg | E. Bartolo | 1959 A. Borg | P. Grech |
| 1953 A. Borg | W. Asciak | 1960 A. Borg | M. Farrugia |

| | | | |
|---|---|---|---|
| 1961 A. Borg | P. Grech | 1969 P. Mifsud | P. Grech |
| 1962 A. Borg | P. Grech | 1970 P. Mifsud | W. Asciak |
| 1963 M. Tonna | P. Grech | 1971 P. Mifsud | P. Grech |
| 1964 A. Borg | P. Grech | 1972 P. Mifsud | J. Lodge |
| 1965 A. Borg | W. Asciak | 1973 A. Borg | P. Mifsud |
| 1966 A. Borg | W. Asciak | 1974 A. Borg | P. Mifsud |
| 1967 A. Borg | W. Asciak | 1975 P. Mifsud | A. Borg |
| 1968 P. Mifsud | A. Borg | | |

## NEW ZEALAND

| | |
|---|---|
| 1945 S. Moses | 1962 K. Murphy |
| 1946 J. Munro | 1963 W. Harcourt |
| 1947 W. Thompson | 1964 T. Yesberg |
| 1948 L. Stout | 1965 L. Napper |
| 1949 L. Stout | 1966 L. Napper |
| 1950 L. Stout | 1967 R. Flutey |
| 1951 N. Lewis | 1968 L. Napper |
| 1952 L. Stout | 1969 L. Glozier |
| 1953 L. Stout | 1970 K. Tristram |
| 1954 R. Franks | 1971 B. J. Bennett |
| 1955 L. Stout | 1972 N. Stockman |
| 1956 L. Stout | 1973 W. Hill |
| 1957 W. Harcourt | 1974 K. Tristram |
| 1958 W. Harcourt | 1975 K. Tristram |
| 1959 W. Thomas | 1976 D. Kwok |
| 1960 T. Yesberg | 1977 D. Meredith |
| 1961 F. Franks | 1978 D. Meredith |

## SOUTH AFRICA

| | |
|---|---|
| 1950 T.G. Rees | 1963 J. van Rensburg |
| 1951 T.G. Rees | 1964 M. Francisco |
| 1952 T.G. Rees | 1965 M. Francisco |
| 1953 J. van Rensburg | 1966 M. Francisco |
| 1954 J. van Rensburg | 1967 J. van Rensburg |
| 1955 J. van Rensburg | 1968 S. Francisco |
| 1956 F. Walker | 1969 S. Francisco |
| 1957 J. van Rensburg | 1970 J. van Rensburg |
| 1958 R. Walker | 1971 M. Francisco |
| 1959 M. Francisco | 1972 J. van Rensburg |
| 1960 P. Mans jun. | 1973 J. van Rensburg |
| 1961 J. van Rensburg | 1974 S. Francisco |
| 1962 J. van Rensburg | 1975 M. Francisco |

## SRI LANKA

| | |
|---|---|
| 1948 M.J.M. Lafir | 1951 M.S.A. Hassan |
| 1949 M.M. Faiz | 1952 M.J.M. Lafir |
| 1950 M.J.M. Lafir | 1953 M.J.M. Lafir |

| | | | |
|---|---|---|---|
| 1954 | M.J.M. Lafir | 1964 | M.J.M. Lafir |
| 1955 | M.J.M. Lafir | 1965 | M.J.M. Lafir |
| 1956 | M.J.M. Lafir | 1966 | M.J.M. Lafir |
| 1957 | M.J.M. Lafir | 1967 | N.J. Rahim |
| 1958 | M.J.M. Lafir | 1969 | M.J.M. Lafir |
| 1959 | M.J.M. Lafir | 1970 | N.J. Rahim |
| 1960 | M.J.M. Lafir | 1972 | N.J. Rahim |
| 1961 | M.J.M. Lafir | 1973 | M.J.M. Lafir |
| 1962 | M.J.M. Lafir | 1974 | Abandoned |
| 1963 | M.J.M. Izzath | | |

## IX Snooker: Women's Professional Championships

| | | | |
|---|---|---|---|
| 1934–40 | Ruth Harrison | 1949 | Agnes Morris |
| 1948 | Ruth Harrison | 1950 | Thelma Carpenter |

## X Snooker: Women's Amateur Championships

| | | | |
|---|---|---|---|
| 1933 | Margaret Quinn | 1959 | Didi Thompson |
| 1934 | Ella Morris | 1960 | Muriel Hazeldine |
| 1935 | Molly Hill | 1961 | Maureen Barrett |
| 1936 | Vera Seals | 1962 | Maureen Baynton |
| 1937 | Mrs. E. Morland Smith | 1963 | Rita Holmes |
| 1938 | Ella Morris | 1964 | Maureen Baynton |
| 1939 | Agnes Morris | 1965 | Sally Jeffries |
| 1940–46 | No contests | 1966 | Maureen Baynton |
| 1947 | Mrs. M. Knight | 1967 | Helen Futo |
| 1948 | Joan Adcock | 1968 | Maureen Baynton |
| 1949 | Rosemary Davies | 1969 | Rae Craven |
| 1950 | Pat Holden | 1970 | Muriel Hazeldine |
| 1951 | Rosemary Davies | 1971 | Muriel Hazeldine |
| 1952 | Rosemary Davies | 1972 | Vera Selby |
| 1953 | Rita Holmes | 1973 | Vera Selby |
| 1954 | Maureen Barrett | 1974 | Vera Selby |
| 1955 | Maureen Barrett | 1975 | Vera Selby |
| 1956 | Maureen Barrett | 1976 | Ann Johnson |
| 1957 | Rita Holmes | 1977 | Ann Johnson |
| 1958 | Rita Holmes | 1978 | Agnes Davies |

## XI Billiards: British Boys Championships

| | | | |
|---|---|---|---|
| 1922 | W. Donaldson (Coatbridge) | | |
| 1923 | W. Leigh (Nottingham) | F. Edwards (Stourbridge) | |
| 1924 | L. Steeples (Rotherham) | G. Cooper (Isle of Wight) | |
| 1925 | S. Lee (Streatham) | G. Cooper (Isle of Wight) | |
| 1926 | R. Gartland (London) | S. Lee (Streatham) | |
| 1927 | R. Gartland (London) | R.L. Bennett (Purley) | |
| 1928 | R.L. Bennett (Purley) | J. Forrester (Taunton) | |

| 1929 | F. Davis (Chesterfield) | H.J. Bennett (Purley) |
|---|---|---|
| 1930 | H.J. Bennett (Purley) | W.H. Dennis (Nottingham) |
| 1931 | C. Desbottes (Brighton) | T. Steeples (Rotherham) |
| 1934 | W. Swinhoe (Newcastle) | |
| 1935 | D. Cruikshank (South Shields) | |
| 1936 | D. Cruikshank (South Shields) | H. Stokes (Glasgow) |
| 1937 | D. Curson (London) | W. Milburn (Newcastle) |
| 1938 | | |
| 1939 | R. Smith (Pontardawe) | |
| 1940 | B. Smith (Wisbech) | |
| 1948 | R. Williams (Blackheath) | J. Carney (Pontardawe) |
| 1949 | R. Williams (Blackheath) | M. Leyden (Armadale) |
| 1950 | M. Owen (Great Yarmouth) | M. Leyden (Armadale) |
| 1951 | E. Parry (Ferndale) | M. Owen (Great Yarmouth) |
| 1952 | M. Wildman (Peterborough) | J. Burgess (Risca) |
| 1953 | C. Everton (Droitwich) | J. Lambert (Pinner) |
| 1954 | H. Burns (Widnes) | D. Deakes (Stoke) |
| 1955 | D. Deakes (Stoke) | G. Waite (Treorchy) |
| 1956 | C. Dean (Bulwell) | A. Gadsden (Bulwell) |
| 1957 | P. Shelley (Stafford) | D. Roots (Penge) |
| 1958 | P. Morgan (Belfast) | D. Bend (Nuneaton) |
| 1959 | | |
| 1960 | A. Matthews (Bulwell) | R. Tumman (Brighton) |
| 1961 | B. Whitehead (Halifax) | K. Richardson (Nottingham) |
| 1962–67 | | no contest |
| 1968 | C. Williamson (Leeds) | D. Ross (Bradford) |
| 1969 | P. Bardsley (Sheffield) | C. Bowden (Matlock) |
| 1970 | W. Thorne (Leicester) | P. Bardsley (Sheffield) |
| 1971 | P. Bardsley (Sheffield) | N. Fairall (Portsmouth) |
| 1972 | P. Bardsley (Sheffield) | T. Wells (Southampton) |
| 1973 | T. Wells (Southampton) | D. Rothwell (Wigan) |
| 1974 | P. Allan (Wooller) | C. Houlihan (Accrington) |
| 1975 | S. McNamara (Cambridge) | J. Barnes (Middlesbrough) |
| 1976 | D. Bonney (St. Helens) | K. Martin (Teesside) |
| 1977 | D. Bonney (St. Helens) | J. Calvey (Middlesbrough) |
| 1978 | K. Walsh (Middlesbrough) | D. Adds (London) |

## XII Billiards: British Junior Championships

| 1949 | G. Toner (Limavady, N.I.) | R. Gross (Greenford) |
|---|---|---|
| 1950 | R. Williams (Blackheath) | J. Carney (Pontardawe) |
| 1951 | R. Williams (Blackheath) | J. Carney (Pontardawe) |
| 1952 | J. Sinclair (Ashington) | B. Simpson (Washington) |
| 1953 | M. Wildman (Peterborough) | E. Parry (Ferndale) |
| 1954 | M. Wildman (Peterborough) | D. Scott (Blyth) |
| 1955 | D. Scott (Blyth) | C. Everton (Droitwich) |
| 1956 | C. Everton (Droitwich) | G. Hampson (Manchester) |
| 1957 | C. Myers (Birtley) | C. Dean (Nottingham) |
| 1958 | C. Marks (Weymouth) | C. Dean (Nottingham) |

| 1959 | P. Morgan (Belfast) | B. Shelley (Stafford) |
| 1960 | D. Bend (Nuneaton) | C. Davies (Derby) |
| 1961 | P. Morgan (Belfast) | A. Matthews (Bulwell) |
| 1962 | A. Matthews (Bulwell) | D. Rhodes (Henley) |
| 1963 | A. Matthews (Bulwell) | M. McCann (Matlock) |
| 1964–7 | no contest | |
| 1968 | D. Taylor (Darwen) | D. Burgess (Portsmouth) |
| 1969 | D. Burgess (Portsmouth) | J. Terry (Ystradgynlais) |
| 1970 | J. Terry (Ystradgynlais) | W. Blake (Newport, IOW) |
| 1971 | W. Thorne (Leicester) | R. Toombes (Skegness) |
| 1972 | W. Thorne (Leicester) | C. Palmer (Lampeter) |
| 1973 | W. Thorne (Leicester) | P. Edworthy (Crediton) |
| 1974 | T. Wells (Southampton) | D. Rothwell (Wigan) |
| 1975 | E. Hughes (Dublin) | I. Williamson (Leeds) |
| 1976 | S. Davis (Plumstead) | I. Williamson (Leeds) |
| 1977 | I. Williamson (Leeds) | J. Barnes (Middlesbrough) |
| 1978 | I. Williamson (Leeds) | J. Barnes (Middlesbrough) |

## XIII Snooker: British Boys Championship

| 1947 | R. Baker (Neath) | |
| 1948 | R. Williams (Blackheath) | G. Hobbs (Chatham) |
| 1949 | D. Lewis (Pengam) | I. Cheetham (Manchester) |
| 1950 | M. Owen (Great Yarmouth) | D. Williams (Ynyshir) |
| 1951 | M. Owen (Great Yarmouth) | E. Parry (Ferndale) |
| 1952 | M. Wildman (Peterborough) | D. Breese (Highgate) |
| 1953 | J. Board (Bridlington) | K. Preston (Cannock) |
| 1954 | D. Bond (Evesham) | B. Allen (Desborough) |
| 1955 | P. Shelley (Stafford) | P. Ferrari (Tottenham) |
| 1956 | A. Hart (Manchester) | D. Bond (Evesham) |
| 1957 | P. Shelley (Stafford) | A. Orchard (Swansea) |
| 1958 | D. Bend (Nuneaton) | D. Trevelyan (Alfreton) |
| 1959 | J. Doyle (Dundalk) | P. Cox (Sheffield) |
| 1960 | N. Cripps (Charlton) | A. Matthews (Bulwell) |
| 1961 | | |
| 1962 | J. Virgo (Manchester) | A. Grant (Poole) |
| 1963 | J. Hollis (Tottenham) | T. McCarver (Southampton) |
| 1964 | D. Clinton (Birmingham) | J. Hollis (Tottenham) |
| 1965 | | |
| 1966 | J. Terry (Ystradgynlais) | R. Reardon (Stoke) |
| 1967 | no contest | |
| 1968 | E. Stone (Exeter) | A. Vincent (Liverpool) |
| 1969 | P. Hughes (Neath) | W. Thorne (Leicester) |
| 1970 | W. Thorne (Leicester) | S. Mays (Derby) |
| 1971 | J. Mills (Bridgend) | R. Dean (Leicester) |
| 1972 | J. Mills (Bridgend) | T. Wells (Southampton) |
| 1973 | P. Bardsley (Sheffield) | K. Jones (Wrexham) |
| 1974 | S. Holroyd (Huddersfield) | D. Battye (Bradford) |
| 1975 | M. Hallett (Grimsby) | P. Hargreaves (Derby) |
| 1976 | W. Jones (Abertysswg) | D. Bonney (St. Helens) |

| 1977 | J. White (London) | D. Bonney (St. Helens) |
| 1978 | D. Adds (London) | M. Jackson (Preston) |

## XIV Snooker: British Junior Championships

| 1949 | A. Kemp (Ynyshir) | L.R. Watts (Treharris) |
|------|------|------|
| 1950 | J. Carney (Pontardawe) | R. Reardon (Tredegar) |
| 1951 | R. Williams (Blackheath) | C. Wilson (Tredegar) |
| 1952 | C. Wilson (Tredegar) | M. Owen (Great Yarmouth) |
| 1953 | C. Wilson (Tredegar) | M. Owen (Great Yarmouth) |
| 1954 | M. Wildman (Peterborough) | E. Parry (Ferndale) |
| 1955 | W. McGivern (Saltcoats) | M. Wildman (Peterborough) |
| 1956 | E. Sinclair (Glasgow) | A. Hope (Edinburgh) |
| 1957 | H. Burns (Widnes) | G. Wright (Londonderry) |
| 1958 | W. West (Hounslow) | D. Bond (Weston-super-Mare) |
| 1959 | D. Root (Penge) | D. Bend (Nuneaton) |
| 1960 | D. Bend (Nuneaton) | I. Rees (Blackwood) |
| 1961 | I. Rees (Blackwood) | T. Clarke (Coventry) |
| 1962 | A. Matthews (Bulwell) | T Collison (Leytonstone) |
| 1963 | A. Matthews (Bulwell) | A. Stringer (Kingstanding) |
| 1964 | J. Fisher (Wandsworth) | R. Dolbear (Denmark Hill) |
| 1965 | J. Virgo (Salford) | J. Hollis (Tottenham) |
| 1966 | J. Hollis (Tottenham) | M. Colleran (Stratford) |
| 1967 | | no contest |
| 1968 | J. Maughan (Consett) | D. Clinton (Birmingham) |
| 1969 | J. Terry (Ystradgynlais) | J. Peacock (Manchester) |
| 1970 | J. Terry (Ystradgynlais) | W. Blake (Newport, IOW) |
| 1971 | J. Johnson (Bradford) | G. Crimes (Salford) |
| 1972 | A. Knowles (Bolton) | M. Gibson (Glasgow) |
| 1973 | W. Thorne (Leicester) | P. Edworthy (Crediton) |
| 1974 | A. Knowles (Bolton) | P. Smith (Hitchin) |
| 1975 | E. Hughes (Dublin) | P. Bain (Manchester) |
| 1976 | I. Williamson (Leeds) | P. Death (Abertysswg) |
| 1977 | I. Williamson (Leeds) | W. Jones (Abertysswg) |
| 1978 | T. Meo (London) | I. Williamson (Leeds) |

# Index